'Through My Eyes'

The Antics We Had

While Renovating

A Doocot

In The Highlands of Scotland

'A very intimate view of our lives'

By *Susan Anne Petty.*

First Edition 2008

Published by Hooper Publishing
ISBN: 978-0-9561218-0-6
© Susan Anne Petty 2008

Foreword

THROUGH MY EYES

Hi, my name is Susan and I would like to invite you to join myself and my husband Roger, on our journey. Seeing things 'through my eyes' and experiencing the antics we had while renovating a Doocot in the Highlands of Scotland.

Taking you from some childhood memories of holidays I spent in Scotland with my mother and father, to battle fights won and lost by my poor brother Paul (*who no doubt still has the scars to prove it from the hands of his 'darling little sister!!!'*). Leading to a promise I made as a child, which was to one day return to this glorious land and make it my home.

From broken hearts to tears of joy, from screams of pain, tantrums and frustrations. To screams of laughter in hilarious situations that hopefully you will see the funny side of.

We also hope that we can pass on things we have learnt over the renovation years, to give you some useful information.

If I bash my toe, I will say "Sod it", not "Oh dear me, what a shame that hurt." This is me as I am, warts and all. (*Of which I must stress I have none anywhere. Just so you know!*)

If I called someone a 'Cow', or have been what may seem unkind, do read on. It may be done in jest, or I may have, in my view had good reason at the time. These times will unfold as you continue on our adventures.

In some situations I have changed people's names. This is because they may have children, and the children are innocent of all things. They cannot be held responsible for what their parents say or do. Perhaps, I decided in some cases one must be discreet.

On that note, I do not wish to offend or upset anyone. It is how I have seen a situation, but if the cap fits, wear it. All I have said in my book is true and, if asked, can be proven by others. If there are spelling mistakes, I'm sorry, but the English language is a minefield to me!!

For example, try explaining to me (*or my brain*) the word PHYSICIST. To me PHYSICIST is spelled FIZISIST and PSYCHIATRIST would be spelled SICIATRIST, I tend to spell things as they sound, so you can see my problem!!

Or poor Pam Taylor's problem, who at times with mounting frustration, gave me help with spelling. But was instructed to leave my grammar alone, so as not to lose my authenticity.

So fasten your seat belts and hold on tight, for what is a roller coaster of a journey. "What you waitin for then ??? Get that bloody bottle open, and let's gets started".

Meanings

Remembering that when you are reading this I have sometimes said things as if I am talking to you in the same room, I shall now translate my meanings in the book.

!!!!!!!!!! = The amount will stress the degree of shock, confusion or mirth, in or at a situation.

Mmmmmm / mmmmmm = Will indicate the degree of pleasure or thought.

.... = Dots or a long space may indicate a pause whilst I am considering how to word something without offending. Or, a said situation that has just simply left me pondering, IE. I am taking a moment.

CAPITALS = Capital letters mean I am making a statement, pointing out something, or highlighting a part. This could simply be a name or description. Also when a word has inverted commas like, 'this'.

Oooooooooops = This is in the voice of Doris Day having a girly strop and sometimes stamping her feet. The length of which will show to what degree.

( ) or using *Words typed in these little ways* = means an inner thought, or I am trying to put my feelings across. Or sometimes trying to put a voice/character into a situation.

I also, as you will see, use commas a lot. This could be because of the way I speak, or just taken a breath etc. Sometimes I get carried away and have to remember to pause for breath.!!! as you will see.

As for the 'etc.' This is a phrase from the film The King and I. .. When the King so rightly uses his famous line "Etcetera, etcetera, etcetera" to cover up his loss of words. Or to let you fill in the rest!!!

Sometimes I have chosen a character played by a particular actor to try and portray how a particular phrase should sound, or be visualised. This I hope will deepen the sadness, heighten the anger or show the funny side of the situation. Also it could be how I have seen someone, or something .- through my eyes'.

Now, I know when it comes to 'Grammar' you will see it will often be misused according to the Oxford Dictionary but that's me, warts and all. Well if your not totally confused by now, I hope this helps you in catching my expressions and feelings.

Dedication

This book is dedicated to
my mother and father in
thanks for all their support
over the years.
And
to my husband Roger
for all the love and kindness
he has given me.
Also
in recognition of all
his hard work.

Events & Antics

DOOCOT 1
In the Beginning - Memories

As a young child my world was sugar coated, full of adventure made in a child's imagination, full of memories that all children should have. Some of my fondest memories are of our family holidays spent in Scotland. Looking back it was clear from the very start that my heart belonged to this wonderful country. I just knew that one day I was destined to return to this 'Promised Land.'

On our holidays each day was an adventure, my older brother Paul and I never knew where our next day's destination would be. In the night time, while my brother and I slept, my father must have spent hours planning the next day's outing, while my mother would be busy making the picnic hamper ready, full of yummy things to eat.

I can remember the taste of the lettuce in the salads we had. It was drizzled in a lemon juice of some kind. This I must say, as a child, made lettuce more palatable. I just wish they could have done something to SPROUTS yuck (*didn't most of us as kids just hate the damn things!!*).

One such outing took us down the long country lanes to a beautiful spot Dad had found on his map, and he was delighted to find that it had plenty of space for us kids to let off steam.

In those days you were able to park up the car in almost any area. People had respect for the country in those days. I mean you never saw rubbish dumped at the side of the road and, as for the dreaded discarded coke cans that seem to be everywhere now, it just didn't seem to happen then. Plus that oh so famous MacDonald's packaging was never seen.

Mind you, in those days, it didn't exist as far as I know, but I suppose the equivalent would have been paper from a local chippy!! I suppose if there was a funny side to it, at least you could have read the page from a newspaper!

I suppose as a child I never saw the rubbish as such, because we were always brought up not to discard our rubbish anywhere except in the bin.

Maybe some people thought that by discarding their rubbish on the streets instead of the bins provided, it helped to keep the road sweepers employed. Perhaps they hadn't noticed that over the years they were seen less of as technology was giving birth to mechanical means of cleaning our streets.

Anyway, my poor brother must have hated me at times. I used to drag him into my world of make believe so many times. In my child's imagination, this land was full of heroes and dragons, with battles to be won and lost. In my eyes, the skirt and blouse I wore became a true Scottish kilt with a top to suit a Highlander going to war, and my brother's jeans and t-shirt would become the Shining Armour of an Englishman, ready to face his death in battle against the Scots.

I guess even at a young age I felt I belonged here, perhaps from a life before. Who knows what it was that made me feel and sense, without being told, that the Scots battled against the English and would lay their lives down in the call for, in the hearts of the Scots, "freedom".

I was far too young to have been taught this in school, or to begin to comprehend what it was all about. Yet I felt this pain in my heart as I looked at the splendour of the rolling mountains, and longed to stand high on the top and scream my name.

On the note of the battles I was to have with my brother, the poor lad must have had a few bruises from when I hit him too hard by mistake, when I gave the final blow of death in battle. Me, well I got the usual grazed knees, but then that was the norm with my tomboy ways. I guess you could say I was more of a brother to Paul at times. Forget the dolls, I wanted to be a driver of a tank or fire engine, not frills and stuff for girls. *(This was much to my mother's disappointment, and led to many years of worrying, by my mother and father, over which part of me I had scratched when falling out of yet another treetop! Usually followed by my brother!!).*

The Haunted House

One year we went to Scotland and stayed in a little cottage bungalow half way up a mountain. To me it was great. Perhaps looking back it had a spooky feeling about it, but that just added fuel to my imagination.

However, my poor Mum got the brunt of whatever was in that place. I woke up one night to the sound of my Mother's screams coming from her room. Rubbing my sleepy eyes I entered my parent's, bedroom, which was only next to mine, to find my Dad trying to calm Mum down!

Dad told me in a gentle and calming voice "mummy was ok, she'd just had a bad dream, she will be fine". He then took me back to my room and tucked me in bed, and said, I was not to worry, "mummy would soon go back to bed, and I'll make her a nice cup of tea." He then gave me a kiss on the cheek and said "goodnight" as he left the room leaving my door ajar, and the hall light on.

My brother was in a room joined onto the side of the house. This he found great as far as he was concerned, as he didn't have to share a room with his darling little sister!! So that meant he didn't hear Mum that night. Years later when talking to Mum about this, she remembered it clearly. She said there was something there in that place. And that night she heard something or someone moving around in the loft. Apparently my Dad went up into the loft and just found an old case full of old clothes. Perhaps it was someone's once and his or her spirit was still there? But I didn't know about it then, just as well!! SPOOKY.

There was also a day when poor Mum was in the kitchen and something spooked her so much she came running out. We as kids didn't want to go in and turn the boiling milk on the stove off. So I guess Dad must have gone in and turned it off? I can't remember this, it's only what Mum told me, but again 'SPOOKY'.

As far as I was concerned the holiday was great. Each morning I watched Robinson Crusoe on the black and white TV that was in the cottage, while I ate toasted marmite soldiers. I can still remember the 'Goosebumps' I'd get when hearing the original theme music to 'Dr Who'. which I would watch while peeping out from behind the cushion I held to my face. I loved it, even if I did scream at times.

That's half the 'fun' of it, being scared and still not being able to wait until the next episode. (I wonder how many of us would admit to playing the "Dalek" and doing the voice?).

Anyway, onward I must go.

The Day I made a Promise to Return to this Promised Land

One of the days we were not going out in the car "We are going to climb a mountain" my Dad informed my brother and I. So we got ourselves ready and awaited our instructions.

Dad had a small rucksack on his back, and Mum was ready and waiting by the door. Mum was a petite lady. So we were amazed to see her dressed in slacks and ladies climbing boots ready to join us.

This was fab I thought to myself, 'Girl Power'. We'd show those boys. "Come on Mum" I said as I took her hand and led her towards the car. I was full of excitement and anticipation, as I fully expected us 'girls' to beat the 'boys' to the top of the mountain when we reached our destination.

But as we set off out the door Dad told us we were to climb our own mountain, so no car journey. This was fine by me and my tummy, as I used to get very car sick as a child.

So off we went at full steam. That is, my brother and I ran up the short part of the road that was left until it turned into a rough track leading us to the beginning of our climb to the top. We didn't realise why Dad was walking behind us. We assumed it was to keep Mum company as they held hands talking along the way.

But it wasn't only that, Dad was saving his energy for the climb, as it was to be a great climb.

After a while Mum had to stop as it was getting hard going for her. I'll always remember the look of love in my Mum and Dad's eyes towards each other as they said, "see you on the way back". At that age it was one of those 'googie' looks we kids giggled at.

Onward and upward we went. You know it must have seemed like we asked poor Dad for a drink every five minutes. I felt him an old meanie at the time when he only gave us an Opal Fruit sweet to quench our thirst.

But I now know Dad knew we'd need the loo if we drank to much, and there was no real place to go if we got desperate. However, as we scrambled to the top I would often look around at the inspiring views. They were, even at my young age, breathtaking.

When we got to the top we were rewarded with a can of pop (between us!!). Yes, Dad was still thinking of the 'loo' problem we may have. Bless him, I realise now what he was doing.

At the very top there was a large mound of rocks. Well, you know me!!! I had to climb it (more scraped knees I could just hear my Mum thinking).

"One, two, three, yeaahhhhhhhhhhhh"..........I shouted with all my might as I stood up and looked at my Dad's face, which by now was ever so slightly wrinkled with just a tad of worry, as yet again the tomboy in me was up to mischief!!!! POOR DAD!!!!!

As I stood on what seemed to be the top of the world, I flung my arms out to the sides and spun round and round. Suddenly stopping, my eyes slowly fixed on a distant blur and as my eyes slowly focused on the view unfolding in front of me, I gasped with shock.

Maybe shock isn't the correct word, but I had never seen such beauty. As I rested my hands on my hips with legs astride like Peter Pan, there in front of me was only what I could call my own "Never, Never Land".

I stood in awe of the land's beauty with nothing but the sound of the wind in my ears. Oh, to have been able to fly like Peter Pan, or like a bird of prey. Being able to swoop down and around the glens below and see every inch of this 'Promised Land' that lay before me now.

It was then that it happened. I made my promise to one-day return to what truly felt like my lost home. A feeling of belonging here overwhelmed me, as if I could hear the land calling my name like an old friend.

Little did I know that the promise, that dream, would indeed come true, but not for many years yet.

It seemed forever until the earth's spell on me was broken by the whisper of Dad calling me, as it was time to return back down this glorious mountain. Alas I had to join the troops as one might say and return to Mum's open arms and go back for tea at the cottage. What a wonderful day it had been. That night I dreamt of flying around the mountains until I must have gone into a deep and contented sleep.

So that's it. Now you know the background of my dreams. I hope you are now ready to join my partner Roger and I in experiencing the laughter, the tears, the fun, the sadness and sometimes heartache over the years of leaving family and friends to renovate a Dovecot in the Highlands of Scotland.

The Hearts of Discontent

Roger had been working so hard on the car in the garage, and the heat was yet again just unbearable. So much so, that one could hardly breathe with all the heat. Down south was just getting hotter each year.

The only escape we had was a swing chair along the side of the garage in the shade, which gave some sanctuary from the blazing sun above. There was also a small breeze that came along the side, but even this was warm air, be it slightly cooler than in the open.

There we sat drinking a well-earned pint of Roger's fabulous home brew for which he was well admired by our friends for many years.

If we had any work to do around the house our friends were well happy to get a few pints in payment. Although we'd lived in this house for over ten years, there was always something else to do.

When we bought the house we had to gut it, it was a hell of a mess. The house needed totally rewiring and decorating top to toe. But we loved the challenge, and learnt so much from doing it.

We weren't truly happy! Our dream was to one day retire to Scotland, but we had been made redundant.

Roger had worked for this company for over fourteen years as did his father before him. His father had worked with this company from before the war, and after the war they asked him to come back. Then many years later in the early eighties, Roger joined the firm in the refurbishment department.

The firm was a small lighting company called SUGG LIGHTING. Unfortunately they no longer go by that name. I joined the firm in the 90's and enjoyed working there.

Roger and I were made redundant along with about ten others. When one of the bosses, who had been away on holiday, returned to find we had been given the 'Royal Boot' he was flabbergasted. There was no one left to do the work he needed. Then Roger got a letter asking if he would do some work at home for them. So we did, I say we, as Roger and I always worked as a team. And if I say it myself we make a damn good team.

Well, as time passed, we could see our savings going down and even with me working in local pubs every day, we still found it hard. To make ends meet was a battle we were fast losing. Our mortgage was getting beyond our control. All people saw was, in their eyes, that we had a big house in the country and that we seemed to live well, i.e. that we always had beer in the house and plenty to eat.

We did have hard times, we just didn't let anyone know. But then again we were better off than some. It all depends on what you expect out of life.

Roger's father lent us money over the years and so did my parents, but still we had to pay this back at some point. So we were well in the murky when our neighbour came up with an answer!!!

There we were sitting supping a pint of Roger's amber nectar when our neighbour, on another hot day, was in the pool in his back garden with his kids.

We got on well with them, so we sneaked up and popped our heads over the fence and jokingly asked the 'noisy git' to be quiet! He just laughed and splashed us, and then said he'd be over later with his architect. We laughed back and asked if he wanted to put a pool in for us? He just grinned!!

Later on he came round with this guy. He asked if he could look at our back extension to the house, which he did. After a short time they were finished looking and the guy went out the gate, Roger called out, "I thought you wanted to buy us out, so what do you need him for??"

In reply our neighbour said, "I'll be back in ten minutes!!!!" And sure enough he came back and joined us for a beer.

Well, I must point out that he had always teased us about selling up to him and (in his words) "Sodding off to Scotland," but we assumed he was joking.

How wrong we were. The bloke only offered to buy us out there and then!!!!

So we thought we'd call his bluff and said "ok".

Our old house

7

Our garden and the bench where it all began

The Starter Gun has Gone Off

Our neighbour asked how much we wanted for our house, and we told him. Then he announced, "You're on". To which he added that he would arrange the money the next day.

"Bloody hell" we thought to ourselves, "he's serious." Well, if he was that serious we'd have to really sit and talk to him. That night we worked out how much we would need for the house in realistic terms. We then got together the next day with our neighbour..... We agreed on a price, and that was that.

Then came one of the hardest moments when we had to tell our families we were going to move in the not so distant future.

It was heart breaking to tell my children we were to move away but they would have been welcome if they wanted to come with us.

However, my son was sharing a place with friends and had a girlfriend, and my daughter had given us a beautiful grandson with her partner. So who was I to ask them to move away in any form?

As for breaking the news to my Mum and Dad, well it just broke my heart. I love them so much and wished they could be with us, but they are too settled where they are. With friends of old living around them, and my brother, his wife and three lovely girls living around the corner.

Perhaps if my brother had lived far away, we may have stayed nearer for longer. But Mum and Dad, although getting on in years, were in great health and good spirit. So I needed not to worry so much.

Plus I kept saying to myself, if we did find somewhere in Scotland, it's not Australia. And we can fly down at the drop of a hat if needed in a hurry. And with Roger's father the same. Peggy, Roger's Mum had died a few years earlier and Dad seemed happy living where he was on the coast. He had made some good friends, and apart from backache he was well.

A few weeks later our neighbour gave us an old computer of his daughter's to be able to get fixed up on the 'net' and look for houses for sale.

We were amazed at the amount of places. But we wanted something we could work on, something we could rebuild a bit.

I was looking into being as self-sufficient as possible. We already had geese and chickens, plus two cats.

We used to have an old dog called Heidi, but we lost her to cancer some time back. She used to belong to a chap called Nick, known affectionately as Baldric. But after a car hit him one night as he staggered home from the local pub in the dark, he was unable to look after her. So in time he asked if we'd keep her, which we were pleased to do. She was a Deerhound, and as old as the hills. She gave us so much love, it was sad the day we had to let her go. She even won a medal at Crufts. Nick put her in for the 'Scruffiest Dog' contest and, bless her, she won. He was very proud of that, and so were we.

Heidi

Nick himself died a couple of years later. You know, we never found the award Heidi got, but we know he had it as we saw it in his house.

It would be a dream come true if we were able to find a run down farm. Nothing too big but with some land to work on would be great. Something out of town, away from all the hustle and bustle.

Call me an old grump if you wish, but I'd had enough of towns. Seeing what green grass was left being bought up by developers just made me sick.

In one of the towns near us there was a large roundabout. Would you believe it, well I couldn't until I saw it They actually built a couple of restaurants and cafés, on the thing. My God what's happening to this world? Every last bloody inch of green will soon be eaten up. I guess there will be one hell of a pile-up one day as someone pulls out from the place into the traffic. I think there must be traffic lights, but things happen.

And to top things off I hear now that the local councils are claiming back the ends of some larger gardens, and yes, only to squeeze yet another house in.

I am beginning to hear myself screaming "GET US OUT OF HERE, YOU'RE CHOKING US'

But at least now we may be nearing our escape from this over populated mass of concrete.

It's a Bloody Tank

Over the next few weeks Roger and I were to search the Net for all it was worth. We went onto tons of sites.

If we found something we liked the look of, there was always something wrong. Sometimes the area and sometimes the price, but we were determined to find our dream home.

We did look into Yorkshire and other areas, but we knew in our hearts it had to be Scotland.

That's where our hearts were truly calling us, and everything we looked at always seemed to point to that.

Our neighbour often asked if we'd found somewhere. He was just champing at the bit to get started on the move.... He had great plans for our house. He was hoping to knock his and ours together to make one hell of a big one.

His wife had a horse that was stabled some way away, and one day he asked if we could clear the far side of the garage out so he could use it as a stable.

Well what did we care, we were packing up like crazy every second we could. And Roger's car business was closed down by now.

We were able to find a company that sold twenty-foot storage containers, so we got one delivered to our house and put it on the driveway. This was to be the first, unbeknown to us, of four.

We had to get these as our neighbour had informed us that he was going to strip the house clean, and we could have everything, including the bath and kitchen sink, cupboards and doors, light fittings and on/off Switches. He meant the whole damn lot was to go.

This was sad in one way because of all the work we had done. But I must say it was to possibly save us money, as we might need to fit out our new abode. We just didn't know what to expect. Plus if we did find a house or farm that needed to be rebuilt, there may not be anywhere to store our stuff in the long term. So the containers would be useful.

One day our neighbour popped in and said the only way we will ever find something is to sod off up to Scotland, and have a look around. Find an area we like, and then look at what's up for sale.

He was right, but what could we do? My car was no good for that. It was a historic Marina, and Roger's car was off the road as he was doing some work on it for when we did move.

"I have an idea," said our neighbour..... Right, that's it!! I can't keep on calling "him" our "neighbour" his name is Dudley. So everyone, you can now say hello to Dudley!!!!

At which point he took Roger off with him, to return about half an hour later with what looked like a TANK.

It was in fact Dudley's old Land Cruiser. It ran well, but needed a few bits replaced and a damn good service. Then a good wash and polish. It looked like new when we'd done.

We later found out it was once Barry Sheen's. Apparently he had it converted to automatic after his big bike crash. This was great for me as, "Ooooops" that sounds bad. (*I didn't mean that Barry's crash was great*), although I passed my test in a manual, I'd only driven my automatic Marina since, and was a little rusty on the old gear changes. It was as if a manual had kangaroo petrol, if you get my drift.

We put curtain wire around the inside, so we had curtains we could pull closed. This was so we could sleep in the back of the car instead of a tent if needed. We packed the car with bedding and a camping stove and kettle. Also, a camping larder to store any food in while travelling around.

We also had a cool-box to store milk and butter in. It didn't have any ice in, but kept things ok out of the sun.

Well, we arranged someone to look after the animals and we were ready to go. With the car full of maps, and a load of sandwiches, mobile phones at the ready. Off we set.

Goodbye Marina

My old marina

My little stories, which show that my old car would not have been up to the travels, and some of the tight spots she got me in to.

ONE FOR THE GIRLS.

Warning. When your dreams come true, they may not be, exactly as you saw them!

In the voice of Max Bygraves	> ***"Let me tell you a story."***
AND Kenneth Williams	> *"OOOOO 'No, Get away."*
Me	> "Yes, really, I did say that!!!!"

Max>"Once upon a time"

Kenneth>"OOOOO' No, now stop muckin about"

Now, recently I had stopped going to a dance class, which I use to go to at least twice a week with my friends, Fiona and Vicky. It was Cerock dancing, and I loved it. It's French Jive, better than going to the gym, and much more fun.

I used to go along in their car and contribute to the fuel, but on this occasion the other girls weren't going. So I decided to go on my own. There was a good crowd there, and I didn't want to miss out on my class. So off I set in my Marina.

On the way I was aware of a faint smell of, only what I can describe, as a fuse burning. I know a little about cars. Certainly enough to know it would need investigating before my next trip out. So I decided that I would have to check this out on my return home that night.

Anyway, by the time I arrived at the dance hall, I was sure the smell was much worse. I put some of it down to my imagination, as I didn't like travelling at night in the car alone, but there was a definite smell.

Max > "Let me tell you about imagination"
Kenneth >"OOOO No, Let Susan tell her own story".

Nearing the end of the evening's dancing I decided to leave early. I felt that if the car had a problem I could at least knock on someone's front door and ask to use the phone if it wasn't to late, as I didn't have a mobile phone. (Good thinking, I thought to myself.)

It was now dark and as I drove back through the town, instead of going down the by-pass where there would be no houses, I noticed some cars coming in the opposite direction were flashing their lights and the occupants were waving at me!!! I knew that I didn't know them as I waved back as they passed by!!

Curious...that I was, to see...why were they flashing? There seemed to be no hazards on the road ahead, so who knows...Perhaps it's because of the car!!! Some people love these old things.

As I drove along I smelled that smell again, but it was getting much stronger!!!!! Still I would be home soon I kept thinking to myself.

Suddenly the front wipers had a life of their own, and were going nuts!!!! Added to this, the car was now full of a smelly haze!!!!! I opened the window and put my foot down to speed my journey home.

At this I notice the lights on the dashboard dimming, and this continued to flash my lights.... Arrrr, hence people must have thought I was flashing them earlier, and even more so now...!!! Bugger, Bugger, what shall I do?

Then at a roundabout it flashed through my mind.... "FIRE...oh' shit..." (Kenneth> Ooooo' I say), that the fire station was somewhere around in the next road.

While trying not to panic I shot off in what I would call 'AS CALM AS A PERSON BEING CHASED BY A HORNET' in what I hoped to be the direction of the Fire Station. I just thought that if this bloody car was going to spontaneously combust, the fire station can put it out. I just hoped it was the right road.

I went as fast as I dare, and considering the age of my car I was pushing it. I must admit that I didn't give two hoots about the speed limit. If the cop's had tried to pull me up, I think I would have just kept going to the fire station, and dealt with it then!!

Anyway, I was relieved to see the fire station ahead, and on approach I swung the car into the road entrance.

At what I hoped to be the right door, I jammed on the breaks, as the car skidded to a halt, and in a split second put the gear in to park, turned the ignition off, and flung the door open. Then ran across the pavement to the door.

Bugger, bugger, oh bloody buggerie the bloody door was locked,......... or perhaps a movement sensor thing was somewhere to open it. 'OH, FOR GOD SAKE... THERE MUST BE SOMETHING, OR SOMEONE AROUND!!!! HELLLLLP!!!' I thought to myself (by now panic was setting in nicely, and I could hear my heart pounding!!).

As my eyes whizzed around in search for a door handle, bell, or something, I noticed a glow at the side of the station door!!!! "A BLOODY BUGGERY, BLOODY BUGGERY DOOR BELL, AT LAST" were something like the words of my now frantic panic that spewed from my mouth in full volume. (Sorry).

As I frantically pressed the button a voice came from what seemed to be the Heavens Above saying "Door Number One"....*God, I jumped out of my skin.* This was promptly followed by a man's head popping out of a small open window above me, just to the right.

With what now was a fearful and trembling voice? Not knowing if my beloved car was about to go up in flames I said, "I DON'T wish to ALARM anyone, BUT I THINK MY CAR IS ABOUT TO SPONTANEOUSLY COMBUST...IS THERE ANY CHANCE OF FINDING A BLOODY FIREMAN???

At which, this head disappeared! Then followed a sound of feet running downstairs, to produce three or four men, who then exited the now open door in front of me. I quickly explained the smell I was getting in the car, and why in my view there was the possibility of the BLOODY THING going up in smoke!

Two of the men checked inside the car, and although there were no flames or smoke at that moment in time, one man did agree that there was a smell of burning....But, NOT a smell from a cigarette.

After the men, who as you must have gathered were Firemen, *Kenneth >* "OOOO' I SAY... Nice".

Max> "Oh, control yourself Kenneth",
had ascertained that the car was NOT on fire at this point. I said there was no way I was getting in it again to drive the distance home on my own. So

they said for me to move the car to a parking spot just across the way, and that I could use their phone to call someone.

"Hey Guys, if you think I'm getting in that Bloody Thing, NO WAY....One of you lot can move it, HERES THE KEY!!!!! Plus that's the car park for the 'Law Courts', AND if my car goes 'BANG' I'll be accused of trying to BLOW the place up!!!... Came my reply.

At which one of them jumped in and moved it, and thankfully not parking it in the suggested place, he parked it a little bit further away.

I followed the men into the building and as we entered the doors automatically closed behind us. Well, I know what you're thinking...*All my dreams come true!!!!! Firemen everywhere*...But believe it or not, until now it hadn't even crossed my mind, I was too het-up about my beloved car.

I was shown into a small office just beside the entrance. This had huge windows and clear panels around it, so I had a good view of my car across the way. The men all disappeared except for one, who said I could use the phone that was on a desk by the main window. I was now left alone in what I assumed to be their reception office.

Well I rang home, and there was no answerer, so I assumed Roger was at the pub just down the road from our house and rang there.

Yes, he was there with our friend Paul. Now I had to explain the where's and why's to Roger...

Now, it was obvious I was going to get a bit of leg pulling over the situation!!! As they know I have a thing about Firemen... But what Sod's!!!!

I tried in vain to explain, and this all came out in one long sentence without a breath....I said "Now, before you say ONE BLOODY THING ROGER I am at the Fire Station in Horsham as my car nearly went up in flames and don't you even dare go where you are thinking it's not BLOODY FUNNY so PLEASE get you Arse down here now PLEEEEASE.........*Deep breath*...

Those Sods, as I put it, creased-up at the thought of me being in a Fire Station, on my own, with FIREMEN all over the place...I could here Roger shouting across to Paul, and for all the pub to hear what was going on, and the pub was in an uproar. They had no bloody intention of rushing their pints to rescue me from my dilemma!!!

But they would come and get me...IN TIME!!!! GITS!!!! It seemed forever.

Anyway as I waited this one chap came back and we chatted about the car. He could see I was not daft when it came to cars, as we talked about engines and things... Then he asked if I'd like a cuppa. Which I was grateful for. Plus to be really honest, now the pantomime had settled, I found myself 'Very' aware of being in a Fire Station...Which until now was not my main concern etc, etc, etc.

Now for a moment of Truth... I have to be honest here and say that I just go all-weak at the knees when I see a man in uniform. But FIREMEN are my real passion!!!.........Not that I've ever...well' you know...It's just Mmmmmmmmmmmm, Mmm. But now there I was standing in a FIRE STATION for the first time in my life, but not as I'd dreamt!!! I was here, hot and sweaty due only to my previous dancing and for no other reason!!!

Well, until then, because I have to admit I was getting just a little flustered!

Anyway, where was I? Oh yes....The man I'd been talking to I now know was the Chief Fireman, and he had now returned with my cupper. He then proceeded to say, "Why don't you come and join the lads upstairs while you wait???"

Max> *"This story may become X-rated!!!"*

Kenneth> "OOOOO, No, She wouldn't, She couldn't, could She, OOOO, I say"

Now a scene from Ally McBeal as a size Twenty foot jumps into my mouth and a zipper then closes it. As before thinking, the following words of thought came out loud before I could stop them....

"No I can't, I've got a thing about FIREMEN". (OOOOOOOOOp's. that thought came out loud!!!!) He just gave me a look and handed me my cuppa before he went back up the stairs...Now I'd done it!! I thought to myself...But maybe he thought I'd said 'I have a <u>fear</u> about firemen...!!' I hoped so.... Then suddenly, as I looked out of the window, I heard the sound of feet running down the stairs behind me!! Oh God what's going to happen now? Well' 'they'll probably only tease me'...were my thoughts, as I turn to face whoever had run down the stairs......only to be faced with three Firemen holding their

Fire extinguishers, *(ha' that got you going girl's!!)*, and while running towards the door, one shouted. "We don't wish to Alarm you Madam, but your car looks to be ON FIRE"!!!!   Christ, I nearly died on the spot and my face must have been as red as a beetroot!!!!!!! Talk about getting hot and bothered!!!!!!!

Anyway, as they ran out the door it closed after them, leaving me inside frantically waving the car keys, in the hope they wouldn't smash the window to get in.

After what seemed forever the fireman, 'Stood Down', I think the saying is. It was a false alarm!!

Apparently from the room upstairs the Fireman could see what looked like the reflection of flames inside my car, so hence the charge of Firemen to the scene.

After investigating they found that where the car was parked in front of a tree, on the other side if the road there was a lamp post which had one of those orange lights in. So as the breeze blew the branches of the tree about, it then gave the impression that orange flames were flickering in my car.

Panic over, they returned back into the station while I, still very red faced, I thanked them.

Shortly after this Roger and Paul ordained me with there arrival...Ha, Bloody Ha boys, thanks for your speed in coming to get me!!!!!! ......Sods...

The chief fireman came and let me out of the station door and after thanking him for all their help I yelled to Roger as he got out of Paul's car.... " NOT ONE WORD, DON'T YOU BLOODY DARE, NOT ONE SMIRK...THANK YOU!!!"

I refused to drive the car, so Roger drove us back while Paul followed in his car, just in-case...You know what....That BLOODY car was fine all the way home....But Roger did smell that smell in the car!!!

I went with them for a pint after we got home....Guess I should have known better!!!! The jokes were flying at the pub....But YOU know I was a good girl...Mores the pity girls!!   *Kenneth> OOOOO' Suzy, did you know that thought came out loud???*.........Ooooo Ooooops!!!

However, after days of investigation, with me still refusing to drive my beloved car, Roger found out what was wrong... It turned out that in the steering column a very small coil spring, (something that looks like it came from a ballpoint pen) had broken of the indicator switch mechanism and was in two bits floating around inside. This in turn was hitting wires causing the shorting out of things, hence the car lights dimming with my windscreen wipers going nuts, and hence that fuse burning kind of smell.

Boy was I glad Roger found this out...I can't tell you how much leg pulling I was getting from all who knew about the FIREMAN thing I have...

MAX > AND THAT'S THE END OF THIS STORY

Kenneth> Arrrrrrrr, Who's a Good Girl then!!!!!!

Gremlins in My Car

THIS ONE'S FOR THE BOYS

After all this I decided to give my beloved car a good clean up, and Roger gave the engine bay a good steam clean with the pressure hose.

At this point I asked the odd question about the working of the engine, for no particular reason, just general conversation.

One question I did ask was 'If I wanted to stop the engine in a hurry, because something had gone wrong, what should I do? *(I was still reflecting on my last experience behind the wheel, and wondered if, on looking back, I could have avoided any further embarrassments!)*

Roger gave me a funny look, and then said, "Only in a real emergency, you could pull the 'HT/spark plug leads' off from here. But that's not good for the car". I in reply just shrugged my shoulders and said "Just asking!"

The next day was beautiful, and I had to go to the bank and do the shopping. So this was the day I was to face my demons, and get behind the wheel of my car again.

As I drove away from the house, I have to admit I was a bit apprehensive. 'But hey' what could possible go wrong today, it's a lovely day.

Just passed the small row of houses before the pub there was a set of traffic lights, which just changed to green on my approach. I noticed that as I tried to slow down, the car seemed to 'rev' high! This I put down to my footwork, and a touch of nerves. *(Silly old me!)* mmmmm.

I drove passed the pub and waved at the workmen, who I recognized from the time they had done some work on the road a few weeks before.

But as I drove along I could clearly hear the car engine was 'revving very high'. So I lifted my foot off the accelerator to see what would happen, plus I was approaching the T Junction.

Nothing....well, put it this way. The engine still continued to 'rev', but now even higher!!!

"Oh bugger, here we go again........What the **** is wrong now? Give me a bloody break God or are you not answering your Sodding phone today???" I said aloud to myself in the car.

I put the car in to neutral and pushed on the brakes, 'Nothing' .So I put the hand brake on......NOTHING....By now fast approaching the junction with the engine screaming as if possessed by GREMLINS..........HELLLLLLLLLLP

I felt myself slapping my face hard, as I really began to lose the plot and panic big time. "WHAT DO I SODDING DO? WHAT DO I DO?' I kept screaming to myself. "Calm down, just caaalm dowwwwwwwwwwwwn' think, think"...(*still slapping myself and talking out loud*). "I know, when I get to the junction, provided the road is clear and the Sodding car doesn't blow up. I'll just turn left and do a complete circuit on the roads and get back to our road. And on approach to my house beep the horn like crazy and hope Roger comes out to my rescue!!! YES, that's what I'll do"......

The car meanwhile was now skidding along nicely! As I tried to stop the damn thing with footbrake and hand brake, it was still revving away to it's hearts content.

My heart was also revving away at 100 miles an hour as I approached the end of the road...Luckily the T Junction was clear so I was able to turn left as hoped...Oh' Bugger this 'I WANT MY MUM!'

As the car revved and screeched away, I was convinced I was going to DIE!....Gremlins are here to get me!!...I even said "SORRY" to my car for anything nasty I had ever said. It wasn't its fault in any way.... (*This last bit of conversation was said knowing no one could hear, so only you know how daft that would have sounded, OK*).

Suddenly the '*Angel Roger*' appeared in front of me sitting on a cloud with a golden glow around him. He then spoke to me in a soft voice and a sound of harp music engulfed the inside of the car.

You could always pull the Spark Plug leads off to stop the car

Arrrrrrrr, of course dummy...that's it...So with hand-brake on full I popped the bonnet, opened my door, and in a split second ran along side the car, reached under the gap of the bonnet and yanked at what I believed to be the plug leads............***BANG...AND OUCH***...as the car ran over my foot it stopped dead. *Phew.*

Now I still didn't have a mobile phone so after I regained my brain cells I walked up to a large country house, which was luckily set back from the road, so hopefully no one saw my antics on this occasion.

A few seconds after ringing the door bell, an elderly man opened the door and was kind enough to let me use his phone. Which, looking back, was a risk he was taking!! As when I explained my car had broken down, (not wanting him to know all the details), I believe I mentioned something along the lines that my car had just run over me, well, my foot!!! He must have thought I was a 'RIGHT NUTTER'!!!

I rang the house but Roger didn't answer, so I rang the pub. Guessed he may be there, or someone may be able to go and tell him I've broken down around the corner.

Time passed and about an hour later I had to face this poor old chap again in the big house and rang home again, and yes then the pub. Only to find Roger and Paul were at the pub having a pint... Mmmmmm.

Their excuse was that they hoped I'd ring back as they had already been on the roads looking for me on the way to town, and as I was not to be seen, they assumed I had got the car going.

They had turned *right*, when I had turned to the left etc, etc, etc.

They came to get me straight away. I explained everything to them and Roger got the car going and drove it back. I went with Paul and in silence we went back to the house.

We all went to the pub, and I got them a beer, and me a stiff drink! There was the usual crowd in there and we chatted away when Paul said " Sue, can I ask you a simple question but you don't have to answer it if you don't want to.......Why didn't you just turn the ignition off?"

As the penny dropped I smiled and replied calmly... *"I will take the 5th amendment on that as I do not wish to incriminate myself"*......Sodding know it all!!!! Mmmmmm.

The result of this event turned out to be the throttle cable was sticking. *Not Gremlins then! I hear you Boys chuckling!*

To Top Things Off – A Moment of Fear for All

Roger said I had to get in the car and go and get some bits he needed for a job he as doing...Mmmmmm the car....OK.

It will be fine Roger assured me. So off I set to Horsham, full of ease, as I knew nothing could go wrong!

All was well and as I approached the roundabout in Faygate I had to stop for traffic. There were road works on the approach road from Horsham, so all the traffic was in the outside lane on to the roundabout, which slowed the traffic down nicely for me.

21

As I saw an opportune moment, I put my foot down to enter on to the said roundabout.

Pulling away into the appointed place of direction. *WHOLLOP!* my foot nearly crashed through the Sodding floor!!!!

(I truly believe someone was watching over me at this point.) With out thinking, and in a split second, I rammed the car into neutral, jumped out the door, *'which I can't remember opening'* and pushed the car back off the roundabout with all my might. As the cars charged towards me, not seemingly slowing down.

You know what? There was a car behind me during all this, and the bugger just drove off with out offering to help...If it was you, all I can say is,......... 'YOU GIT'.

This time to no embarrassment I phoned from a house, where bless her heart, a little old lady even offered me a cup of tea.

For once Roger was at home and he came to collect me with a solid towing bar. Oh, I was towed once with a rope... *(No really, believe me, you just don't want to know that one. OK.)* Anyway, Roger hitched me up and off he set. He had put the car on a short towing bar, and as he sped off in what he thought was a sensible speed around the roundabout, it felt like 900miles an hour 'Shiiiiiiiiiiiiiiiiiiiiiiit'. I screamed as we were back on the road home. Blasting my horn at him to slow down.

For those who have never done this. Basically you just follow the car in front and you're not driving as if you're on a bungee rope, but set at a set distance from the car in front. Which in principle is better, but it can be very unnerving as you can't see the road ahead so clearly...Oh' blarr, blarr. That's my excuse, and I'm sticking to it.

Well, we got home safe, and as Roger diagnosed on the spot, the accelerator cable had snapped.

Thank you whoever was looking over me that day...*shame you weren't on a couple of other occasions, but hey' guess you were busy at the time!!*

Even after all this, and other adventures I had thanks to my car, I really loved my Marina but I knew I had to say 'goodbye' soon. *Sob, Sob.*

Scotland Here We Come - Our First Adventure North.

No going back to where we were. After everything was checked and double-checked we set off after rush hour the next day full of excitement, heading towards Yorkshire. This was so I could visit my cousin Keith.

I'd spent a couple of summer holidays there as a young teen, too old to go with Mum and Dad anymore, but too young to be left with my older brother. They were fab holidays. Getting up early milking the cows and haymaking, although hard work, it was fun. So it would be great to see the old place.

My Auntie Mona and Uncle Arthur had passed on many years ago, but Keith still ran the farm, and as we were going all over the place it seemed a good time to re-visit.

We got around London, and after a while I took over driving, I'd already had a drive of this throbbing tank at home, but now it seem to be driving me. On the motorways it was a dream, and as we drove in to the more countrified areas, it was lovely not to have to change gear every five minutes.

On the map I marked our route with little black arrows, and was to mark in red any area we liked.............But none so far took our eye.

Don't get me wrong, there are some lovely places. Just not for us, we didn't need to be near schools and we could travel if we needed shopping, perhaps it would make a days outing, who knows.

Things down south were just too expensive for us. Also, we would have to keep in mind how much we had to spend, and that we would need to find work at some point

Well when we got to the farm my heart broke as we went up the short lane. What a mess, the fields that the cows used to graze in were full of old broken cars and lorries. As for the farm-milking yard, the byre had fallen down and the cows had all gone.

We stayed for a cup of tea and chatted to Keith for a few hours, but I could see he was a broken man. A family had moved their mobile home onto his land. For some reason Keith had said they could live there!! Hence I believe, all the cars, and it was so sad to see the mess.

God knows what my Auntie and Uncle would think if they could have seen it. I shall always remember Keith with affection, but was glad to leave the farm as I wondered how long I could hide my tears.

On our drive we had picked up a map that showed all the campsites, so we headed off to find one. To be honest I can't remember where at the moment. But when I find our old map you will be able to see our stopping points and our route in full.

What I do remember from the map is that, if you think of the beginning of the TV program 'Dad's Army'. Those little black arrows going around by themselves, well that's what our map looked like.

If at that point Roger and I had been married, well we would have been divorced 100 times.

The car air was blue to say the least. Map reading is not my forte, but it wasn't my entire fault!!

Often, I would say to Roger "turn left", and yes you guessed it, he'd turn right!!!

But I suppose one could say it added to the adventure, plus we saw many places we may not have seen if we had a proper route.

We told a bit of a fib at campsites on the way up to Scotland. We told the site owner that someone, no names mentioned (at which point we took it in turns to take the blame) had left the tent behind.

They were very accommodating and let us sleep on site in the car. We always laid it on how tired we were.

Most people were sympathetic, and knowing the dangers of driving when one is tired, they were happy for us to stop there the night. We stayed in some beautiful places, clean and tidy. Some had cafes, and some had a pub on site. If not there was usually a country pub near by.

We would mainly park up and have egg and bacon cooked on the gas stove, and just chill out after the drive. We'd talk about the places we'd been through, and sometimes stopped to look in estate agent shop windows. Sometimes we were able to get a local paper to see houses for sale.

Almost There

We were following the map to Perth as we felt this would make a good starting point for looking for our new home. This was because we didn't know Scotland in any way whatsoever, and felt that after Perth the map indicated the land may have more countryside places. The main Route Planner map we were looking at seem to show far less major roads, so we felt it may be a good indication that there were less towns etc.. This was just what we were looking for.

After we had left the farm in Yorkshire we headed towards Edinburgh and the Forth Bridge.

As we crossed the border on the A68 from Darlington to Galashiels we let out a cry of "Hooray, we've made it!!"

We travelled through Jedburgh, and carried on around Edinburgh and went over the Bridge. We had to pay a toll to cross over. God what a nightmare. There were roadwork's going on and traffic was Hell..... But we didn't really care, we were here.

We went onto Perth and parked up there for a few hours. Looking in estate agents windows. Well, we actually went into the first one we saw and enquired about properties for sale in Scotland in general.

This was when we were told all about the Feuing Laws in Scotland, and that estate agents are also solicitors. Bloody hell, after the Feuing Laws were explained to us we could see why the agents worked with you when buying and selling a property or land. Also here in Scotland, property and land is advertised as 'Offers Over'. In these cases the owner would gather all the 'Offers' and on a set date called 'The Closing Date", all offers would be viewed. Not always the highest bidder would get it. Sometimes the sellers were looking for someone who would keep the property in a certain way. Perhaps an old family home they wished to stay the same with out any structural work done to it.

As for the Feuing Laws, well they are so long and complicated. But in brief they are laws of old, that have been handed down over centuries. For example, there may be 'Water Rights' if the house had a private water supply, which many properties do. Or Fencing, even when and if trees can be put in or removed, and rights of ways with paths. There is just so much involved that I could not explain.

But although some laws as such seem on the outside to be out of date, it can also work for you as sometime they can also protect you.

We left our address down south with the agents we went into that day, and enjoyed a lovely summer's day in Perth. It is a magnificent town, most of the building made from granite. We found this to be amazing. I mean the size of the blocks compared to the normal brickwork, and the designs of the buildings were of great interest. We'd never seen such architecture, it was truly magnificent.

After studying our faithful map, and looking for a campsite to stay at we found a place called Huntly. It was placed off centre on the map, and seemed to be set between Aberdeen to the right and Inverness further up on the coast. Inverness was also not far from Nairn where I had been on holiday with my parents as a child and would love to see again. I phoned the campsite in Huntly and booked us in. With no more ado we set off from Perth on the A93 to Braemar. I'd heard of this place before from my Dad.

Also looking at some of the houses for sale from an agent, there was a small farm house for sale with outbuildings in Blairgowrie. So this was to be the first one we ever looked at as such.

The first farm we looked at

We found the farm down a small lane off the main road. This was already something I was sad to see as the road was very busy. It looked as though there were developments in progress, and it looked as if these could possible grow into estates in years to come!

Anyway, we went up to the house and knocked on the door, and yes I know the thing to do would be to phone the agent to arrange a viewing. But we didn't have time for all that. Plus in my view if one wants to sell one's place, surely it wouldn't matter. I mean if you were busy when someone came or the place was untidy, people wouldn't mind waiting in their car for a viewing. Well, that's my view anyway, perhaps not the right one, but mine.

As it was there was no one in, so we had a peek around. We were ready with our paperwork from the agent, and some I.D. Just in case the owners came along. We weren't intrusive on their privacy, we were very careful to respect it. But as I said, if they want to sell, we just may be the ones who would buy it. So the ball was as such, in their court.

The house looked in good order, and there were plenty of outbuildings that we could use for the animals. Plus another outbuilding of good size. Roger and I grinned and both came to the same conclusion that it would make a fab play room. Maybe a bar-billiards room and a drinks bar, separate from the house. Like our very own little pub. With enough space to have guest rooms for our friends if they came to stay, giving them independence. This still had room left for garaging.

We found that there was a small cottage on the edge of the land that could be done up as a holiday cottage we could rent out to get an income.

But more importantly it would make a lovely home for my parents, or Roger's father to come and stay for holidays. Or even more of a prospect is that they may want to live with us in later years, but still want to be as independent as possible.

But as we left and drove around the area, it was clear that the surrounding area was to be highly developed. Trees had been felled in readiness, and land cleared, with marking posts in the ground. This we assumed was that houses were to be put there. It was a great shame, but with that on top of the road near by, we decided it was not for us.

So off we went to Braemar. This drive was out of the world with beautiful views, getting more and more remote as we drove. We didn't stop at Braemar on this day as we knew we would be back at some point. Plus time was getting on, and we didn't know how easy it may, or may not be, to find the camping site. Well, you must know by now about my map reading!

Plus I have come to believe the Scot's have a warped sense of humour!!!....In a funny way that is!!

I shall explain....You can be travelling for miles, following sign to, for example, "Perth", and then 'BANG', the bloody sign disappears. As if the place has vanished, and little villages and towns appear from nowhere.

Many a time I would launch the sodding map into the back of the car!!, muttering to myself " Oh bloody ha, ha. Here we go again, I guess the aliens took that place away during the night just to give me more fun, Ooooooooooooooo, bloody har-de-har!!!!"

Still on the A93 we went towards Ballater and turned off at Bridge of Gairn onto the A939 to Corgarff. This drive was hair-raising to say the least. The beauty was breath taking, but at times the narrow road would take my breath away with fear. At times the road was only really one-way even with what was called a passing point. You had to have you wits about you. There was also the added fun of blind corners. You just couldn't go too fast, but we were happy to drive at a slow pace. Even so, some people were so impatient. They overtook at the most scary of places. We just held out breath at times, and it wasn't always the youngsters. Nine out of ten were the older men.

As far as I was concerned, if they wanted to meet "Him" upstairs now, that was up to them. Me, well, I'd like to hang around a bit longer, thank you.

The mountains were so beautiful, they had funny markings on them. It sprung to my mind that it looked like a giant had smoked a joint and climbed aboard a huge lawnmower and raced it around, leaving strips in different colours, mixed of brown, green and some purple.

I nicknamed them the Val Doonican Mountains, after the well-known jumpers he wore on television years ago. I remember my Mum used to knit jumpers the same for my Dad.

The area was lovely. As the sun began to go down it sent beams of light that caught the tips of the purple heather. It seemed like a sea with waves dancing, as the wind blew down the sides of the mountains into the valley below.

We had climbed a little way up on the roads and had now started to descend. This part was a good road, but we had noticed that there was never any fencing around. Which sometimes certainly added spice to a car journey! Often we found ourselves on a blind hill, not knowing which way the road might go and felt as though the car was going to topple over the top. It was something we were to get used to on our travels.

We'd also noticed there were often tall poles at the side of the road, with reflective red markings on one side and white on the other. We assumed these were to show you the edge of the road at night because of the lack of fencing, and there usually being a big drop the other side.

So as we came to the end of the road which was a T junction we turned right to the direction of Huntly. Yes, I suppose we could have gone the other route upwards towards Aberdeen, instead of Perth, and stuck to the main roads, but where's the fun in that?

Oh God, this is beautiful here. We travelled along this road, the A944 passing through a small village, the name of which we didn't notice, as I was too busy taking in all the sights, and Roger was concentrating on the road.

Suddenly we just had to stop. We got out of the car and marvelled at where we were, and what we had just driven through. Taking a deep breath of pure clean country air in to our lungs, we both agreed this was what we were looking for. If only we could find our dream home here, or near by.

There was a river that we had been alongside for some time now and the mountains were all around us, covered in places with huge pine trees.

If an artist had painted all the trees we could now see before us, you'd be very tempted to say he'd used his artistic imagination with the colours. One just couldn't believe there were so many different shades of green in the world.

Time was now getting on and we had to tear ourselves away to continue our journey to get to the site before dark was upon us. Little did we know that at that time of year, in the summer, it didn't get dark until very late.

We drove for miles and went through some beautiful little villages, most of which consisted of only one main street with a few houses laid back along the side of it. Perhaps a small local shop, and some had a very small village school. Some even had a little pub, much to our delight. One or two seemed to have a small inn or hotel, which would have a bar.... (*Goody !!*)

In the early part of the evening we arrived at Huntly. The site owner had given me directions and for once we went straight there without the usual mystery tour of the area.

We were thankful for this as we were so tired of driving. There was so much to take in, one's brain could go into overload at any second. After explaining our predicament with the tent, we were able to stay on the site. They gave us some keys so we could use the showers and toilets on site, and the washer room had a washer and dryer which we could use.

It was heaven. The site had well kept gardens, with little areas set for caravans to park in. This meant no overcrowding, and one got privacy.

After parking up we went and had showers. (Oh what bliss!) That night it was early to bed.

Our New Friends and Huntly

As we opened our eyes we could almost hear our brains whizzing around our heads, full of excitement of the pending day. Our brains asking, "what will we find? Will we find our dream home? What are the people like here ?" etc, etc..

These thoughts were only interrupted but the sound of hunger pangs rumbling around our bellies, and the sound of movement outside on the site.

I pulled on my dressing gown, and pulling a curtain apart I could see people starting to get themselves on the move as their mornings begun. Some children were playing ball, while their respective parents we organizing their cars for the day's outings.

I didn't even notice the time as I opened the car door. But as I clambered out of the car I had the most odd feeling...!!

As I stretched my arms out I could see the other occupants of the site trying to discreetly glance over in my direction in disbelief that someone had slept in the car in the first place. So in seeing the kids eyes open wide I reduced them, and the mums and dad's, to laughter by crying out "Let me out here, I'm a GRANNY". Somewhat looking like a deranged woman with PMT. I followed up by saying in the direction of one young mum, "You think I look rough, just wait till you see the 'GRANDAD' when he appears!!!" I tell you the place was in fits.

After a morning shower and retuning to the car, a little more respectably, we set off on foot on a short walk into the town. We had been shown a short cut to the town on a path through some woods along the side of the site.

We decided to see if there was an estate agent, or if not get some local papers, then find a place to get some lunch. Time was now getting on and we were starved.

We found the little town had three estate agents in, so we got everything we could to look at and gave our details to them.

There were two banks, so I was able to get some cash out, and we saw a pub. Well, what a choice, we could (1) go back to the car and have lunch there and read the paperwork or (2) go to the pub.

Only one vote please!!!!!!

Yep, option one, out voted by a majority of TWO! So the PUB it was...Mmmm.

We saw a pub called "Cheers", and crossed the road and went in. The pub was nearly empty, due to the hour I think, about 12.30 now, and we were greeted by a middle aged man behind the bar.

He welcomed us and we ordered drinks and food, whilst holding polite conversation, then found a corner to sit at a table. The place looked clean, and looking around we could see it held lots of functions as posters were dotted around on the walls, with some wooden tables and chairs around the edge.

The chap behind the bar came over with our cutlery and bits, and noticing our paper work he sparked up a conversation with us. He introduced himself as Trevor and told us he and his wife had come up from down south a few years ago. His wife worked in the kitchens and her name was Sheena, and he said he'd get her to pop out and say "hi" later. He seemed a nice enough chap, and it was nice to be made to feel so welcome.

His wife came out after a short time, and we all chatted for a bit and we seemed to get on well with them. We became friends over the next few days as we popped in for lunches while still making a list of places to see.

As we went through the paperwork and saw something we liked the look of we marked the local area map in a red cross. Then after we'd found a few in a certain area we marked the paper work, one to three to plan a route as close as we could to view in turn.

Over the next two weeks we found some we thought were not too far away to look at.

Now something we hadn't realised is that anywhere you go here takes forever. Places may not look far on the map but with all the roads being like country lanes, it was very slow going.

Even the main roads were like this and hardly any traffic. There were of course farm vehicles on the road which slowed people down, but we weren't in any hurry. Besides we wanted to take it all in.

Some of the house adverts in the papers didn't have pictures so we never knew what to expect. On that note some we saw were just, how shall I say, "beyond our wildest nightmare"!!!

But these were soon crossed off the list with notes to suit. We found some places you walked into very carefully and crept out without daring to breath in case the bloody place fell down around our ears. These, to be fair, in some ways were advertised as derelict buildings, some suitable for conversion, but some were just the last remains of walls. It can be funny what some would call suitable for "conversion"!!

Some however were suitable in our eyes for conversion. At least there were walls in place, be it needing a lot of work. Most estate agent adverts had written on for viewing (go along to site) so there was no need to get the owners to be with us. This we found much better as one could have a real good look at the structure and surroundings.

The structure was the most important as we were to do the work ourselves. We didn't have money to throw at builders when we felt it was something we could tackle.

We'd note all we could about the building, the pros and the cons and note any questions we may have had. We would have taken into account the land and area before we even looked at the building, so had already decided the location was fine.

We found some places we liked the look of, but nothing overwhelming. We found some beautiful places and had some lovely pub lunches. Sometimes we'd have a picnic, all depended on how we felt. At the end of each day's outing we'd set back to Huntly.

Back at the site we'd lay a blanket out on the grass and down a good few beers while looking over the day's viewing.

Now the days were passing and we had to think about setting off back down south. God even the thought of going back to all that concrete made us cringe.

We had places to ponder over so we went to 'Cheers' one last time for lunch. It was a beautiful day, so we thought we may get one more outing in, but this time, just to enjoy the views.

At least now we had a good idea what you got for your money, and we'd seen a lot of the areas around Huntly up to Inverness and around the coastline back down to Aberdeen City, then criss crossing across the country and back.

Aberdeen City was amazing. It was so clean and again the architecture was out of this world. It was daunting when we first drove along the High Street trying to find a car park. We found one and spent a day in the city. So many shops. We walked down one side then back up the other. It struck me it looked like New York with all its side roads, and the building towering above you.

But we were glad to return to the countryside at the end of that day. You know what, the city is only about fifteen or so miles from Huntly, but it seemed much, much longer.

But our plans changed at the last minute. Trevor was in the pub this day and told us that if we go to Aberdeen and find the ASPC building they have huge magazines full of places for sale that cover the whole of Aberdeenshire. Plus he found out that you can use the computers in the building to view the properties online.

So off we set to the city one last time. We found the building easily and set to work. We found out the properties all have their own reference code. We found tons of places. We found we were also able to order the paper to be sent to us down south so we could go on the net when we got back.

We decided to stay just a few more days and go up the country further to view some interesting places. We went all over the place armed with maps and notepads as before. This county is full of surprises, around every bend there is such beauty. Don't get me wrong, I don't live in cloud cuckoo land. There were a few places we just wouldn't even think about.

This day we'd been out all day and thought it best to set off back to the site. Yes, you guessed it, again we got totally lost. We even landed up going down lanes that ended in dead-ends, or at some remote farm. Most embarrassing was one such lane that took us to a larger field in the middle of nowhere. And to top it off, as we turned the car round to drive out, we got stuck!!!

That's not all. As we struggled to get the car free lights came on in a farm house not far away. It lead to a scene resembling John Cleese as Basil Fawlty when he lost the plot yet again with his old car and beat the crap out of it with a branch. We pushed with all our might. As we were panicking to free the car, we could hear the local farmer coming across the field.

God, he's going to think we're young lovers looking for a spot to......you know what.!!! How would he believe us. Oh please God help us, I'll just die. I thought to myself.

Suddenly the car moved forward. "Quick" Roger yelled as he jumped in and slammed the door. I didn't need telling as I shot around and jumped in.

The car wheels were nearly smoking as we took off at high speed back down into the darkness of the night and hopefully in the right direction out of the lane. We felt like a couple of school kids as we burst into laughter when we could make out the end of the lane.

It was getting so late and we wouldn't be able to get back into the site, the barrier would be closed with the keepers in bed, so we couldn't drive in. People who arrived late would park their cars and walk in, but we were now stuffed.

As we searched for somewhere to park up off the road we went through a town called Keith. Suddenly we saw a door open to a hotel, and the lights we on. We pulled into the car park and I ran in to find someone. The hallway itself was empty, but there was someone in the bar area I could see through some massive wood and glass panelled doors.

So I ventured in, to find a pleasing smile from the barman. Asking about a room, he told me the price and that there was a room we could have.

On returning to the car I tentatively told Roger how much it was. He groaned at first, but then I pleaded as it was a soft bed for the night and there was a bar still open. Guess that did it for him, THE BAR did it!!!

We were shown to our room and then we decided that, as the bar was open, it would be a shame not to have a nightcap.

As we walked into the bar, which had been empty apart from one barman we noticed a large well dressed man at the end of the bar. He had a definite sway to him as he drank only what we believed to be a very, very, very large whisky.

We ordered drinks and offered the barman one which he accepted as he said he was due to close up soon and he would enjoy it.

At this point the chap at the bar came over and started to talk to us. Christ we couldn't understand him. Partly his accent, mainly I believe he was ratarsed.

He was truly terrible, but I suppose he was happy. He kept on insinuating that "I" should be tired and should go off to bed. I told him I was fine but he kept pushing.

Now, you should know that I don't like being told what to do. Least of all by a stranger, who was by now beginning to 'pee' me off a tad.

Then he became more forceful in his voice. As luck happened he went to the men's room, at which point we said goodnight to the barman and did a runner to our room.

We locked the door and turned the lights down. After a bit we guessed the coast was clear and settled in. We put the TV on and both had a hot shower.

We watched some old black and white movie while drinking the remainder of our drinks from the bar. After a cup of tea we must have dozed off to sleep as the next thing we knew it was seven in the morning, and we could hear movement on the landing as people must have been going down for breakfast.

After we had our breakfast we set off back to Huntly as we had to settle up at the site and say goodbye to Trevor and Sheena.

This we did and then set off back down south. We'd miss Huntly, it was a lovely little town but we felt we would be back soon.

We travelled back at a slow pace, I think we just didn't want to return there plus all that packing we still had to do.

As we drove down, the sky lost its blueness to a dullness that seemed to cover the earth like an overcoat. The further down we drove the more you could see the pollution hanging over the towns, and the air seemed to almost thicken with its choking fumes from the cars and industrial estate that would have chimneys blasting out their smoke.

More and more houses were on the horizon and the traffic becoming more aggressive as each mile passed.

We could see a big difference in the speed people drove the nearer to the south we got. Everyone was in such a hurry to get to their destination. Some of course were going to and from work but the sheer madness of some drivers, overtaking at fast speed, just to get one space ahead was just crazy to us. They would be risking others in trying to make a move that only the best driver in the world, Sterling Moss, would contemplate doing at Le Mans.

It seems to me that the most docile of people seem to suddenly think they are "Formula One" racing drivers when they get behind a wheel. And as for the "Young Pups" as I call them in their zoopped up Fiestas with what resembles a can of baked beans on the exhaust!! Well I'm saying nothing.

Anyway we drove around London and headed towards Gatwick and arrived back at our house in the early hours. We went straight in and after a cuppa we went to bed.

As I tried to get to sleep I tried to imagine I was still in Scotland, and instead of counting sheep, I imagined counting the beautiful mountains we had just left behind...............

(Didn't work. Took me sodding hours to get to sleep!)

'Oh' My God

Well as we opened our eyes to the reality of being back in our old bed it struck us how much packing we had to get done and in such a short time if the house sale was going through as fast as it should.

We gathered our brain cells together and made a start on the day's work, on what was to be the daily routine for some time to come.

As the weeks passed by we were set for another trip to Scotland. We'd found some more houses to view on the web and we're keen to see them.

I tell you what, God help anyone who says we'll move house again one day, I'll bloody shoot them!!!

Everything nailed down was slowly being taken out the house and put in the container and another container was due to be delivered the next day, the first one was now full.

We sprayed No1 on this as it was full off things we felt we would need first, tools and bits of wood, building materials/electrical wiring and stuff, some suitcase of clothes and bedding.

We got rid of a lot of things, but as I said we just didn't know what we would need.

Dudley popped over and asked if we could do with taking a caravan up to Scotland because he was selling his. So we took it off his hands and took the price of the house. The caravan was in good condition and ready to roll.

That day our friend Lindy came over to see us and how we were getting on. Lindy is like a sister to me, we'd known each other for years. So we asked if she'd fancy a holiday and come up to Scotland with us this time. She thought it a great idea and the date was set for a few days time.

Later that week Lindy stayed over a night and the next day we packed the caravan and had a sleep in the afternoon. We set off just after 8pm to avoid traffic around London and have a good start on the journey into the next day. We felt that the trip was dull until we got a fair way up country.

By daybreak we were well on the way and found a campsite in Appleby-in-Westmorland to park up for the day. We refreshed ourselves in the showers and had dinner that evening in the camp restaurant. We stayed up fairly late and chatted about what we were looking for with Lindy, as hopefully she could look at them with an outside point of view. It's too easy for one to be swept away with ideas, and not always see what others may see. So we would value her view.

When morning came we couldn't wait to continue our journey. So after another shower (not wanting to miss out on the luxury of hot water) we set off on our quest.

The car started to overheat after a couple of hours so we were concerned as to what may be wrong? So we took it easy, stopping more often than we would normally.

We went across country towards Aberdeen and around the outskirts towards Huntly. We stuck to the main roads this time as we had the caravan and didn't fancy the mountain track we took before. I'd phoned the campsite earlier to book ourselves in, and looked forward to getting there.

As we were about ten miles from Huntly the smell of hot car was getting very disconcerting. Suddenly we could smell burning and then what looked like smoke bellowed out of the front of the car! "Holly dodos. We're on fire!!", we all shouted at once. Roger pulled in like a rocket.

As the car screeched to an abrupt stop in a lay-by Lindy, Roger and myself couldn't get out quick enough as what looked like smoke bellowed out from under the bonnet.

Lindy grabbed the fire extinguisher like a real pro. As she held it ready Roger lifted the bonnet, meanwhile I grabbed the camera. Partly instinct in not wanting to miss this 'historic' moment in our travels, and partly I just did it automatically in the moment of adrenaline rush.

We hadn't realised we had pulled into where there was a side café and what people were now staring at must have looked like something from a movie. A comedy movie. We were running around like the 'Marx' brothers on speed. Plus although we were sort of laughing and yelling instructions to each other in all the panic in what seemed perfect sense to us, it must have sounded like some kind of alien language from the planet Zorb to any onlookers.

After what seemed like ages the smoke began to clear and there were no flames to be seen. Roger had told Lindy to hold off using the extinguisher until he gave her a nod. Suddenly, as we stood in silence, over the sound of our hearts pounding in our ears as the adrenaline rush began to subside, we could hear a hissing coming from the engine bay!

After a few seconds it was a great relief to hear Roger saying "PANIC OVER GIRLS, it's a pipe burst" and we all began to laugh uncontrollably. Guess it's nerves that do that.

Anyway, realising that we by now had a small audience. I turned to our viewers and gave a very large bow and declared "This performance is now ended, and I am pleased to say there will be no encore today."

I hasten to add at this there were a few giggles from folk and one man even gave a standing ovation. We all gave a slow bow to him, and I shouted "Autographs will be given later!"

Roger found it was the heater pipe that had burst so he was able to bypass the heater. We hoped it would get us to Huntly. As we needed to fill the radiator up, the owner of the café let us have some water with enough to fill a huge water container to have as standby. We had a cup of coffee while we waited for the car to cool down before setting off.

We hadn't been pushing the car engine, but continued to Huntly a lot slower than we would have, getting very paranoid at the slightest smell from the engine. We were glad to arrive at the campsite with only two stops on the way just to let the car cool off a bit.

We parked up and decided to go into the town as it was late afternoon and just get some food for the evening and, of course, some booze. We felt it was something we all needed.

As the evening came in we had got the caravan set up with Lindy's bed up by the door and Roger's and mine at the far end. Our bed had to be folded up until we went to bed as the dining table went over it and the seating was part of the bed.

We had bangers and mash for our supper that night and then played cards for a bit. After a few beers we started to laugh about the day's adventure and could see the funny side of things that had bypassed our sense of humour on the last part of the drive worrying if the car would make it to the site before spontaneously combusting

As we settled down that night part of me was tired, but part of me couldn't wait till morning to get started on the house hunt.

What would we find, what would we see, what, what, what? was flying around my head as I drifted off to sleep.

As dawn came I opened my eyes to the smell of coffee. Lindy was up and dressed ready for action. "Bloody hell Lindy, you must have been up at "the crack of a sparrows fart"!

She handed me a coffee and to my surprise gave me a cheeky kiss on the cheek and said "NO THE SODDING SPARROWS SNORING GOT TOO LOUD!!!" ....Sorry Lindy I thought to myself, knowing I was to blame. Oooooooooooooops.

First Love

We got ourselves ready for a day of searching for our future home. We packed a hamper and some hot water in a flask to make tea/coffee and set off with paperwork on places to see.

At one or two Lindy just laughed and sat in the car. Even we knew there was no way we'd even think about looking at them to buy, but Roger and I just wanted to blacken our noses.

We came across a couple that had good potential, but really the setting was wrong or there was no land to speak of.

Then after a few hours we were up near the coast. Not really where we were looking for somewhere, but who knows. We stopped in Nairn and I could remember it from when I was a child. Well, some of it. Just flashes of memories came to me at certain points along the way around the town and later along the sea front. We took a long walk along the water's edge. It was fab.

I love the sea. I have a good, loving but fearful respect for her. She, the sea, once asked me to join the mermaids below but thanks to my father coming to my rescue I was able to decline the offer as she took me in her arms and tried to lead me to her city beneath the sea's surf! I was only about five years of age then at Herne Bay. A wave came over my head and the current began to pull me under and away. But I remember it as if it was yesterday. I also remember very clearly that I was not afraid. I just remember the sound of the waves above me and my eyes being wide open looking up through the dark green sea. Then suddenly hearing my father's voice calling me and the sound of what must have been him running down the pebbled beach towards me. Then my father sweeping me up out of the water.

I must have only been a matter of feet away from my family, sitting in at the edge of the water. Playing, I mean I had arm bands on and it was, as I remember, a beautiful day with a calm sea. Guess I was very lucky.

The Skies Opened

(Getting back to our day in Nairn)

After a walk along the sea's edge we went back to the car and got the hamper out and went on to the beach for lunch. We managed to find a spot that was a little sheltered from the winds that had picked up a bit.

The skies suddenly began to gather in a strange darkness and as if by magic conjuring up a blanket of darkness that seem to be disconcertingly charging in our direction. Then down it came, I mean we didn't even have time to think much about it when the heavens opened and we had to grab our stuff and legged it back to the safety of the car.

Thunder and lighting were all around us at one point. It seemed funny at the time. As we sat in the car Lindy and I continued to drink a bottle of wine, we had earlier opened, before we were rudely interrupted by the now increasing storm. Even on a picnic I insist on wine glasses for wine not plastic ones. So there we were in the car. Now, you have to try and picture this scene as I tell it. (The capital letters are us shouting above the storm.)

In one's very best posh English lady's and gentleman's voices.

Scene 1.

Sitting in car, dripping wet and sipping wine from glasses.

Me>>>I SAY OLD GIRL LINDY-LOO...DASH IT ALL...I BELIEVE YOU'RE DILUTING YOUR WINE WITH NATURAL RAIN WATER....DOES IT IMPAIR THE FLAVOUR??? >> flash of lightning and a loud crash of thunder with rain crashing on the roof like bullets, then a waterfall down the windscreen>>>

Lindy>>>NO MY DARLING...IT SEEMS THAT THERE IS ALSO A DELICATE AROMA OF THE SEA AIR IN IT'S NOSE.... FASCINATINGLY MAKING...>> bang goes another thunder crash>> ONE FEEL QUITE AT HOME BY THE JOLLY OLD SEASIDE>>>flash, flash flash>>>

Me>>>LINDY LOO, HAVE YOU SEEN ANYTHING OF OUR OLD FRIEND ARCHIE, NOT SEEN HIM FOR AN ABSOLUTE AGE...>>>>> bang goes a whopper just above us>>>>Oooooooo crumbs...that one was close...>>>

Lindy>>>NO DARLING DON'T FANCY AN ARCHERS NOW, THE WINE'S JUST SPIFFING FOR NOW..>>>>bang crash flash bang.>>>>

Me>>>NO, NO MY DEAR I DIDN'T ASK IF YOU'D LIKE A DRINK OF ARCHERS, I ASKED>>>>>bang, flash bang>>> OH SOD THIS DARLING LET'S GET OUT OF HERE BEFORE WE, DON'T, HAVE TO WORRY ABOUT THE DRY CLEANING.!!!!!

At which point Roger was very happy to drive away from the seaside storm and get us back to reality, even if he did find our little play amusing, the storm was getting a little too close for comfort.

We decided to go back to base camp and get a hot shower before we all caught our deaths of cold. Lindy found a couple of towels in the back of the car so off we set.

Then to top it off, the car started to overheat again. Roger had been able to put a bit of pipe on the car but it really needed a new one. So the next day he would have to order one from a car parts shop in Huntly. We managed to get back without stopping, and I think if cars could speak it gave a sigh of relief as we drove in to the parking space beside the caravan.

In Nairn we had picked up some more housing papers to read that night so after our showers we sat in our jimmies having a beer while reading the papers.

There it was an ad, for a "Steading.. suitable for conversion to dwelling." And blow me down when we looked on the map it was a stone's throw from Huntly.

So with a couple of others to look at not far away, the Steading was first on our list in the morning. Plus the estate agent selling the place was in Huntly so we could get details from there. But it was odd we hadn't seen anything to do with it before. We just couldn't wait til morning and for a change I was up and about first.

Now let me remind you, if I haven't told you already my nickname is Crabbie. This is, I have to say, because I am the most crabbiest person in the mornings... So be warned anyone talks to me before I have a cup of tea..... Ok, you've been warned! ha, ha.....and if I have told you before.....well there's no excuse not to remember to stand at 50 paces before my tea....ha, ha.

A couple of others we viewed and walked (sorry ran) away from!

A New Day

This morning the sun was shining brightly in the skies and one could almost forget the storm from the day before as we stepped out of the caravan, and took a deep breath of fresh clean air into our lungs.

We didn't bother with a hamper today as we felt we would probably come back to Huntly for lunch and then decide where to go next.

We set of with Lindy reading the map for a change. I felt with relief that perhaps we'd get to the place without getting lost this time.

We drove out of the small town and headed onto a main road up towards Aberdeen then after a short drive we turn off and headed down a very narrow lane. It was a beautiful drive when suddenly I noticed a road sign which could take us to another house on our list.. So Roger said we may as well go there first.

We found a very small cottage at the top of a hill over looking more land of some kind. There were the usual sheep in fields around, and farmland with other farmhouses near by.

The cottage had planning permission for an extension to the back of the building, which, looking at it, would need something done. Or maybe not as there was only Roger and myself. But we would need to build barns for the animals and the tractors we may need to work the land in future.

We spent some time there as we needed to give the building a careful look and had to assess how much land came with it.

There seemed to plenty of land for what we would need. There would have to be water put on and electric but that would reflect in the price, seeing electric was across the road at another farm. So there was somewhere we could join on to. As for water, we would have to find out details.

The building itself was tiny as I said, and was in need of total restoration but it was in the middle of nowhere which was a big attraction to us. We agreed the place was rather small, but had potential.

We took appropriate notes before setting off to look at a steading, not far away, according to the map.

We set off looking around at all we could to get an idea of the area, which seemed good on first impressions. But we would have to look at planning for the area and all kinds of questions would have to be answered before doing anything like putting an offer in. Plus we had plenty more to see.

As we drove along the lane we could see what looked like the steading we were looking for. Roger stopped the car as we studied the pictures on the paper work to confirm that this was in fact it.

It was massive. Well with the outbuildings, it seemed to fit what we were looking for. The instructions on viewing were to 'go along to site'. This meant we didn't need to contact the owner to arrange for them to be there. As before this we preferred, as one could have a good look etc.

We parked up in a small lay-by at the entrance to the gate and walked down the small track. It was looking good. The old outbuildings were in need of much repair but there was one that could easily house a mobile home for a few years while one worked on the steading if needs must. I reckon there must be tons of spiders who found it a nice home, there were tons of webs, and every now and then Lindy or I would let out a screech as a mouse ran across our view.

Roger was taking notes on the size of the buildings and would ask us to hold the tape from time to time and we were all taking into account the state of the buildings. There was a lot to think about but at that point there seemed to be plenty of outbuildings for workshops, for farm machinery, plus there would be room to build a small living area, i.e. a granny annex of some kind if Mums and Dads decided to move up, which is something we were keeping in mind.

Now for the steading, well this was a different kettle of fish.

The outer structure was in need of a lot of work. It would have to be re-roofed for a start, and the granite work had a kind of white plaster on it. Sorry I should say there were bits left of the covering, most was on the ground were it had fallen off over the years of neglect, and the weather getting to it.

We couldn't get in the door and the windows were not much help. As I tried to see through, suddenly Lindy popped her head up right in front of my peering eyes......"SHIT," I yelled as I fell over backwards in fright...Lindy just roared with laughter as I declared she was trying to kill me off!!...COW BAG....

Bless her she'd found down at the far end there was a way in! Not joking, the whole end of the building was open. Gave a fab idea for patio window of some kind. The view was great, over looking more farms and land then up over a hill in the distance. Still just a fleeting idea at the time.

The building was just one big open void, the wall structure was the same inside as out, and any partition walls had been long since removed. It was simply a shell.

This was fine by us as we could design our own place from scratch and boy did we have some ideas running wild through our heads. Lindy came up with some great ideas, and in that moment I jokingly said she could always come and live with us. I mean she was always at our place down south, and she was like a sister to us. Bloody hell, she said she'd think about it!

I sketched the outline of the building the same as the outbuildings and with Lindy's help we measured everything. We spent a good few hours there and decided that if it was possible this was the one we would go for.

'First Love' near Huntly

We got back to the car and pondered over the views, there was one hang up. There were some electric pylons near by but far enough away from the buildings on the far side of a field not to cause any overhead interference etc. It was something you could ignore in time.

The property only had about a quarter of an acre with it, so we would be looking into buying extra land if possible, that would make it for us.

Over the next day or so we contacted the agent and the owners agreed to let us purchase an extra seven acres if we made an offer. Well we gave a verbal offer and found an agent to represent us.

This they then put in writing to the Seller, and they were pleased to except our offer. There was no 'closing date' on the property, so we were a little surprised when we were told our offer had been accepted so quickly but we weren't too bothered as we'd got it.

We went to the council offices and got the relevant form to fill in for planning. This was because it would need an architect's drawings done for the building interior, as well as water/sewage and electric.

Well we had to get back down south by now, and we still had packing to do etc., so we left it in the hands of the agent to work out....meanwhile we were already full of ideas.

We were able to leave the caravan on the site for however long we wanted, of course with a smaller pitch fee as it was not in use.

And so once again we set of back down south...

Planning and a Torn Dream

When we arrived home we had plenty to do and plenty to think about. Dudley by now was full steam ahead on removing parts from the house and clearing the garden. I'd already emptied my pond out the back and given the fish to a friend call Paul, affectionately known as 'Plonka'. I loved my pond, it wasn't very big, but we enjoyed watching the fish and the wild life it gave a home to.

Anyway not ever having taking on a project like we were going to, there was lots to find out and lots of hidden fees to deal with. We found this out when reading all the paper work involved.

We filled in all the forms (in triplicate) and I did drawings of our ideas for the 'steading conversion', if you can call it that. This was so that when we found an architect we could 'hopefully' give a clear picture of what we wanted.

I went on the net and downloaded drawings from architect books so I had an idea of what planning may need...Plus I didn't want to look a pratt. I wanted them to think we had some idea of what we were about to take on.

I did drawings of site elevations NORTH/SOUTH/EAST AND WEST as the buildings were at that time. Then elevations with the changes, this included replacement windows 'LIGHT FOR LIGHT.' This meant, according to the paperwork I had read, the windows would be replaced with the same design as the original windows, so as to keep the original look. This was also to be for the doors.

I also had an attempt at showing the interior design we had in mind, it was to be a big project, but the idea was brill. Or so we thought. The architect would have to do it properly with all the plumbing and electric things in place. Plus a septic tank and water supply.

The buildings were all to be restored on the exterior. None of this new updated look that so often loses the character of so many buildings. Don't get me wrong, modern can be great if you are in to that, but we're not. We much prefer to keep things the same and restore.

I know I mentioned the building lent itself to some kind of patio doors at the far end, but this would be made to look old fashioned some how. Plus this end if the building could not be seen from the road. But that was something to look into later.

Ok, I must admit my drawings were very basic, and you could no doubt take the Mickey at my attempt. Especially an architect, but at least I tried. I just wanted to show that we had ideas for the planning etc...oh,blar,blar blar.!!!!! you know what I'm saying.

We posted the forms to planning and awaited some news.....

Two weeks later we received a letter asking us to contact a planning officer in Huntly. So we contacted the planning and were asked to make an appointment with the officer.

We assumed this was good news and decided to beat it back up to Scotland, armed with all the drawings and information we had. We were able to see the officer the following week.

With the same routine for the care of our animals we set off, leaving Dudley free to continue with his part of the move. By now we had 3 containers with a storage company and still more to clear out.!!

We arrived the day before our appointment so we visited the steading again, just to be sure the drawings I'd done were as correct as possible. There were a couple of points I'd missed but nothing a pencil mark couldn't correct.

That night we could hardly sleep, and come morning we were on a full buzz.

As the town clock struck 10am we were asked to follow a lady up some stairs in the planning offices and led to a small room on the second floor.

A young man in his 30's introduced himself, and asked us to take a seat. He was formal in his address to us at first but freely spoken when asking questions. He had read our paper work and showed great interest in our drawings. We knew of course that if all went well we would have an architect do proper drawings and yes, I admit it, he did have a little giggle at my drawings, but he wasn't rude. He just politely said in a firm voice "you would have to submit proper ones for planning" and I think he gave a small smile as he looked over the rim of his glasses at me.

The officer said there was much to still consider but first he asked for a STRUCTURAL SURVEY REPORT.

OK this was something we knew would come up, so we agreed to get one done ASAP. We arranged to ring him as soon as we had this, and thanked him for his time.

We were out of the office in time for lunch in the pub, so as one does, we forced ourselves in the door.

Over lunch we looked in the yellow pages and found a couple of surveyors and after lunch started to ring around to find one that could do one now.

I gave them my mobile number to ring back. Then we found one that could do a survey on Monday morning. Well I mean it was now Friday, so that was great.

So we planned to go touring for the weekend, or just chill out.

Then it happened...The survey man rang back. He had bad news. He informed us that looking back at his paper work, because the name of the property rang a bell, he had in fact looked at it before.

He advised us that if we hadn't signed anything to back out now!!! The recommendation would be to pull the whole thing down and start again. The structure is deemed unsafe.!!!

At that point our own world began to crumble, so we thanked him for his advice and yes I openly admit we went to the pub. God we were so down, it felt like a kick in the guts...But we had to think, and think hard and fast for our next step.

We were able to get an appointment for the Monday to see the officer again and by then we may have thought of a plan!

We looked at all the evidence, and decided that we would take up the Gauntlet that lay at our feet and except the challenge. God help us.

We weren't stupid, we knew it was going to be hard work and also hard work to deal with planning, but we decided we just had to go for it. We'd have a mobile home to live in, and plenty of time to rebuild.

We knew we would have to have help...so here goes...

The weekend went by so quickly but we did go back to the steading and have a really hard look at the facts...Bloody Hell we must be mad. But others have done this type of thing, so I'm sure we could get advice, and go on the net. We also had some books on renovating old building etc...we kept a positive, but open view on it.

Monday arrived and we were now sitting in the planning office. The same officer studied the paper work again and asked more questions. We told him the truth about the surveyors report from before, and sat in silence as he pondered.

Then he said it. He told us he was sorry but planning just wouldn't allow it. We'd have to get consent to knock it down and rebuild it as a farm building then apply for full planning to convert it to a house.

Which, in his opinion, planning would be refused. Well, what can we say !!!! that's it.!!!over!!!!lights out!!!!

It was as if our legs had been cut off. We were able to ask what we should do about buying the building, and advised to pull out. Nothing really sank in.....just an over whelming feeling of total loss swept over us. As we stood outside the office on the street it was as if our world had collapsed.

We contacted our agent to see what we could do to get out of any contracts, if there was a way.!!!!

The Law and Hidden Costs

The laws in Scotland are very different to England, these were things we had learnt about on the net, and from our agent.

For example, if you find say, three properties that you like and want to put an offer in. Only offer on one of them at a time. Because if you put offers in on all three, and all three accept your offer, you have to buy ALL THREE..!!!! It is very important when putting an offer in on a building/house that you make sure you understand this law.

Plus some places are up for sale with 'subject to survey.' Now there are two ways you could look at this. If you've had an offer accepted 'subject to survey' and the property is not in the condition required or stated, you can withdraw your offer.

But the other side is that each time you have a survey done it is solely at your cost, which cannot be refunded, thus be sure you really want this property before going ahead. These are some of the hidden costs.

Other hidden costs....

Checking water supplies. If the property has mains water that's good but if you have a private water supply this will need testing. Or you will have to find a water source on or near your site

Water Testing; (this is to test that the water supply is not contaminated in anyway>>i.e. It is fit for human consumption etc.....This can be got over by having special filters put in to your supply. Two I know of are, one is a particle filter and the other is a UV Light. Then the water has to be retested, (more money).

If you need a septic tank put in, this again has to have tests. There has to be a 'Soak Away' test done on the land. Here a large and deep hole is dug and a certain amount of water is put in. The surveyor/tester will then asses the time it takes to 'soak away' (more money).

Mains electric, the same thing, if there is no electricity supply to the building, check where the lines are near the property. This is where a supply could be tapped off from. But keep in mind the further away, the more cost and it costs a lot (and the same for phone lines).

These are to name but a few things to keep in mind but please don't let them put you off. Just be aware of them. I hope the knowledge and the experiences we encounter will help you and perhaps save you time and money.

Two days later our agent phoned and informed us that there was a way out. Now keeping in mind that although we hadn't given a written offer our verbal one had been accepted, we were still committed as the paper work was being processed.

The solicitor/agent pointed out that the paper work for the sale of the property states in large letters 'STEADING SUITABLE FOR CONVERTION TO DWELLING'...When in fact as we found out it could not be 'Converted'...the Bloody thing would have to be PULLED DOWN and rebuilt etc

So I suppose we got out on a technicality in our favour, as it was, but it could have been far far worse and we learnt a hard lesson.

The following day we just packed up and went back down south, our hearts were sad and our spirits low, but we had to find somewhere soon, our house sale was almost through.

A Dream becomes a Reality

Back in our old and very empty house, we decided one day to have a re-look at the places we'd seen. So onto the net we went.

It was raining for a change, and this didn't really help our mood. We were very low, and as for carrying on packing, forget it today.

I know, I know, it's just that we had such high hopes, guess that's one bit of advice we can give you.

Make sure that bubble you're in doesn't get too big before it bursts.!!!! get my drift. Mmmmmmmmm

"O' POO", sorry just so low at this point. Still "Lar-de dar" as they say !!!!!

We went through them all one by one and, to be honest, we did try and look at them from other angles but they were really all in the same category, just beyond repair or the area was a definite 'no'.

Then Roger noticed an ad in the column for 'Building Plots', but it read 'Building Plot with granite building'. This sounded interesting, but most times it was just the remains of an old farm building/shed type thing. So we didn't get our hopes up.

As the screen began to reveal the advert our jaws hit the floor, surely there must be a mistake we said to each other, I was sure I'd put the correct details in...... God it's out of this world !!!!!...........

Roger said to type the info in again and make sure...........

I punched the details in again, very slowly with Roger checking each bit so we knew we were now looking at the correct item......

There in front of us was a magnificent building. A bit like a small Gothic Church, in what looked like a wood in the middle of nowhere.

A strange feeling came over us. This was it....this was our home we'd been looking for...this place was calling to us....I can't explain the tingling I felt and Roger the same. Guess you could say 'IT DID IT FOR US'..!!!!! you know "FLOATED OUR BOAT " and all those saying come to mind.

We read all about it, then printed the details off from the computer, we sat an read it over and over. Yes this was it.

We just had to have it, we knew the rules, but we then broke them.!!!!! mmmmmmmmmmmm

A very, very risky thing to do, but we had to get this building. There was something about it, I just can't explain it.

We could see there was repair work to do on the outside and roof and windows but this was the one. mmmmmmmmmmmmmm.

The advert said to contact 'The Sellers" for viewing. So we phoned them....We told them we were 99.9 percent sure we would buy it. They were English and we were able to arrange that IF we wanted to buy it we would give a deposit as Good Will...This they agreed to (keeping in mind the Scottish Laws on buying, we felt this may stand us a better chance with the sellers).   If they had any others interested, plus paper work can take ages, plus remembering our last 'Bubble Burst' etc and why.

We got a move on and arranged everything once again to drive up, but the urgency was electrifying, we couldn't get to Scotland quick enough.

When we arrived in Huntly the caravan was a blessing, we were knackered, we had stopped over and camped the night in Appleby as before but it wasn't just the drive, our brains we working overtime.

We'd travelled up around Stonehaven and across through Alford and on to Huntly this time, so were in for a shock when we set off to find the building the next day..!!!!!!

The next morning we set off along the road to STRATHCOVE, and we began to recognize the road more and more.!! We went through a place called GLENCOVE, and then passed the Glencove Arms, well need you ask!!, we'd been in this pub for lunch on our travels

A little way further we passed the spot we first parked up in months ago and wished we could find some thing near here.

Then a few miles down the road we came across a village shop which seemed funny to us all the way out here, it also had a post office. But very handy as we would find out. There was also a bank.

We had arranged to meet the owners at 2 o'clock. It was now only 1pm.

We stopped at the shop and asked directions. Just as well, the plot/building was up a side track off the main road and we would have missed it otherwise. Well in fact we did pass it once and had to back up.

Plus technically you could say we missed it once before on our first visit here, but then again we didn't know about it then.

But with the helpful directions we found the track and BOY O BOY, it was as we hoped and much better, as it came in to view through the trees (forest).

Then as we got near the top of the lane our hearts sank to the floor. We could see some other buildings near by, a few small steading conversions. We will have to look into this.....

But the draw the granite building had on us outweighed that, at the moment, as we parked the car out the front on grass a bit away.

Armed with paper work we walked over to the building. You could almost say you could hear it saying hello to us like an old friend we hadn't seen for a long, long time. It was a feeling of peace and calmness.

We stood looking at this wonderful building. It was mixed pink granite with greys and specks of black. It was a long building. If you were facing it, it was as follows...to the left was what looked like a bricked up window a gap then a window. In the centre of the building was a Dutch Front which had a door, to the left side, then another window. This frontage was slightly protruding from the main building

Then as it recessed a little there was another window, then another door. Interesting mmmmmm.

Above the central door there was a small four pained window and above that four Dove holes in a recess. This just added to its interesting character.

At the back there were four windows to be seen, it had a narrow back path or gap all along the back. There was what we thought could be a dog pen along side this..!!!

As we went to the front again we could see there would be a fair bit of pointing work to do and, as for the roof, well it would need retiling a least...Plus I forgot to mention there was a tree growing out the right-hand part of the roof. It wasn't big, but big enough to be a possible problem, we'd have to be carefully in removing it. On closer inspection we found the roots around the window and in the granite work in other frontage bits. Still can't jump the gun yet..........Lets look inside.

As we opened the door dust and crap blew up in the air, but as it settled we found ourselves in a small room with a tongued and grove partition wall. There was a ceiling with a hole in it which had a small ladder up into we assumed the roof area. A few benches lay around in disrepair.

Roger carefully climbed up and stuck his head through the hole. There was a very small window each side of the roof, and he could see there would be need to change some roof joists. It looked like kids had used it as a den.

We then went in the middle door, it was very dark inside, it didn't help the windows being of frosted glass, well the ones that weren't broken that is.

The building was called THE GENERATOR HOUSE.??? We were very mystified at why it had such a name, this ornate building with dove holes.???

On the far wall was a huge amount of fuse boxes and strange wiring.!!! Guess we would find out later. The were two huge concrete plinth, one at each end of the room, with two smaller ones in the middle of the floor.

This time the ceiling was open to the roof with only beams across the top of the walls. This led us to think of bedrooms.

We poked at the wood work and granite work to see what state they were in...By now time was getting on and we closed the doors and waited in the car for the sellers to arrive.

Shortly a couple walked up towards us from a grass lane that led from the woods along the front of the building.

We climbed out of the car to greet them. They introduced themselves as Andrew and Sylvia, and we in return introduced ourselves.

They were a lovely couple, and we chattered as they showed us around asking questions. We had to admit we had looked at it earlier and in doing so we'd like to make an offer.

However wc would like to buy some extra land with it if possible. They agreed this could be possible, but they would have to arrange this..

So that was it. The deed was done!!! So we parted ways and they walked back from whence they came. (Down in the woods somewhere!!) Guess we'll find out later. We arrange to meet them again in a few days.

To Billy or Not to Billy, that is the question?

As we left what looked like to be our future home in this glorious wooded area the car died on us at the end of the lane. We joked about it not wanting us to leave.

Roger popped the bonnet and after a bit he found what he suspected it would be, a split in the fuel line so it was taking in air.

He tried to clamp it with a make shift sheaf and ties, and we set off in hope of getting back to the site.

Off we set, fingers crossed but as we went up a hill the car started to die again…We were able to pull off the road and we came to a stop. "Sod it" Roger said, "we'll have to ring the AA."

Now I know what most of you are thinking, Roger's good with cars so why the AA. Well the fuel pipe had had it, and we were stuck in the middle of nowhere. If they could get us back to the site Roger could get the parts tomorrow from Huntly.

Luckily I was able to get a signal on my mobile phone, we'd found the line we were using didn't work very well in the mountain areas, so it was a relief it was working now.

We were able to get things sorted, and now we just had to wait…………… And wait, and wait and bloody wait.!!!!! Time was passing and we were getting cold, plus I needed the loo, which didn't help my mood.

Looking around I noticed the huge gates we were parked in front of, thought hey looked a bit grand!! Then I noticed a young blonde girl playing down the driveway in the distance. It suddenly dawned on me…."O, cryppes….Billy Connolly lives here somewhere, if this is his driveway, O.GOD, he will be bloody mad if he thinks we're autograph hunters or reporters"!!!!!

I told Roger my concern and I decided there was only one thing for it. I'd take my ID and AA card and go down and tell whoever what had happened, and why our car was stuck right outside the gate way.

Nothing to lose really, only might get told to " **** off " by Billy….Only joking in one way, reckon he'd understand if it was his place…..I hoped !!!!!

And as much as I am a great fan of his and his wife Pamela, now was not a good time to meet one's hero's as such. I was covered in oil and dirt from the day's events.

I hadn't taken into account that the girl playing was too young to be theirs at the time. Their children would have been older…

I asked the little girl if her mummy or daddy were there as I wanted to talk to them and she went to get them..

A man came around the corner and I introduced myself and showed my ID etc explaining all.

It was fine….. And of course partly to my relief it wasn't Billy but I must admit I was a little disappointed it wasn't them.

As I walked back to the car it was getting dark and the temperature was getting colder, it was also a bit spooky with all the trees rustling in the breeze.

We could hear owls over head and got the odd glimpses of bats as they whizzed past us, it was scary how close they got. You would think the bats would stay away but I reckon they were dive bombing us for fun . Wooooosh, as another sodding bat just seemed to swerve away at the last second.

As we waited for the AA the mobile rang again. The AA wanted to try and pinpoint were we were, we could only describe this roughly and hoped they could find us soon. But it came to light they were sending a van. I had to explain this would not be good as the car was an automatic and would have problems being towed. And I explained again the fuel pipe was broken beyond repair etc..

So they said they would send a pickup lorry to get us back....GREAT....

Suddenly from the darkness of the drive we could see a tall dark figure heading towards us then a huge bellowing voice called out..."YOU'VE F****** BROKEN DOWN IN MY DRIVE THEN !!!!!!"

Ok, I can forgive you for thinking it was the man himself, Billy, as we did, until this statue of a man was in view.

The man introduced himself as Iain and he gave us a welcoming hand shake followed by a well needed invite to a hot cuppa and most important for me, the loo.

It was now nearly 8 o'clock and we were beginning to wonder if the AA would ever find us. We left a large note on the car to say where we were, and Iain left his phone number on it.

We were welcomed by his wife Mary at the door of their house, which gave a warming glow in the night sky around it. It smelt of open fires and home cooking and there was a small light in the lounge area to the right hand side with a large stone floored kitchen, there were candles all around giving a wonderful atmosphere.

We were made very welcome and given hot tea and coffee. We felt like we had known them for ever, they were so easy to get on with...After a time we were offered wine and nibbles, which went down well.

After a bit longer we were laughing and joking with them, and found out about the area and all kinds of things i.e. Who was who in the area, important people to know. Like carpenters and local traders etc., it was all very informative, and of course the vino began to flow.

Mary and Iain had run their home as a B & B for years, and had a room we could use. They said as it was too late to try and get in touch with the AA again, as no doubt, they had been unable to find us

True, time had got very late, but just as Mary and Iain insisted we stayed as their guests, and the sound of a hot bath and a warm bed was calling to us the phone went.

The AA were at the gate entrance and although we were pleased in one way, we were cheesed-off to miss out on such a lovely gesture by our new friends.

We said our goodbyes and arranged that we would pop in when we were to meet the owners of the place we were looking at in a day or twos time.....

Ooooooooooooooo, as we left the house with Iain the amount of wine we'd drank hit me like a sledge hammer. The fresh mountain air just seemed like a waterfall rushing over me. Weeeeeeeeeeeeeeeeeeeeee, as my head hit the skies above.....Still we weren't having to drive.

Funny thing was the driver had been told we were going back down south so I think he was relieved when we explained we were only needing to get back to the site at Huntly.

Two days later we met Andrew and Sylvia at the Generator House and all was agreed very satisfactory all round. We also found out that the building was originally a Dove Cote which explained the dove holes, then it was used for the generators to supply the estate with electricity, hence it's name.... THE GENERATOR HOUSE.

Andrew and Sylvia left as we asked if we could have one more look around, and take measurements. They were happy for us to do this.

We had done all we needed, but as we were about to leave one of, what we assumed to be, the neighbours came along. She said we would probably be refused planning permission due to the water supply!

She wasn't what you'd call hostile, but you sensed she didn't like us being here. So we just thanked her for the information and said we would look in to it.... Can't explain it perhaps the natives aren't friendly!! We shall see.....

Now we really had to move on things back down south, the house was empty apart from our bed, and the house was now Dudley's in full. We had the last bits to empty from the workshop where we had unloaded the last house things into, before we left to get the house clear for him to get on. It was kind of him to help us out. We were going to stay with our friend Paul (Plonka) for a while. The chickens and geese were already there and he was feeding them at the moment for us, there were just the two cats at our place.

We arranged for the agents to contact each other etc, and do their thing. Then seeing Mary and Iain again and telling them, we were persuaded to stay the night with them. It was great. We also found out that the people in the house next to the building we were now buying had been there a long time. Perhaps they didn't want anymore neighbours.

Anyway the next day we went back to the caravan site and arranged to store the caravan there until whenever.

Well this was it...we'd done it...we had our future home......God help us, now the work begins..

Time to Leave the South

Back at our old place we spent the next few weeks going back and forwards to Plonka's but we were itching to get to Scotland, and were uneasy all the time.

The summer months were now over and in the distant past, it was taking so long for the sale to go through. We were constantly being told "any day now" but it was now November !!!!

We contacted Andrew and Sylvia and we arranged that we could come up before the sale of the property had gone through and start to (make safe) the building i.e. block up the window and tidy up.

And do the tidying of the grounds around the building etc. it was over grown, and rocks everywhere to be moved out of the way..

We arranged with them that we could live in the caravan on site, this would allow us to continue as much as possible. It would also help if we were able to get the tree out of the roof and do some makeshift repairs before the winter snow set in. As I said it was now November, we didn't know when the Scottish winter set in.

December arrived and we decided to make the move. Even now I get so upset when I think back to just before Christmas when we left our Mums and Dads and families behind and close friends. We just couldn't wait till after Christmas in case bad weather set in, and of course we had to collect the caravan and set it up on site.

If you look at the photos I hope to have in the book at this point you will see that we looked like "Billy Smarts Circus" as we drove up to Scotland. Actually we were lucky not to be stopped by the 'old Bill', we were loaded up so much. You couldn't have squeezed a mouse in the car, mind you in saying that you'd have been hard pushed to find a mouse willing to go in there. I mean in the back, something resembling a three stories high hotel, were the geese and chickens in their travel containers and in the space left near the front seats, were our two cats in the baskets, facing the front of course, so they could see out on the long journey ahead.

We left at about 9pm and as dawn broke we were in Scotland, we had been sticking to about 40/50 all the way. We took turns at driving, and stopped every 100 miles or so for a stretch of legs and check of the animals.

We got plenty of 'Honks' from cars as they past waving and giving a thumbs up!!!! Some were clearly students moving base. They cheered and waved. It was quite good fun seeing them smiling at us in a way of wishing us good luck I suppose. They must have thought NUTTERS!!!!!

As we approached Alford the skies were getting dark so we headed straight to the Estate. We would get the caravan the next day. We had to unload the animals and set the trailer in place first.

Since Perth we had been very tired. There was no way we could park the car with the trailer left unattended if we stayed at a Holiday Inn, plus the animals. We had let the cats out on harnesses on the journey, but you could tell they'd had enough by now.

Now I'd been videoing the journey and at this point I put it on to say... "I am not recording the view here, but would like to make it very clear it's to warn of the PEUWwwwww. Warning, don't travel in a car with cats for toooooooo long without a GAS MASK", one of them had wind, !!!!! PHEWwwwwww

The geese and chicken were fine in that regard. Because we covered their (hotel) in a sheet they thought it was dusk time, so they just settled down as if ready for bed until we uncovered them on our stops. They had plenty of fresh air as we had the two back windows ajar all the way, (just wish we did at that moment!!!!!).

After we parked up outside the house we put newspaper in the holes in the windows and put the animals in the left hand area with corn and water for the night.

We set up in the other side!!!!! We cleared the floor and put the frame tent up with the blow-up camping mattress inside, it just fitted. We got the cats in and let them free. We had a cat tray we left in the corner. First they wouldn't come out, and then the little sods use a corner full of leaves we had swept up for a pee. 'O' thanks girls...!! We gave them some food while we had a cup of tea done on our little gas burner. We also had a Grand Feast !!! A pot noodle.. Which was great fun as we couldn't even find a spoon. Have you ever tried eating one of these things sharing a ruler ????.. It's different.!!!!! but don't get me wrong we like pot noodle there fine.

We were so tired and now it was pitch black outside, although it was only about 5.30pm, so we put a note on the other door saying not to open because of the animals inside and we went to bed.

We had Artic sleeping bags and we put thermal jammies on. I kept my hat on as I had a stinker of a cold. We must have dozed of quickly, next thing we heard was a car coming up the track, then car doors going.

It was late and we gathered it was one of the neighbours. Was this a sign of things to come I wondered to myself!! Mmmmmmmm.

Now, just a small tactical detail, but a bit private. As for going outside for a pee during the night, I confess I took one look at how dark it was and "pee'd" in a bucket indoors. Sorry but that's the truth of it. But I won't tell if you don't!!!!

The one other disturbance that night was at about 2 am we heard what we thought was someone going into the animals in the next room. Roger jumped out of bed, got the torch, and ran to investigate.

As it was it was only the geese flapping there wings, it just sounded as if the door was being opened. But all was well, be it apart from our heartbeats.

First night camping in the house

First snow

Gooooooooood Mooooooooooorning Scotland

(Picture Robin Williams from the film Vietnam shouting this)

Now we had no idea that living here could mean WAR at this time but there was a sense of hostile activity about to unfold over the coming weeks as you will see.

The day was fresh and you could almost smell snow in the air, if you get my meaning. As one inhaled the fresh unpolluted air, it tickled the inside of your nose like champagne bubbles. And I noticed for the first time, that God must have been doing some of his artistic work over night with his magic paint brush. As the trees were glistening with gold and magnificent autumn colours.

With a sprinkling of diamonds dropping from the tree branches as Jack Frost's art was being slowly melted by the rising morning sunbeams. I could have been content just to stay looking at this beauty all day, but alas we had to go and collect the caravan from Huntly......This was to be our home/accommodation for some time to come.

We left the birds in the building, with the note not to open the door and wrote on it that we would be back soon!! We put the cats in their baskets and set off to get shopping and animal feed, then the caravan.

We arrived in Huntly for an early lunch in the pub and were pleased to meet Trevor and his wife again, telling them the news we were here to stay now.....

After doing all we needed we got back to the Estate in good time. After about 2 bloody hours of pushing and shoving we got the caravan in place.

We had also been able to arrange a PORT-A-LOO to be delivered the next day. Trevor told us where the local firm was in the town for that kind of thing.

Queue the music for Dr Who

I spent the rest of the day setting up the bed in the caravan and putting the supplies away before darkness fell. We put the gas fire on and it soon took the chill out, this was flued out side. So there were no real fumes.

While I did this Roger had moved the trailer contents into the building/house. You know it's difficult to remember whether to call it a building or a house. I mean it is a building now, but will be a house, so you'll just have to forgive what ever I call it....ok...And at the end of the day it's 'OUR HOME'

Roger set the trailer up behind the caravan out of sight and put the small generator in it ready to wire up to the building first thing. This was to be a God send that we managed to bring along, with strip lights to hang in doors. There was no electricity in the building at the moment.

There was however water. This was a blue water pipe just in the entrance of the land. This was our water supply and Roger was able to connect some more water pipe and he laid across to the building, and fitted a tap etc. He knew this had to be done so he made sure we brought some with us.

The next few days I would be busy patching up windows with glazing we had brought along, with Roger fitting lighting and doing the wiring to suit. And sweeping all the debris out of the house.

The weather was in our favour at the moment, but the first snow had arrived!!! Just a sprinkling cover the land but enough to remind us what it was.

We hadn't seen 'hide nor hair' of any of the neighbours, but we often heard them going in and out in their cars!!

Well it was the day we were to try and remove the tree from the roof, and make repairs.

Roger got the ladders ready and started to remove dead leaves etc and clear away tiles, passing them to me below. Now Roger you must know hates heights so this was as far up as he was happy at for now. He would work himself up as he went along. Slowly but surely he started to uncover the roots and remove some lower branches.

Tree in the roof!

Santa Claus
'Does he bring gifts of joy, Or a Bundle of Trouble'

As we were doing all this, a car came up and parked just outside the entrance to our land. We watched in amazement at, what I can only describe as a very large version of Santa Claus, peel himself out of the car. He had a stern face as he proceeded to come towards us, (fully expected as scene from the film Miracle on 34th street at that point.... But this man was not in Red!!) Oh and of course there should have been Reindeer instead of a car.... Well that was first impressions, and they should never count.

We could see at a glance it was no one we knew, who was this tall and rounded man?? What did he want???? Perhaps he'd come to look at the place, as we had been informed that the building would still be in the property papers until contracts were complete. So who knows who it is? Mmmmmmmmmmmm?

As he arrive at where we were, he introduced himself as the Local Councillor, and we in return introduces ourselves.

He then asked "Do you really know what your taking on??" in an abrupt voice. Ooooooooooooooops, I could hear by his voice this was trouble !!!! and Roger felt the same hostility in his voice that I had!!!

Roger's reply was firm but polite in saying " Yes, we we're fully aware, thank you. Who are you again please.???"

The gentleman then said "You know of course, you will never get planning permission don't you "

Well,. I'm sorry but that just got my back up.!! His hole tone of voice was so ....Bloody POMPOUS and OUT RIGHT RUDE, as far as I was concerned, and I could see Roger biting his words.

The man then just left and drove away...and left us 'peed off'....but we would hear from him again.....

Anyway we took turns in clearing the roof of roots, and then we tied some rope around the tree..

As I posed on the ladder for Roger to take some film I called out "eat you heart out Alan Titchmarsh I've got my own roof garden!!!" then I climbed down and put the other end of the rope around my large waist so I could have one of my hands free to video this momentous moment.

1, 2, 3 HEAVE, 1, 2, 3 HEAVE, 1, 2, 3 HEAVE .....again and again then wooooooooooooosh, was the sound I heard in my ears as I was bungeed above the snow to fall slap on my ass!!!

Roger just fell about laughing as I sat covered in snow from the fallout from my impression of a cannon ball let loose. Oh, har-de-bloody-har is all

I could say sarcastically, before assessing there were no broken bones, and could see the funny side of things!!!

Anyway the tree was out not broken. We had found out it was a Rowan Tree and it was bad luck to cut them down i.e. you get cursed....so we planted it in the garden. And I openly admit I begged it's forgiveness in having to move it, and hoped it understood. I said it would be far better here in the sunshine. Blar, blar, blar and said we could then see its true beauty. No I haven't lost it, I'm just respecting the tails of old...I try to respect folk laws and saying....plus one just never knows!!!!!

The days passed and the weather got worse. I'd found that if I stood on a large lump of granite in the what was top be garden area I was able to get a signal on my mobile, just long enough to let my Mum and Dad know we are ok, at that was it. But by now it was damn cold standing out there in the snow...but I did phone as much as I could.

Now, if you can remember we ordered a PORT-A-LOO, well it hadn't arrived yet, so I rang the company. The company thought we had ordered it for this week, not the following day of our arrival. So they were sending one today. We been lucky enough to have the Chemical Loo in the caravan so far

A pickup truck came up our drive about lunch time with what looked like a Tardis in the back, and parked up outside the building.

The men unloaded it and put it on the ground area in front, but away from the building. Well after they left we decided there was no way it could stay there. I mean every time we went to it people would see you...plus it was not the type of thing you wanted on view in your so called garden!!!

We put some scaffold plank down to help us push it across the ground, bloody hell we were getting really stressed pushing and shoving the thing. It was surprisingly heavy and clumsy to move, tempers were getting up, but we managed to get it around the side of the building out of sight, and tied it down before filling it with water.

The Winds of Change!

When dawn arrived this day and we awoke in the caravan, there was a sense of unease in the air around us, all we could hear was the roar of the wind howling around us. As I pulled the curtain to one side, and wiped away a small porthole of condensation from the bedside window, I looked in horror at tornado in its early stages.

I know now that this was nothing to what was to come and to us it seemed far worse, as we'd never seen a snow storm before. It may have even been nothing to talk about to a Scot as they see it all the time.

But I can assure you that, at this exact moment in time sitting on the bed in my jammies, if I'd had my pants on' what I was seeing from the window was enough to scare the pants off me.

Suddenly the caravan shook !!!!!!!!!!!!!!   I froze for a second and then heard Roger pipe up as he was making a cup of tea.. "DID THE EARTH MOVE FOR YOU TOO..!!!!!"......

At that we both looked out the back window to see a birch tree had come down along side the caravan, just missing us...."Bloody hell, Roger, that was close...and no the earth didn't move.!!!!ha,ha,", was my uneasy reply as we looked at the tree.

In some what of a hurry we got dressed, well, I mean to say, if a tree hit the caravan we didn't want to be in our jammies.

There was no let up in the winds as it began to shake the caravan about and you were hard pushed to see two foot out the window as the snow swirled around.

At one rare moment of ease, it was as if the snow was being drawn up into the skies above into a kind of 'Black Hole', a huge vortex high above the trees only to be spat out back to earth moments later as if from nowhere, leaving a fresh heavy pile of snow that seemed to be only waiting its turn to be taken up again and again as the storm increased its anger on the earth.

'Mother Nature' can be such a wonderful and beautiful thing but she can also be your killer if she is not respected of misused. And I suppose that as we understand 'Mother Nature' to be a women, 'well like myself and all women, we do have our off days!!!!

But boy 'o' boy has she got 'PMT' to-day, she's really making it know that she has the hump with things today.

You know I can't help but think we've upset the some of the neighbours in some way. I mean when we have seen them, we've always said hello and been polite. Yet as the hours passed and there was no sign of the winds easing, there was no indication that they may wonder if we were ok in the caravan.

Don't get me wrong, I didn't expect them to come over every five seconds to see how we were getting on. But in this bad weather, if it had been the other way around, I would have been over ages ago to see if people we ok, and offered a place of shelter and a hot cup of tea. Even if only just the once, you know what I mean, you're not interfering or being nosy, it's just to be neighbourly but I guess that there's 'nothing as strange as folk'!!!

All we could do was sit and wait for the storm to pass and in time the wind eased enough for us to go and see to the animals, and let the cats out for a much needed pee, etc.

We got our coats, boots, hats and scarves on and stepped out looking like something for a Star Wars film as if about to go into battle. Battle it was, as we took our first steps out on to the crisp white snow, one felt as if you were the first man on the moon leaving ones foot prints. But the difference being that a few seconds later the snow covered them, leaving no trace that man had in fact even been there at all.

Later on in the afternoon Mary and Iain came up to see us and very kindly invited us to stay at theirs for Christmas. I must confess that I was relieved not to have to think of Christmas dinner any longer.

I had tins of Turkey, Ham, Veg and Spuds that I was going to cook up, and make some kind of stuffing and a ready cooked Christmas pud, but they weren't going to be the same as a good old home cooked Christmas Dinner with all the trimmings........in time when the electric is on in the house we will get a small oven and microwave from a charity shop but until then I only have the two gas rings in the caravan. It's not that I can't cook, in fact I've been told I'm very good and artistic, I've been cheffing for many years in pubs.

Sorry I'll rephrase that, I'm not a chef, I'm a cook. If I work with a chef I do things his or her way and give input when asked....but I do confess that I break all the rules, I mean I know you should have red wine with red meat and white wine with fish etc., etc., etc. but I my view, where is it written in Law that this must be!!!!

I feel that when giving a dinner party one should put red and white wine on the table, and let your guests choose what they desire. I feel that if you have a favourite wine, then that will enhance your enjoyment of the meal you have before you. And I have no qualms if anyone wished to have a beer, it's what ever they enjoy. There must be nothing worse that having to drink wine, if you don't like it, so have a damn beer and to hell with the rules.

Ok in saying that, sometimes wine is better for the pallet with some foods, but that is your own choice......JUST DON'T LET THE CHEF SEE....!!!!!!!!!!!!

Over the years in the past Roger and I had always gone to my mother and father's for Christmas and then Roger's dad would come to us, or we'd go to his but this year was not to be. Oh how I was missing them, my heart was bursting with sadness as I thought of them back down south, I wished I could wave a magic wand and have all our family here.....but I guess the pain would ease in time, we're not in Australia... (I kept thinking to myself we will see them again soon, but it still hurts to this day.)

Anyway, with cats and all, we had a great time down at Mary and Iain with their kids and Mary's mother who lives with them. They extended our invite on and off over the next few weeks for New Year, and we'd pop back to feed the geese and chickens each day and do odd bit around the place when we could.

We made one very Big mistake in all this...!!!!....not knowing what was what when it came to the caravan we left the fire turned off. When we came back to the thing it was frozen solid.

We managed to get the door open, and it was so cold and damp the water taps had icicles hanging from them and the windows had ice around the rubbers.

And to add insult to injury, the wine and beer was as frozen as it could get sitting in a box under our now very damp feeling bed

As for the 'Port-a-Loo', WELL, one just learned to scream silently in one's head before being unable to hold it off.

We lit the fire, and opened the bedding to warm up and went into the house, there was nothing we could do but get on with it. We were warm enough as we had to tidy the animals area and we had tons to keep us busy. So no sitting around for us, besides you'd freeze if you stood still for too long!!!!!!!

Every now and then I'd go to the caravan and change the cloths we had put around the bottom of the windows to soak up the water now collecting, and replace it with dry. Then as the day passed we were able to wipe the windows as dry as we could. The bed soon warmed up and I put hot water bottles in it. We'd been lucky enough that over the years we had got hold of earthenware hot water bottles, they really were a Godsend, and with the knitted covers my mother had made us they were to keep us cosy in bed.

Shoot the Messenger!!!

The days passed and we settled back into the work, and we took tons of photos as we went along, perhaps this was to one day let the kids see what nutters we were on the one part !!! Also to show our grand children what can be done if you put your mind to some thing etc.

But also I always had in mind to do this book and as I said before, if it helps someone else by showing them what we learned along the way that's good. Show people you don't always have to go to the big companies for parts....go to local people, and go to the auctions etc, every penny counts.

After the New Year we went to Huntly and did some shopping, and met up with Trevor and Sheena in the pub at lunch time. We had tons to talk about, it was as if we'd known them all our lives, they are a really nice family.

We stocked up on corn and hay for the animals, and shopping before heading back home and by luck the local pub was open!!!!

Now, the pub was owned by a great couple called Peter and Kim, they were a fab couple and an absolute scream. After they had finished food for the evening they would join staff and punters in the bar. Peter would often burst into song later on in the night and we'd all join in with the fun. You were always made to feel at home. The food was out of this world, and the 'ambiance' was great.

A Little Note ... We've met some really great people there, who over the years have become good friends. There was a lady who worked there called Mo, she's just fine, very funny, and she and her other half Hughie are some of our closest friends to this day.

We stayed for a beer this evening, but left early to get the shopping in and the weather again looked like snow.

When we arrived back we found a note stuck to the caravan door!!!!!!!!

It was a note saying to, "stop all work on the grounds around the house", and that we needed 'Planning Permission' to have the caravan there, followed by a contact number for councillor!!!! Oh Yes, it was the same councillor we had met before! himself again! Now what!!!

The next day I rang the councillor and asked what he was on about.?!?!

He told us what was meant by the note. He claimed we could not do any work on the (garden/driveway area) and that we needed planning permission to have our caravan there!!

I had however double checked with our now architect, who in turn doubled checked with a member of the planning/council.

Come on now!!!!! do you really think we hadn't looked in to this!!!

I mean with a set up like we were possibly going to have for at least a year, it made sense to check first.

So I was able to tell the councillor to check his facts etc
Number 1   The garden area does not need permission from planning.
Number 2   The caravan was a 16 foot touring caravan and also did 'Not' need planning, plus we had the consent of the owners to park it there.

I also added that we had a Port-a-Loo on site that is emptied each week...so I then "Thanked" if that the right word (O'ooooooooo) him for bringing this all to our notice. Sodding bloke is getting on my tits already, was this a sign of thing to come from him? Mmmmmmmmmmmmmm.

We then settled in to what we hoped to be a peaceful renovation of our future home........

Let there be Light.

We had a great time removing the granite and bricks from the window that had been blocked in years before.

It was hard work and some of the granite blocks were huge, heavy or what....we borrowed a small digger with a bucket to help lift them down.

The granite work was ok to work with, but out hands began to suffer with dryness, oh, and of course the knocks they got along the way, I was always in the wars in that regard.

You know what really bugs me beyond words sometimes. WHY 'O' WHY, does it seem that if you have a sore finger, hand or foot it always seems that the lump of granite..(or whatever) lands on that part.....

Just as well I wasn't one of those ladies who had manicured nails, there was just nothing left, and the skin was so sore around my fingers. I wore gloves when I could, and used cream on them but it was difficult.

On the one part you wanted to keep your hands looking reasonable, and keep them from getting sore. Yet, if you used too much cream to keep them soft, your hands were too soft for this type of hard work

The granite work around the window was not damaged, just some pointing to re-do, and cleaning of the old cement.

We put a cut out of ply wood in to fill the hole, and an old blanket we had got from the charity shop nailed inside to stop any drafts.

Hopefully we would be able to find a local carpenter to make the windows later in the year. We still have to wait for the planning and building warrants to be done.

But our main work was to get the roof done before winter returned, and the months were flying by.

We were also hoping that Lindy would come up for Christmas, as I said she was like a sister to me, and we both missed her very much.

So we hoped that at least the roof would be on and a bit warmer inside the building. I mean, once the roof is on, we can get the chimney made and get a fire in the place.

The one heavy thing we did bring (it was an absolute must, on our 'first needed' list) was our Log Burner....and we would need it.

It would be a God send to get the building above its dampness as soon as possible. Plus the house would be heated by this in future. We would also have our Oil Raeburn in the kitchen for cooking and heating the water.

Cancel Dick Van Dyke.
There'll be No Need for a Chimney Sweep Now!!

We got very disappointing news from our architect today. We had put plans in to build a granite chimney at the end of the house.

All in keeping with the existing building as far as looks could be. We felt it would be the only addition to the building, and it would not look out of place i.e. crofts and such like had chimneys at the ends.

Well, planning was saying "NO" to this....... You know what, !!!! The Crazy planning wouldn't allow the above because they felt it changed the look of the building ?????

YET, they wanted us to put TWO of these, (*the only way I can describe these*) stainless steel MacDonald Chimneys....sticking out the roof..

We did try to get them to see reason, but to no avail.....

It's beyond us. I just can't believe the sense of it... Well, there is none.....

One thing was for sure though....We'd paint them black or a very dark grey somehow... We didn't want to look at them sticking out like sore thumbs.

Meeting Frank

As the weeks passed we were able to remove the wooded partition in the house, this we did very carefully as it was 'tongued and grooved' old pine. We also took the remains of the ceiling out of the side that we'd spent our first night in the tent.

Cleaning off all the dust and cobwebs, we hoped to use it again in the house, or if it was past it, we could use it to make a shed for the animals.

We had plans to do the inside of the house like an old wooden lodge of some kind, with wood panels etc of some kind, we weren't sure how as yet, but the idea was there.

So anything we may be able to recycle would in turn save us money. As you will gather we'll reuse all kinds of things. Things that some people would just chuck out, we grab, sometimes much to their amusement.

The thing is regarding this, we have always been the same, hence all the containers full of odd thing we hoped to re-use at some time of other. This can sometimes be a pain in the butt, because we find it hard to pass a skip without having a nose, but we have also found some fab stuff, so it works both ways.

We put some scaffolding up indoors and I started to clean out any loose pointing around the walls, while Roger attacked the wall and window area where the tree roots had driven themselves well into the pointing around the granite blocks. He also had to make the roof leak proof where the tree has grown on it for so many years. The damage was really bad, and Roger had to remove huge lumps of granite so he could get to the roots as much as possible. He had a strong mix of root killer that he pored down everywhere he could.

Tree roots growing in the walls of the house went everywhere.

On one corner he began to remove a huge lump of granite. He put a support under the top line of the wall, and slowly edged this limb out. As he did this it suddenly slipped and we then realised it was much larger than we first thought. Next thing, Roger was stuck!!!!!

He got this granite to slide on to a scaffold plank, but even though the plank was strapped down it moved, and Roger was left holding this ton of stone on his own. There was nothing I could do before he 'Very gracefully fell on his Arse', with the granite wedging itself on the scaffolding and his leg. The bar even bent. We'd have been in the murky if Roger had broken his leg up here, the nearest Hospital was Huntly.

When I say 'luckily' he only had some nasty bruises, I only mean how lucky he was but I know they must have hurt like hell.

It slowed him down a bit for a few days, but he kept going, bless him. I would often write to Mum and Dad, but I never told them of any upsets or bad things that happened. We didn't want to worry them, but I know they didn't think it was all roses. When I was on the phone to them I was always cheerful to them, even if sometime I just felt I needed a hug from them, hearing their voices picked me up.

Don't misunderstand me, I was 100 percent in love with what we were doing, and very much in love with Roger, I just missed Mum and Dad, even at my age.

The top of the walls had to be cleared out, they where in need of big repair. The wood joists went across the roof area and rested on the walls, and between these the granite had lost most of the lime mortar and it was like dust or sand. As I cleared this away I had to remove tons of small granite stone and save it to rebuild this later. We would have to rebuild the granite then put a plastic membrane on top for the joists to sit on to stop water getting to the wood.

We treated the end of the wood with Cuprinol, in preparation for later. God what a mess it made.

We kept on with this for weeks, each day getting a bit more done and in time we finished stage one. It was a messy job and you had to wear a mask because of the dust. God knows what may lurk in the particles after all these years.

By now the animals had ventured out of the house and seemed to stay nearby, so it left us room to carry on indoors without upsetting them. However the cats seemed to have cottoned on to staying in the caravan, where it was nice and warm compared to the snowy outdoors. Something of a shock to them the snow was, they'd never seen snow.

Now all this time our Architect had been doing her stuff and we were often at her place going through things. She had given us plenty to work on as regards a list of things that must be done, i.e. surveys, drainage tests, water tests etc.

We'd also been given a phone number of a man called Frank Taylor, he did ground work with his diggers, and was the man to see about a water supply pipe to the house.

I contacted him and arrange for him to pop by at some point, which he did the very next day.

A tractor came up the drive, I think it was a Friday, I'm not sure. Anyway this strapping man came over and introduced himself as Frank. Yep he was our man.

We told him what we needed, and he was able to do the work when we were ready. He seemed a nice chap, and he was able to advise us on the work that was going to be done, and explain the 'Where's and Why's 'etc.

As he was talking to us another van arrived, and this was to be his son Robert, he helped his father in his work and on their farm, a few miles down the road.

It was so funny watching Roger's face as Frank was explaining things to his son!!! Roger just couldn't understand them, the Scottish accent was too strong. I however found I could understand them, just the odd word miffed me, and that was usually a Scottish saying or phrase I didn't get. But we would learn in time.....

Frank must have said something to Roger, he just looked blank shaking his head them smiled at Frank. I smiled and brushed my hand over my head to indicate that what ever he had just said, went over Roger.!!!!

Frank and Robert burst in to laughter, then frank slowly said it again, and Roger got it. Bless.....

Most of the Scots we had met were easy to understand, but one or two....Well one just hoped you laughed at the right point........But it became easier...And Frank always seems to slow his words to us. Or it could be that over these next few months we sussed it.

Months passed and we were getting on well in the house. Every second we had we just worked and worked. It was all preparation on the walls and wood work. There were thousands of nails in the beams we had to get out.

In the centre of the house there were about five rotten beams that would have to be replaced but we decided to remove them and have it open plan upstairs, with a landing between the two bedrooms we had decided would be there.....i.e.. One each end of the house, about 15 foot by 15 foot each, with a 10 foot landing between in the centre of the house.

At this point we were going to have a spiral staircase in the opening as you went in the front door

In the centre part of the house this went up into the 'sticky out' bit where the Dove holes were, this gave plenty of head room as the apex of the roof was in a more open area.

The thing was because the "Building" had never been lived in as a house, it was classed as a "NEW BUILD ', not a conversion. So we have all New Building Reg's to go by. This meant the spiral stairs were going to take up so much of the ground area, so we may have to re-think this as a later date.

Each day seemed to be getting longer now, but our eyes were getting strained as we had to us the strip lights run by the gennie in the house most of the time, so it always seemed so bright when we stepped outside.

One day Frank popped in to see how we were getting on. We were in a bit of a spot really and were unable to tell him a time when he could start work for us!!!!!

You see the thing was that we **still** didn't own the place!!!!!! We kept being told any day now, but it was just not happening...The solicitors were trying to sort out the land area at the back that we were going to buy with the building......We just had to wait...We had given our solicitor the money for the house and land to keep in their trust until all went through....Two reasons for this..(1) was to reassure the sellers that we would not back out....although by Scottish Law we were "Bound " to buy...and (2) at least that way we knew what money we had in the bank was all we had...i.e. there was no chance of dipping into the money for the property etc..

The still owners Andrew and Sylvia were really great about it....They were happy for us to carry on with the work....And by now the garden area was begging to take shape....

When we saw them a day of two later they agreed to let Frank lay a drive way up to and around the front of the building. It was getting hard to drive across the rough land at the front and we all felt it would tidy the place up..

We rang Frank, and he and Robert were over the next day, and made a grand job of a driveway for us. Frank, talking to Roger over the next couple of hours, found out that Roger was good on mechanics etc, and asked if Roger would have a look at one of his diggers. So we arranged to go to their farm the following day.

A Family Welcome by All

We arrived at the farm the next day at about 11.30am and were met by Frank, who took us to an open barn and showed us his tractor. He explained all to Roger, and at this point we met his wife Betty as she had come to tell Frank he had a phone call to see someone later, or something like that anyway.

Betty was a lovely lady, what Scots would say 'Bonnie' with a smiley face and rosy cheeks from the cold winds of the day, she invited us up to the house for a cup of tea later on.

To Catch a Fly!!

After about half an hour passed and Frank had to go to the house for something, and then Betty appeared and called down. "COME AND CATCH A FLY"!!!!!!!!!!!

We weren't sure if we heard right!!!!!!!! But we assumed there was a big ' BEE ' or ' WASP' in the house that Frank needed help in getting out ?????

So we dashed up to the house. What pratts we felt when we found out that the saying "TO CATCH A FLY " means to have a cup of tea and food etc.. NOT to chase the winged species. Betty made us so welcome, and as

73

we sat talking to her and Frank, Robert arrived to have his lunch as well.

'Bang'

Over the next few weeks we met Frankie, their other son, and Heather, who was one of three sisters in the family. They all made us very welcome, it made a big difference having them around. It was as if we had a new world beginning, new friendships forming....And we were to find out over the years how much they were able to help us.

One such time was when Roger, myself and our friends son Struan had been digging out behind the building, where the ground was full of rubble and built up dirt. We had moved much when Frank arrived.. He saw what we were doing and said it would be quicker to use his digger.....Well, I for one wasn't going to argue with that....So Frank began to clear it away.

We carried on in the house, then Frank appeared in the doorway looking a bit stressed!!!!!!!!

Frank said we had a bit of a problem!!!! He'd gone throw our power line, but he could see we had the gennie going for our lighting, so he was even more confused?????

Frank knew we had no electricity to the building, as it was originally the Generator house that building were sticking up inside, and we all knew they were dead because we'd removed all the iron work and fuse boxes weeks ago.....!!!!!

Yet one hell of a Flash had arced at the back on our building, thus making poor Frank jump just a tad out of his seat.

On looking at the ground out the back it could be seen that there was the old original thick electric cable, then a joining box of some kind, then new cable which we found led to next door. We think....

Bugger, that's all we need............Yet this cable was right next to the house with only rubble and dirt chucked over it. It was not laid properly in my view and there was no black and yellow stripped tape, or any kind of warning to say it was there..

Frank rang the Hydro people, and they sent an emergency van out to our place. Well, the guy was very surprised to see the cable there and the way it was laid etc...

I tell you, watching him fix this wire was something else....The wire was 'ALIVE' when he worked on it, just standing on a rubber mat and wearing huge rubber gloves.... "Sod his luck" Roger said, as we all stood back......

Still we survived this, and thankfully Frank was unhurt, bet it made his hair stand on end though!!!!!!

Still at least the guy was able to fix it, and he put a join in with our electric lead of point at the same time....So I guess it saved us time in the long run.....

Frank finished the clearing and we were able to get the wire deeper and marked up properly but what a day.....

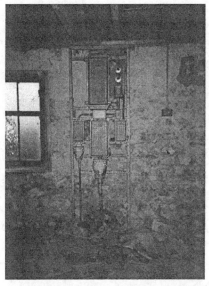

The fuse boxes left in the building

The electric cables outside

The Shower from Hell

Now until now we had been very lucky in the shower department, Mary and Iain were very kind in letting us shower at their house. We were also able to get our washing done at the same time, which was a God send.

It usually ended in us staying for dinner, and the night in a lovely warm bed. Personally I enjoyed a long hot soak in the tub......mmmmmmmmmmmmm it was beautiful, with tons of bubble mmmm

Anyway we didn't want to abuse this kind gesture by them, so when Peter and Kim at the pub said we were welcome to an old shower unit in their back shed, we jumped at it.

I mean, Roger likes to shower every morning, and has had to forgo this for some time. Because of the situation we were in, I had to have a strip wash each day. Well, one it was very cramped in the caravan, but worse still it would not make a pretty sight!!!!!! Well that is if you could picture what would resemble a Elephant trying to have a bath in a washing-up bowl. !!!!ha-ha.!!!!!!!

(SORRY, *perhaps you might not want to exactly picture that scene!!!!!!*)

Roger was able fix the shower unit together in the house in a corner and what a set up it was. The unit had to be on a wooden coffee table we had got a week of two back at a charity shop. This was meant to be my one luxury as such, i.e. the coffee table was to be a dinner table in all the mess, just to give a small feeling of being human, a bit of normality etc...

Still, never mind!!!!! It was used so we could get the shower high enough to let the water drain out the bottom into a bowl. As for using the shower I shall now explain this 'Very High Tec' procedure!!!!!

Now you have to close your eyes to visualise every intricate part......Come on you're not trying hard enough.

Here follows a list of instructions to follow. AND SOME NOTES...

First put on Cannon Heater to warm house above bloody freezing !!!!!!!

1. Fill bucket with water from outside tap (in rain or snow).

2. Place bucket on small gas burner to heat up (this will take about 10 minutes to get nice and warm !!).

3. Undress behind wooden makeshift screen (just to hide what's left of you dignity).

4. Enter the unit...... Remember don't jump around, it's no time for a 'Table Top' dance !!!!

5. Ask the outside operator the drop the small submersible water pump, which was removed from the caravan, in to the bucket of water.

6. Simply press the shower button to on.

7. Shower as fast as possible in case Sodding water runs out. (But hopefully the outside operator will top up the water in time for it to heat up as you go along.. (HOPEFULLY !!!!!!)

8. Finally.....Remove yourself from shower and dry off to suit.

Oh, and do remember to wear ten million coats as you go back to the caravan through the snow.   Oh, and your wellie boots!!!!!!!

So endeth the lesson in the shower department store for today. M mmmmmmmmmmm, think I'll have a break from typing and get a hot cup of tea...For some strange reason I feel all of a shiver...Brrrrrrrrr!!!

But seriously we got used to it.........!!!! Well there is just one small story I have to tell you!!!

Now, Now....Don't get all hot under the collar, it not a saucy story.........ok.......

We had been spraying the woodwork in the roof all day and until now I confess to Not using the "SHOWER" in the house...I hung on having strip washes in the caravan each night, and used Mary's bath at her place.

But I was covered in spray from the work, and my hair was thick with it...So, Yep, I had to use the shower.

Oh, God help me.....Brrrrrrrrrrrrrrrr

Well it was all set, and in I went.......mmmmmmmmmmm.....It wasn't as bad as I thought. Well, Roger forgot to warn me the first bit of water would be cold as the water came along the pipe, but I forgave him....The water was fine....lovely and warm.

Then it happened........I was enjoying the shower so much I did realise the heat out side the shower unit had warned up just enough to cause a kind of vacuum in the unit.....

Now, with the distant sound of the music from JAWS in the surrounding air, unknown to me the 'FREEZING COLD' shower curtain was sucked into the unit, and suddenly it clung to my behind.

'OOOOOOO" came the only translatable screams from my mouth.

Roger couldn't control his laughing......Sod......

I was out in a flash, dressed and storming back to the caravan OOOOOOOO I was bloody mad,

And then to top it of as I could still Roger almost crying in laughter I fell on my bum in the snow......
OOOOOOOOOOOOOOOOOOOOOOO.!!!!!!!!! I just stomped my feet in a paddy

I must admit that by the time Roger came in after his shower,, I was able to laugh about it... Well, just a little bit,...HAHA...!!!. (Roger fixed a curtain wire in the middle, so it wouldn't happen again.)

The shower from hell!

Meeting the Natives Friends or Foe!!!

On yet another snowy day, one of the neighbour's children came over to ask if we'd like to go over for a cup of tea!!!!!!

This was a first.........So we said we'd love to.......Maybe this was a sign of friendship??? We took a bottle of wine along to give them as a show of friendship on our part. We put our thick winter coats and boots on as the weather was blowing like a mad, then set out along the track to their house.

We were made welcome by the woman we had met before and she offered us tea and coffee. Any hostility we had felt from her before had gone. She was very nice, and a bubbly person. Perhaps the first time we had met she was just having an off day! She informed us that her husband was due home soon. We assumed he was at work.

The afternoon passed very quickly, and we enjoyed her company, and after a while her husband returned. As evening drew in we made our excuses to leave, but we were invited to stay for a few more drinks with them.

They seemed a lovely couple, and we hoped this would be a new friendship forming. Now time passed and it was getting late.

They invited us over for 'Brunch' the next day. This was so we could show them our plans for the house, and hopefully put any worries to rest... They must have worried what we were going to do with the building etc....Well, I would have....

Plus we were to discuss a privacy hedge with them...you know...discuss what type of hedging, bushes, trees etc.......This was something we had to do in accordance with our Deed's, so it would be nice to let all the neighbours know what we intend to do in time.

It was nice to be able to discuss this, as we wanted to put in something we would all enjoy looking at.

The next day we went and talked it over, hoping to get along with them now, and put everyone's minds at rest.

Unfortunately, until now we had felt there had been some hostility towards us. But as I said we now felt this may be a new beginning, and we could have a fresh start.

I mean to say, we were not two headed aliens from the planet Zorb!!!!!!!

I wanted to put conifers there, all different colours, you can get them in dark or light greens, yellows and there was also a lovely bluey one. Plus they are evergreen and easy to maintain.

Our neighbours wanted Hawthorn, but with the kids I felt it was a bad idea...with all those spikes. Hellish to prune and not evergreen. Other native plants we'd have to find out about....

So as far as we were concerned the 'meeting' went very well, and we had a nice time. Hopefully we had put their minds at rest regarding the work we were going to do.

A couple of days later we just caught them as they left a note in our post box, and they called over to say they would see us when they got back from holiday.......

Fine no problem.............The note was to say they'd been on the 'Net' and found some plant companies and prices, plus he agreed with what we'd said about the Hawthorn, he did say however he didn't like Yellow conifers....Also they said not to dig the holes for the trees etc until we were to put them in, as the frost will get into the ground and damage the roots...... This was very kind of them to look into it, and we felt at ease.

Oh how wrong we were..............Two days later Heather our Architect phoned me on my mobile. There had been an (get this)...... an " OFFICIAL COMPLANT ', by one of our neighbours saying they wanted to have a 'PRIVACY HEDGE ' put in straight away.????!!!!!!!!!!!!??????????!!!!!!!!!!!!???????

WELL, that did it for me! We were hoping to do this in time, but what the hell could we do right now???????

Anyway WE DID IT... We found a company through our friends and got 150 Laurel bushes and put them in before the neighbours were back. We could add native plants later, Laurel is fast growing and evergreen.

Guess the neighbours that had been away got a surprise when they drove back up the lane from their holiday..

Why do some people behave like this????? Surely it wasn't anything we'd said or done. We thought we'd come to an understanding all round......It's beyond me how some people can be...

Rabbit proof, newly planted privacy hedge

Time passed........

All was calm for a few weeks and our Planning Application was in and building warrants being sorted.

Then Heather the architect rang for us to go and see her. She had more bad news??????

We sat in her house and she explained all.........A local councillor is saying there is not enough water to supply another property, so he was putting a block on planning...(*if that's the right word??*).

Basically some of the neighbours had complained to the councillor about the water etc......*Here we go again............*

We'd checked the water supply when we looked into buying the place, we knew from the owners the water is fine, and plenty of it...

We knew the only time that the water had problems were when the old piping had split or broken and it was Frank and Robert that fixed it.

In fact I think it was Frank's late father-in-law that laid the original water line many years ago.

We had also been shown the water tank storage point up in the mountains by Andrew and he owned the water rights....... So we knew what was what.........

This whole situation was seemingly getting very personal....But we shall see......

In fact the whole situation went on and on. As for the neighbours, well, we rarely saw them...And if we ever passed on the drive, we just waved, or if they were in their gardens we politely said hello.

In the end Robert and Frank came to our rescue as such. They had heard of our troubles with the councillor, and how we felt that he was taking sides. We felt he just wasn't doing his job and he was in our view digging his heals in on things he hadn't looked into.

Plus I must add that the councillor never once came to see us to talk about any of it. If he, or anyone had, had the decency to come and just talk to us; I'm sure all this hassle could have been amicably settled all round.

In the end we contacted our Architect and told her we were going to see the MP who was having a Mobile Office down the road that week so anyone could go and talk to him about local things etc

Plus Frank and Robert, *how shall I say,* 'Invited' the councillor to SEE the water tanks etc.....!!!!!!

Very shortly after the phone call, and his 'Meeting' with the above we got a call from our Architect to say the councillor was signing the 'house off'....'passing approval'.......(FUNNY THAT).

"Knickers"

Now I have to admit, my hand held high.....I went out and bought the biggest pair of joke bloomers from a shop in Aberdeen.....And once we got it in writing that the plans had all been passed....Well, Yes you guessed it. You should know me by now.!!!!!!!

I HUNG THEM UP HIGH ON A WASHING LINE TO SAY 'KNICKERS'.......

Mmmmmmm.......Just for anyone who, 'may' look over our way when passing!!

Charlotte's Holiday

Now, remembering we were new to Scotland, and didn't really know how long it took to get to places. We would set off in what we hoped would be in good time to reach a said destination.

So when our friend Charlotte announced she was to be our first visitor we were delighted. We'd been getting on at her to come up for a holiday, but to remember our set up here.

She'd have to share the caravan with us. We would set the other double bed up at the other end, and it would have a curtain she could pull across for privacy. Also to take into account our setup for the loo and makeshift shower.....We had however been phoning her and keeping her up to date.

Just to re-cap for a second...

A few years ago when we first started to seriously talk of moving to Scotland, Charlotte was living with her long term boyfriend Mike. They both decided that they may join us in buying something big with lots of land, and doing B&B.

We talked at great lengths, and Roger and I hoped to get a really big old place and do it up, and do Haunted Honeymoon weekends, or with Murder Mystery weekend and Henry the Eighth Banquets etc. So all our ideas were beginning to come together.

But sadly Charlotte and Mike split up suddenly and all that idea was lost....Poor Charlotte was heart broken.

She said we were to carry on working on the building, as all she wanted was peace and quite, and just rest.

Well, the day of her arrival came and we set off in what we hoped to be in good time to find the airport and be waiting for her...Her flight was landing at Dyce Airport in Aberdeen...And thinking of Gatwick or London's Heathrow Airport we didn't want to get lost in the terminals.

The drive was like a knife slicing through a sponge cake....So easy, and smooth was our drive we were there in no time at all...For once not getting lost on the way, and taking 4 hours to do a 1 or 2 hour drive....Mmmmm, well you know me and map reading!

What pratts we felt when we'd parked up the car and walked across to the main entrance and went inside!

The Airport was so tiny.....Oh' please don't think I'm being rude, it's just that being the main airport we assumed it to be much bigger... then we all know what thought did!

Well, in fact we were in good time! ....In fact '3' sodding hour in good time...Mmmmmm Then to top things off her flight was delayed.....So all we could do was drink cups of tea and coffee...Lots of sodding cup.......

In the end Charlotte arrived and after the 'hallows' we headed home in the chill of the now darkness that covered the skies at night.. We all just went to our beds that night, and looked forward to showing Charlotte around over the next few days. In fact Charlotte was to stay for two weeks, and during that time we took her to many places, but true to her word, she really just wanted to put her feet up with a good book and a bottle of wine, now and then.

Charlotte and Roger

83

The Wasps from Hell

Over the long spring months we'd seen a subtle change in the weather.

The days were getting longer, but there was still a definite air of winter...We still had days of snow, although it was now well into April.... This was normal for here for the time of year but in saying that we did have some lovely days.

The winter seemed to go on far longer here, it was something we were to adjust to in time. We would have to change the way were lived in many ways as we learnt the ropes.

We had by now started to remove the slates from the roof and each one we removed we stacked in doors to be reused....Some broke so we would have to find some more later but on the whole they were ok......We tried very hard to keep the area tidy, and the scaffolding was never left with loads of rubbish or tools on it over night, we cleared up each night.

This was partly because we didn't think it fair for neighbours to have to look on to a building site mess, and partly pride on wanting to keep it tidy for ourselves.

Over the next few weeks we worked flat out on the roof, we hoped to finish for the next winter.

Little did we know how much work was involved and added to that, the sudden changes in weather kept slowing us down.

The sarking boards were knackered, rotten through, so we had to order new ones for the whole roof.

This was expensive, but had to be done. Luckily the joists were not bad all things considered, but we did have to change some and we doubled up on the end ones. This was because although the end ones were not too bad, it was a tone of work to remove them form the granite work around them.

We also sprayed them in tons of Cuprinol, this was the wood treatment to protect the wood from all kinds of little beasties that can destroy your house very quickly if not detected in time.

Plus it was in the Building Regs this had to be done.........

Also, soon my Mum and Dad were coming up to stay for two week at the end of May and into June........   HEYYYYYYYY..DON'T PANIC>>!!! They were staying at the Hotel down the road, not with us !!!!! They couldn't wait to see the place.......Oh Boy, were they in for a shock.!!!Although we told them all about it. And they must remember the pictures of the outside from when we showed them the For Sale add, I had never sent a photo or video, as I wanted to tidy it up a bit first.. Didn't want poor Mum to have a breakdown over it.!!!!

It was a beautiful day to-day, the beginning of May brought some lovely days and we were doing well on the roof...Roger had worked his way up to the top over the time and was 'kind-of' ok being up so high. (Remember Roger can't stand heights of any kind.) So I was very proud of him going up there, each day it seemed to get easier for him.

We would have a pint or two during the days work but we never drank much because of the risk but this day I truly wondered if I had.!!

And it went Buzz, Buzz!!

As we worked up on the roof I kept hearing a very faint rustling in my ears...?? On mentioning it to Roger, he sarcastically said it may be my little 'pee-brain' rattling around, or the wind going though my head as my brain had perhaps gone out for the day .!!!!OH<HA<HA<HA

Ooooooooooooo,I love you too dear.!!!! I will treat your comment with the contempt it deserves.!!! was my reply to that one.......

Thing was as I turned round in a friendly gesture of a female huff... *THERE IT WAS !!!!!!*

Spread out on the scaffolding board was the **BIGGEST DAMN WASP** I'd ever seen or would ever want to see again.

I just froze on the spot, and tried to get Roger's attention....Now although I am a lover of most things in nature's world **WASPS and all things that can cause pain,** are **NOT** on my list of thing I would wish to hug.!!!!!! If you get my drift....

And this **THING** was heading my way, slowly creeping towards me, I tripped over my own feet and fell onto Roger - who was now standing with his back to me, just behind me.

I hadn't realised that as this **THING** was creeping towards me, I had been creeping toward Roger, thus there was nowhere to go now.

At this point Roger turned to see my 'distressful' look of fear, and I pointed to 'IT'..........

"Bloody Hell", Roger roared as he too began a hasty dash for the step ladder. At this the **WASP** took off in our direction.

It must have looked like a scene from Benny Hill, all in fast forward as we dashed down the ladder and ran in the house, slamming the door behind us.....

You know this damn thing only followed us in the house, so we ran out at a speed unknown to man, only to see it bloody follow us.!!!

In the end it seemed to just hover in front of us...as if to study us...Then it flew off into the woods.

HA.....How rude ...I shouted after it......!!! Saying "I wasn't scared of you anyway" cough, cough.....

You know, the swine came straight back as if to say "O'YER"....Needless to say I was now running away looking like a demented bird flapping my arms around like a pair of wings after taking speed, and screaming.. For once Roger was not laughing too much.!!!

The next few days we were on lookout for more of these things...They kept on dive-bombing us from time to time.

It looked something like a huge fluffy wasp, but with wings like a dragon fly. Orange/yellow in colour and the worst thing was, what looked like a ¼ inch sting on its bum....Now we felt that "MAY" just hurt a bit! But we weren't hanging around to study it long!!!

A week later and after investing in two squash rackets to fend of the enemy from above, we had got about six of the buggers...But they seemed to disappearing on a set route now to and from the woods. So we just avoided that area as much as possible, unless ready for battle..

Robert came over at the weekend to see how we were getting on, and we told him about our problem with *"THE WASP"*. Robert was very polite in explaining what they were, (while he grinned a sheepish smile)...they were in fact a thing call a " WOOD WASP ", and does not sting. The spike at the back end is used by the females to boar a hole in the wood and then lay their eggs in side the tree.

We felt very sorry that we had killed some, but we just didn't know......But I can tell you the truth, with no embarrassment or shame.....That is we still *'RUN LIKE BLOODY HELL'* When the little darlings fly anywhere near us......Oh, believe me....Roger starts by making fun of me running and flapping, Mmmmmmmm But he soon joins me when it turns on him......SO THERE>!!!!!

Silly pair, I hear you saying but I 'dare' you to shake hands with it.......mmmmmmmmmm

Not so brave when you see it, I'll bet.............!! Ha.ha.

Now after these events we were all set for my Mum and Dad to arrive. The next day we spent tidying up the building and we had got four Rhododendrons in lovely pots around the edge of the garden area (they were in full bloom, just making the place look more habitable). I'd also put some primroses around the edge.

Mum and Dad Arrive

Dad and Mum were driving up, stopping over night half way, then on to us. Dad reckoned they would be here at 3 or 4 pm the following day...Well Dad is an ex-army man, and I mean from the War, not as a courier. But he was very regimental when it came to paper work, and time keeping.

You know,.....as a child I could let you know what he would be doing at a set time, on a set day of the week, any day of the year. And as for his cars...He kept a record of mileage and fuel use each time he used the car etc, and that was from his very first car.....It's just the quirky things some people do, I for one wouldn't have Dad any other way.

In fact I think it would make interesting reading.....It's like a record of someone's life....where they were on set days in time. Where they were on national or historic days in history.

How many can remember where they were when the first man walked on the moon, or what they were doing when Kennedy got shot.???? Interesting to see......

The next day arrived, and yep, Dad was on time......Now ...I have never heard my Dad swear. The worst he's ever said is 'ruddy' but as we gave hugs and kisses to welcome them my Dad said "Bloody Hell", as he looked at the building/house for the first time." You've got your work cut out, haven't you!!!!!!"

YEP...................came our enthusiastic reply......

Mum and Dad arrive.

First Impressions Don't Count

Dad was amazed at the structure of the building, but you could sense he was trying not to show he was worrying about the work that he could already see we were taking on.

As for Mum, she just said "Well, rather you, than me", followed by a big smile of interest as she asked to look inside. She also laughed and said she hoped I'd done the house work.!!!! Joking of course.

We went into the building in the far door, and said to be prepared for a bit of a mess. .i.e. remembering the building was in need of total renovation etc..

We had made it as tidy as possible, and I think they were surprised at all the work we had done so far. The building was always damp, but this was due to it being only granite walls etc at the moment. But in saying that, it had dried out a little over the past few months as we had aired it as much as possible.

We had put blankets up at the around what was left of the windows to stop the winter winds blowing in, but we had left this in place to stop people looking in, as we had our tools and all our worldly positions it the building.

Problem after Problem after Problem

There had been problems in buying the building and extra land.!!!!! Believe it or not, we still didn't own the place.!!!!!!??????!!!!!

It was all solicitor jargon, to do with the Land more that the building. But the two parts were being dealt with as one....Lots of legal stuff and nonsense that was being drafted out to suit the Sellers and us before we could sign etc....

But we were able to continue the work as the sellers were happy for us to do so, they would often come up and see us and took great interest in our progress...We got on well with them, and it was nice of them to show so much enthusiasm in our work.

But because the property was 'Not Sold' as such, it was still advertised in the papers. We had many people come up and want to "View" the building and we had to tell them we had bought it and it should not have been in the paper still.....

Most people were ok about this and wished us luck in our work, we even showed a couple around as they showed great interest in what we were doing.....However one guy was hopping mad...He had come some way to have a look at the building....Ooooooooooooops.......

We said we were sorry and offered him and his family a cup of tea but he wasn't interested and just got in his car and drove off at speed down the track. OOOOOOOOOOOpsssss.

There was nothing we could do really, but be apologetic to them..........

This was mainly why we left the blankets at the windows......just in case anyone came up when we were out....

Mum and Dad stayed for two weeks and although it rained 80 percent of their holiday, they had a lovely time with us....We went out every other day, this meant we had time to still do some work on the roof...

They would sometimes go off out on their own to see places, other times we went with them. But they understood that time was of the essence. We had to get on as much as we could, they just couldn't wait to come and see how we were getting on, and to see us again......

One day we were in the hotel for lunch and I heard one of the many jets that often flew over the area coming in our direction.....I grabbed Mum's arm and started to warn her about the horrific noise that was about to happen when WHOOOOOOOOOOOOOOOOOOSH....The bloody thing went over the hotel very low..........Poor Mum just cover her ears and called out in fear...........reckon she nearly had a heart attack on the spot...it was so loud.......it should never have come over that low...Sodding thing......

I just hugged Mum, and said it was ok.....and explained what it was.......she was a nervous wreck for a bit, but settled down after a cup of tea and some lunch. It made Dad jump a bit too.

Their holiday went too fast, and it was soon the day for them to return home...Oh how it hurt to say our farewells......In the end we just said "No goodbyes,....Lets just say.."See you soon". It didn't seem so final then to us..... And on parting Mum and Dad said they would be up again next summer to see how we were getting on.....This we said would look forward to but perhaps make it a little later in the year...i.e. July time....the weather may be warmer....We still didn't know when the summer started up here.....

The month of August arrived and we had some beautiful days, we managed to get on well with the building work and each day seemed to have a little adventure of some kind....But luckily the *'WASPS FROM HELL'* now weren't to be seen anymore.., but they were around...I just know they were...spying on us from the woods.!!!

All summer in different towns and villages there are huge meetings of the Highland Games, and here they had the famous "Lonach Games"....It was a grand event, and to start it off the local men and their sons would take part in the famous 'Lonach March'. with a Highland band to suit.

Now I don't know all the rules, wheres and why- fores, but I assumed that to be in the March one would have to be born here, or at least be Scottish....So how our neighbour got in (being English and all that) would be interesting to find out......But if one was asked to join the March, perhaps just for one time, as a guest, it would truly be an Honour, and not one to be taken lightly...The Scottish code of dress is very forbidding...in the sense that it is very heavy to wear, and on a hot day in August you would find it hard work if you weren't used to it.....But the Men look so proud and gallant as they would march along the road to start the Games.......There would be much to learn about the traditions of this land......

However, we didn't get to the Games this first year.

We were going to go, but decided to carry on with the roof while the weather was good, and the next thing we knew our neighbours we back and asking why we hadn't made it down to the games. ??

Blimmey, the day had gone and we'd missed it all. Well, not all.......we could have gone down to party all night ...but to be honest we were knackered..........Still we'd go next year, when we will have time to enjoy it all.....

We did get our neighbour to give us a twirl in his Kilt,, he looked great. He was wearing the Wallace Clan attire......

Friends in Need

The weeks went by and we got a call from a very close friend down south, they were in trouble!!!! I shall not name them for personal reasons.

They had lost their jobs some time back, but they never told us, they had got behind with their mortgage and bills, and were hoping to get a loan..But although they had now got good new jobs, the mortgage company was not going to wait.

So we offered to lend them some money. In fact it was a lot of money, but when the loan came through they'd pay us back with interest...

So it was the same as having the money in the bank. Plus it wouldn't be for long....We trusted them...

And what are friends for if you can't help them when they need it.......It was all done in writing though...to keep it formal. Regarding money you must do it....But we didn't bother with solicitors because of extra costs etc....

Gerry and Sheila

We found a goose house for sale in the Scot Adds paper and went to see it.......We met a chap called Gerry and his wife Sheila...We got on well with them and found out that Gerry was a carpenter mmmmmmmmmmmmmm. Great we would be in need of him when we have to have the windows made.....They all needed new frames, in fact the whole thing would need doing.....It's not something Roger could do... So again we would use local people.

We arranged for them to come over once we had any news on what we wanted.....so he could measure up etc.....

Windows

We got the 'Building Warrants' and were amazed so see that the window replacements we stated to be "SLIDING SASH AND CASE' ??????????????????????

This must be wrong, the windows were meant to be exchanged "LIGHT FOR LIGHT", keeping the

widows the same as they were now.!!!!!!!!

Surely this would change the character of the building ?????????? So we challenged this......We battled it out for weeks....We sent photos to planning, and it was like hitting our heads against a brick wall.

In the end planning, or who ever, said we could have "SLIDDING SASH" with out the weights.

Well, thanks for nothing,................... whippy- do -dars.......

There we were trying to keep the building looking the same, and some***, who probably has never seen the building is telling us what we should be doing.....!!!!!!!!!!!!

Anyway we had to get on with it....So we got Gerry to come over and after a good look he said he could do the windows for us......He was to make them from oak,...... so they will last.......and once in place with be coated in oils......Not painted......At least planning hadn't said we had to paint them.

The house next door has white painted windows and doors and to be honest they look like modern double glazing. It just looks too modern for the age of the building....We have been led to believe that part of this was originally the old mill, which was used for milling the corn etc and part of it was the stables. This is something that we will look at when trying to gather some history of the area.

Just Like Pulling a Pint

Now indoors we had put the slate from the roof leaning against the walls, each row was kept neatly in order...This was to hopefully help when putting them back, as each row of slates had a slight variation in size.....

Next I used a scrubbing brush (*not too firm bristles and not too soft*) to clean off all the loose dirt and slate. Then I would drill two holes, at the top end, one each side, these had to be in the correct place for the new nails. The original holes were nine times out of ten, crumbly and too large to use again.

We had to shell out on 'Copper' nails, this is in the Building Regs., dear God they cost a bit, but it had to be.

After this, I dipped each slate in "Silicon Brick Sealer", and let it soak into the slate...We hoped this would hold off the slates from "Blowing"... Or shall I say, help to stop the slate from flaking, slate tends to flake into layers (and these were very old).

After doing over half of these laying the slate on a flat bit of wood, Roger borrowed a 'Bench Pillar' and was able to fix the drill in it. So hence I felt like I was pulling pints in the pub all day..

Just a shame there wasn't a few pints of beer at the end of it...!!!!

Containers

Back down south we still had our storage containers!!...It was costing a small fortune to keep them there. So after a while we were able to find somewhere to keep them near by...The agreement was that as soon as they were empty they would go to a farmer for keeping their farming equipment in, and animal feeds etc...So time was of the essence.

They came up by train and then by road on huge lorries, plus we had to have a huge crane to lift them into place.......On the day all seemed to go well until the last climb up a hill and the huge crane lost it's 'six wheel drive' thing !!!! Not sure what it was.....We had to go and get a farmer to help pull it up the hill....But they did it. And there they sat, at peace after hundreds of miles, and there they would stay for now.

There was no way we could even attempt to get them up the track, we also didn't have any room for them. Plus I don't think we would have been able to keep them here very long because of planning etc., plus it wouldn't be fair to have them here, I mean we were trying to keep the place not looking like a building site.

It's a Baby Fergie!!

Today was the day....Roger, myself and Iain went to the containers and we spent six long and gruelling hours in hard labour....

NOW HANG ON.....before you think this is some enchanting birthing thing *PLEASE* let me explain....

We spent six hours getting everything out of one of the containers for Roger to '*PROUDLY*' appear driving our "Grey Ferguson" tractor.........

This was to be a God send, as there was so much heavy lifting to do....Originally we got it when we were hoping to get the farm/steading near Huntly. But we knew we would need it here...We hoped to have the land at the back as 'farm land'. So we could still try and be self sufficient and keep some animals, apart from the geese and chickens

This would all happen in time, we had a plan for the next few years ahead. But still we were waiting for the sale to go through..........................It was a very worrying time for us........................

Still life carried on, and we were much too busy to think on what might be....We just had to wait, and hope things went through......

We would enjoy going to Huntly each week or so, mainly to get supplies but it made a break from the building work.....One also tended to be a bit of a 'Hermit' living away from it all.....We must admit that we loved it......We get on very well, and we always had something to talk about, even though we were never apart.

Some people would go nuts not meeting other people, or going shopping in the towns, but we just loved being away from it all..... If we had to go into a town, Huntly was it for us...It's not like towns down south.....It's more like a village, and so pleasant to walk around. Also if you need help in a shop, the people seem to take time in talking to you as a person, not just a punter.

After 6 hours hard labour we had a baby Fergie.

The Money Worries Begin

Remember me telling you about our friends who we leant money to......Well, yep, it's hit the fan.

We received a long letter from them explaining that the loan had fallen through at the last post, but hoped to get one from somewhere else very soon.?????????????

Oh   God help us......what have we done........??????????????????? We would need the money soon. We were getting low on our funds...

But they would send a cheque up as soon as possible to start paying the money back, they were so sorry, but what could they do now.....

When we were at Mary's the next day we rang them. This they had asked us to do...to catch them at home in the evening.

They were both at full time work during the day, and he was working in a pub in the evenings, but he was off that night so we could talk.

We had a long chat, and we were satisfied that they were doing all they could to pay us back etc, and would send some money soon....

At the end of the day they were going to pay us all the interest lost from not being in the bank, which seemed fair to us...

However it didn't help us for now.....We had to open an account at 'Timber Centre' so we could get wood etc   but it meant that we could pay on a monthly basis up to a set amount.

Because we didn't have the cash, we couldn't go to the auctions that were on in the area that sold all kinds of thing.   That would have saved so much money on building materials...

The best local one is held at Thainstone Market in Inverurie, about 45 minuets away, it's held the first Saturday of each month. It sells from buckets of nails to roofing, granite/brick....basically any thing and everything...and farm machinery to caravans and cars etc

I know I needn't have told you what Damn idiots we were, but I want you to understand that it wasn't all a bed of roses..

We know it was stupid of us to get in this situation......Believe me, we don't need reminding.....It's been a long hard lesson......We had very hard times because of it.....We did live on beans on toast and much to Roger's disgust the dreaded pasta. (*he's not a great lover of pasta*)..I love the stuff, but even I got fed up with it some days.

And we nearly became the "SOUP DRAGONS" of Scotland......Mind you I'm a whiz at making soup now.....!!!!!!!!!!!!!!!!

During all this time we never told my Dad and Mum about the

money...Two reasons...The first> I knew darn well my Dad would tell us what 'TWITS' (to use a phrase of Dad's) we were in the first place, and second > We didn't want them to worry about us being, how shall I say "struggling". ....Even if it was our own fault for lending the money.

My Dad and Mum have always said something like "Never be a borrower, or a lender".....Wish we'd taken note of their years of wisdom.......*Bloody Fools we were..........But they were friends in trouble..*

To be Really corny now......We had each other.....and we would make it together...Hard work never hurt anyone........besides, we were building our home together.....LITERALLY......

Nature Leaves the Woods.

As the summer had almost passed it was now our area of wood to be "thinned or racked".

This was where the Forestry Commission were removing areas of the huge pine forests in Scotland, the wood that was planted many years ago to be used in time for making paper...

Big estates would have been given grants to plant the seedlings, and to later have them taken down by the government etc.

But when this was first done, I expect no one would have dreamed that instead of workers from the estate doing the work over many years, there would, in their place, be a machine of such a scale to do this.

The machines that took the trees down looked like a cross between a long single armed digger on huge tank wheels, and an robotic alien from NASSA.

It would grab a tree, some times a 100 foot plus in height, and a blade would then slice through its base like cutting butter.

It was as if it was as light as a feather turned on its side, then the tree was drawn through what can only be described as a kind of clamp that had millions of teeth, or blades.

This in turn, with the horrific sound of shredding, was then spat out at the other end cut into a specific length and naked of all branches, leaving just the trunk.

The mess left was dreadful, it seems it is just left to rot over the years......What a bloody mess.

Now in my view..........You'd think it could be shredded right down and taken away. Then somehow dried, then compacted into say 'blocks' and sold to use as fuel...i.e. for household fires etc....

And perhaps if the Government could see fit, that the money could go back into Scotland to develop/help in preserving the countryside, or give the rural communities the money back to use in their villages etc......Give it to the people who live in these areas, places who have had to lose their trees, put it to the locals to vote on what to spend the money on....Not some pen pushing person sitting behind a desk, who has probably never been to see the devastation it causes.....Or in fact doesn't even live in Scotland.

Ok, so perhaps I shouldn't get on my soap box, because I'm new here (but I do live here).

So it does make my blood boil when I see all the mess and devastation. And as for the wild life.....**Forget it**.....there's nothing left apart from bugs and beetles...(*which are fine by me, they live here too. They all have their place in natures land.*)....*But, all* the birds are gone and the squirrels

SO THERE   *I've said my bit....sorry* ....*I SHALL NOW GET OF MY SOAPBOX !!!!!!*

The extra land we were buying was to be racked, and a border left between us and next door. This was still not our land, but we were given the choice, and after seeing what "clearing' left, we wanted to save what trees we could.

There were a lot of fallen and damaged trees, and the Harvester felled or removed them for us. This was the areas we hoped to build the barns on for the animals, and grow crops for our own use later in years to come......

Affectionately Grumbleweed

It was now September and Roger's father had come up for three weeks holiday. He came into Dyce Airport, and this time we timed it right.

For once he didn't grumble about anything to do with his flight, or the distance we drove back to the Glencove Arms where he would be staying. Dad is affectionately know to us as 'Grumbleweed', as there is usually something he would 'grumble' about during the course of the day...It's never anything much, it's just his way.

It was great to see him, we missed the old boy very much, and he was now considering moving up to be near us. Peter and Kim who owned the Glencove Arms were just great with him. Pat always took time to talk to him while he waited for us to pick him up each day, and a woman called Annie was very kind to him. Then there was Peter, and he and Dad would share a joke or two.

Roger and his Dad

We were able to carry on with the house on some of the days, as Dad knew we had to get the roof done. But we had some lovely days out with him while searching for a place for him to possibly buy.

Now at this time we were having to do a lot of work on the 'Dutch Front' part of the house. All the mortar was coming away, and it was very unsafe. Roger had to sit astride the apex of the roof behind it, re-pointing it all. He had to remove a lot of the granite work. And re-seat it on to new cement etc. It was very heavy and dangerous work.

We had a scaffold tower up at the front of the house, strapped through the window and around the wall, then through the door. There was no way we wanted it to move, plus Roger had to rest the lumps of granite on the platform of the tower.

Plus to my horror, because Roger couldn't handle heights, I would be the one to climb up the tower and help from the other side.

We had to remove the very top of the Dutch Front. (*This was a Fleur-de-Lis, and also heavy granite.*) We put two bits of wood across the top of the tower, and gently started to ease the fleur-de-lis across to the wooded shelf. But as Roger eased it towards me to slide across, it wouldn't rest on the boards for some reason !!!

So there I was, ten billion sodding miles in the air, unable to move an inch in case I dropped this granite...I thought that I was holding on to the world in my arms, the weight, just sat there.

Roger climbed down and found another lump of wood, and on his return he was able to get it under my arms on to the bars. But as I removed my arms it still just stayed hovering, just above the shelf!!!!

We found that there was in fact a metal rod up the centre. Which was now bent over and holding it up......*Plonkers !!!!!!*

After this we carried on until teatime, and just as I was about to descend from the tower it jilted! I just froze. I've never been so scared. I physically couldn't move....my hands went white as I gripped to the bars.....it was as if my whole body had cramp.....a cold sweat made me feel quite sick..

Roger's dad tried to sweet talk me down, but it was as if my body was not mine, it just wouldn't move to my command, not even a finger.

It seemed ages with Dad and Roger trying to get me to relax and come down....In the end Roger joked at me and said he'd have to ring the Fire Brigade to get me down!!!! Every time Roger tried to get up the tower it moved (*only an inch of a wobble, but it felt like a mile*). Poor Roger wasn't too keen on the tower height but, bless him, he did try to help.

The tower was not going to move, or come crashing downing in any way, it was safe. Dad tried to show how safe it was, but my brain was not having any of it.

Now at this point I have to be honest and let you into a secret... *I have a thing about "Firemen"*...They, how you say, ' *Float my boat* ' etc.....But on hearing Roger saying he was to phone to them, I cried out for him not to.......just wait a minute more...give me time...Pleeeeeeeeeeeeease Waaaaaaaait..........

It would be so embarrassing in the first place...and to top it off, our friend Robert is one of the local Firemen.....*Oh God I'd just die* ....

Strathcove has its own fire station and the locals are in the Brigade there, so we knew or had met most of them.

After a short while I managed to sit down on the top platform, and very slowly climb down. I had to just look straight ahead...you know. Not look down at all.

Dad gave me a big hug when my feet were back on the ground, and Roger laughingly said he never thought I'd want to miss out on seeing Fireman, and he gave me a big smile...(little bugger!!) ha, ha.

Me on the scaffolding.

The next day however Robert and Frank started to put in the Septic Tank and drains (not in his uniform I might add!!!!).

Anyway, Robert went up the tower and helped to re-seat the Fleur-de-lis, and later helped Roger to take the tower down.

A day later it all seemed funny, and now it seem funny to have a 'loo' in the house. It was on a pallet with curtains around it for privacy....One just had to sing loud!!! And to flush it we had to us a bucket of water... (Very grand it was too!!!)

Roger and the Loo!

A septic tank!

A Life Ends and a New One Begins

It was a very sad time, as our old cat Minnie had a cancerous growth in her neck, and she was losing the battle. We knew we would have to take her to the vet soon to be put to 'rest', but we, like all of us, hoped she would slip away in her sleep but she was putting up a good fight.

For the past few evenings after dropping Roger's dad off at the Glencove

Arms, we had seen a tiny kitten on the side of the road, and this night there was a hell of a storm, it was chucking it down.

There again was this tiny thing, but all wet and cold, looking more like a drowning rat. We went to drive passed, and yes you guessed, we just had to stop.

This poor little thing was frozen, but it had a real strop as I tried to hold it by its scruff...There was no way I was chancing it getting its claws into me, or getting loose in the car. The poor thing must have been terrified, poor thing. But I was playing safe.

Still we'd take it to the vets tomorrow or cats home... Mmmmmmmm, (or perhaps not.!!!)

This little kitten was a character.. It was a stripy ginger and by its attitude, I reckoned it was a tom. I'm going to call him 'TIGGER' I mean the poor little love can't be called 'IT' !!!!.We put it (sorry) Tigger in a cat box, with a warm blanket, and some tepid milk, in the hope he would settle once a bit warmer.

Boy was Tigger mad at being in the cat box...it threw what I can only describe as a humongous tantrum. Yes you guessed it again. I gave in. I sneaked it in to our bed, wrapped in its blanket....It (Tigger) fell asleep in seconds....*Bless him.*

In the morning Roger woke up with such a jump!!!! Tigger was licking his nose, and patting his face to wake him up..... Roger was bemused to find Tigger had been able to open the cat box door all by himself!! *(What a clever little pussy cat you are Tigger!!!!)* shhhhhhhhhhhhhh.

Well we just fell in love with this little stripey thing, and ended up keeping it. We decided that as we think it was a boy it would indeed be called Tigger, or Tig for short. Or when Roger thought no-one was about

(I believe much to Tig's embarrassment) he would get called **Tiggi-wiggi.!!!**

I really believe that Tig was what I'd call a 'Pete's Dragon', as he came along at a time when we were to lose our cat Minnie, and Tig gave us so much to laugh about *(**as you will see later)*** it helped us in our time of sadness.

Tig

102

It's Our Home at Last

The post arrived this day and we were overjoyed to find that at last the solicitors had completed the purchase for the house.

We went to Mary and Iain's that evening for a celebration dinner, we left the cats in the caravan with food and a 'litter tray' as we were staying over. We were going to get very, very drunk that night!!!!

(LETS   PARTY... ON.....) hip, hip horary...............................

It was such a relief, after what was coming up to a year and we had really put our souls into this place...

Day in and out we would be working on the roof to get it done, as well as all the other work inside that we were doing on rainy days.

We needed some good news, as there was still no sign of any money coming up from our friends..

Yes, they were still our friends......We knew they were doing all they could to get the money back to us.

Anyway we had a great evening and we slept like a dream in the lovely warm bed Mary had made up for us.....(and she put the heated bed blanket on) 'Oh' it was heaven.

Oh, and I have to confess......The 'Jumbo Knickers' went back on the washing line fist thing when we got back to what we can now call

OUR HOME

The summer was now over and we'd finished the front roof of the house. We had in due course removed the slates from the back roof as before and had just finished putting the roof sarking boards on.

The "green membrane" was now on with batons to hold it in place for the winter.

We had three Velux windows on order for this side of the roof. They had to have a stripe down the centres so they looked like the window you got in barns and this type of building. They also had to be Fire Escape ones....Yep...Building Regs. again....

Mmmmmm; Blimmey,   with the size of my bum, It would be like popping a Champaign cork getting out of these.!!!!!

SORRY>DID THAT THOUGHT COME OUT LOUD. Ooooops

Anyway, our friend Lindy was due up soon. We hadn't sent any recent photos to her as we wanted to surprise her with the work we had managed to get done.....But then again she may have changed her mind about coming in the first place

In just a week or so Lindy would be here. Outside the BT men were fitting new poles and a phone line in for us.....So in due course I gave them teas and coffees.

Just the other day I'd spoken to Lindy and confirm flight time etc.....She was to have an "assisted flight". This was for someone to help her with the steps as she was still getting over a knee opp and was still using crutches. We laughed at the fun we would have getting her around......

We had got a set of temporary stairs in by now, and the plywood flooring was put in just two weeks back, so it was beginning to look a bit more homely......The BT men were amazed at the work we were doing.

As we'd said 'See you soon" to her she wished us luck until we saw her next and finished by using the famous saying "Brake a Leg".

As I was in the house sweeping up and all that it happened......There was a piece of wood sticking out from behind something leaning against the wall.   So I tried to pull it out.......BAD IDEA....!!

As if in slow motion the piece of wood I was trying to remove from behind, knocked whatever it was......and in a split second this *THING* fell at me........I tried to move my feet out the way.

But **BANG** IT CAME CRASHING DOWN ON MY LEFT FOOT.....

was the words that spewed from my mouth like the Devil himself had possessed me. Although I think I am quite 'lingual' in that I can adapt to words......I NEVER knew I knew words like that, or even say them in one LONG sentence in one LONG breath......"**OH GOD FORGIVE ME**".

Roger came in the door as I rolled around on the floor in absolute agony, I was trying my best not to scream out loud as the workmen were just outside in the driveway...they would have thought the Devil had risen from the depths of hell if they had heard my language..

I'm so sorry for the tender tears, but it just came out.....

Roger ran over to me and asked what had happened?? He said not to move, as I pointed to what ever it was had fallen over,....... "Oh, Bloody hell Crab......That's the fire back plate, it weighs a ton. Bet that bloody hurts!?!?"

"OH Darr" came my muffled reply,.. HURT,... my God I thought I was going to die....!!!!!!! The pain was on a scale of 1 to 10... Mmmmmmmm.. About '9.9'..................

Roger was very good, he helped me to my feet, or rather foot, and sat me on the bottom stair.

Jesus, I'd flattened my food big time....There was no blood, and no bruising which I thought was odd as normally I bruised very easily. Perhaps I was ok....!!!!!

I tried to walk on it, but it just hurt too much.......One of the workman must have heard and came in the door. He assessed what had happened in a second... He reckoned I'd have bust it for sure....

"Oh, ...No shit Sherlock..!!! "........(sorry, just one of those sayings.!!).

I blame Lindy....Well, she was the one who said "break a leg"....

Our friends came over the next day, they came over to invite us all over for Christmas dinner, which was gratefully received.   Sheila took me to the doctors, while Gerry stayed and helped Roger check the window sizes.

The doctor gave me some crutches and sent us to the hospital in Huntly with a letter for an x-ray. The hospital confirmed it was broken, but I had to go back after the weekend to see some 'Bone Doctor' of some kind...... there was still no bruising, but you could see a line appearing where the edge of the 'Cast Iron plate' had fallen across.   It was now in a kind of wadding and thick tape to hold it in places. Not a cast, but very similar.

Thing was Lindy was due to arrive on Saturday morning....So we'd both be on crutches...Oh, whippy-do-dars......

Roger could help Lindy around, she was tiny, but I'm a big lass,...I'd just have to get on with it......Luckily the loo was down stairs.

Lindy and Roger

The pain at night was a little better as I was not standing, but I still had to get on with things, you just do..... Anyway, nothing a few beers can't help to get over.

Santa's Grotto

When we went to get Lindy, she really thought I was taking the Mickey, you know, having a laugh: It took ages to convince her it was for real. Anyway, we went into Aberdeen to show Lindy around, and to get any last minute shopping for Christmas. While we were there we got a call from Sheila to say there was bad weather and we should, if not already head home......so we did as there was snow in the air....

By the time we got to Alford the snow that had been coming down heavily, as we set back to our place, had eased and when we got to the Glencove pub we stopped for a beer, and to say hi to Peter and Kim....

Now, as we left the Airport we got Lindy to put her watch forward a hour.!!!!!! We told her that's why Scotland gets dark earlier than the south.......HE, HE.....the time difference......(there were to be a few more windups on her stay with us...Only a bit of harmless fun.......But it didn't take long for Lindy to suss out the time joke...The clock in the pub gave it away....

When we got back to the caravan it was nice and cosy. Well, to us it was, I think Lindy was just too tired to notice it was a "tad" chilly.

We got the hot water bottle in to the beds before we went to collect Lindy in the morning, so we just boiled up some more water and re-filled them.

All the way home I'd comment on how sad it was that we wouldn't have any Christmas decorations in the house this year, and when we saw the lights in peoples gardens and houses. I'd give a small groan.

Now came the surprise for Lindy....We said she just must have a quick peek at the house before we go to bed.....

I covered her eyes as Roger led her into the house, and on uncovering them she found a 'Santa's Grotto'.....We'd done the house out in every decoration we could lay our hands on.....

However the 'Christmas Tree' was rather LARGE....15 foot plus... in a metal rubbish bin wrapped in paper, sitting on the floor, it went up to the roof and then bent over at the top, with a fairy dangerously stuck on top..... Lindy cried........It was fab......

We didn't really show her the house, it was too dark and late...So we went back to the caravan.

We sat chatting for a bit but now we were all tired so we settled down for the night.....

Lindy was one for mucking in, so she was happy to help us with our work.....It was great to see her. I really missed her. She can be an absolute scream.

There Were Three in the Bed and the Little One Said, Rollover, Rollover!!!

A few days into her holiday it was really not letting up with the weather, and on this night it was freezing.......

I woke up and I heard a strange noise. It was Lindy's teeth chattering.. Poor cow must be frozen. So I called over to her and said "for God's sake Lindy come in here with us and get warm"!!!!!! She was frozen, we snuggled up and went to sleep. What else could we do, we'd have to arrange something tomorrow. Roger was half asleep, when I just told him to 'roll over darling' I'll explain in the morning!!!!!

Next morning I awoke to find Lindy's face against mine, with her arms thrown across.....

Ok, that's it ....Roger we have to move into the house, the beds just too small for three, mattresses on the floor upstairs...I don't bloody care how!

The Haggis Hunt!

Bless her, we got Lindy on the old 'Haggis Shoot'.....We convinced her that at this time of year they have "Haggis Shoots." We told her it was true what they say...The Haggis, was a four legged creature, very illusive......and a cross between a sheep and a badger.......and to keep a look out for them....

Deep down I'm sure Lindy knew it was a wind up, but she went along with it....I mean, if you don't know what Haggis is, well, it just could be what everyone jokes about.

We suddenly stopped and made out there was a 'Haggis' up a field.......we tried to get her to see it. But she didn't!!!!!!!!!!!! Wonder why, ha ha ha!!!!!!!

The U.F.O.'s?

On one outing Lindy noticed a group of circles in a field in the distance....We just couldn't resist this opportunity to wind-up the poor girl again....

"Oh yes, that must be where they said there were strange lights in the sky last week and there was a thing in the local paper about it, they said that it was a U.F.O that landed there...!!!!!" came my reply as I reached for the map pretending to try and find the spot, when really trying to hide my face as I was beginning to smile out of control......

But this time we couldn't hold out long, as we had to confess to the wind-up....There were too many in other fields. ......We had to tell her it was the marks left from where the farmer has his hay feeders for the animals....   (*I think she forgave us.*)

Now we were in the house for the night times, we got the bedding out of the caravan and put them upstairs......It was a lot better than the sleeping arrangements we had!!!! There was plenty of room, and with the log burner going it was warm enough upstairs...Still a little chilly downstairs, but we still only had the bare granite walls and boarded-up windows.

So we went to the containers and dragged a carpet out and put it on the floor at the 'lounge end' near the burner....Also Sheila and Gerry came over with a two seater settee and two single arm chairs, it was just like home from home!!!!!!!! They would do us for now, it was very kind of them....Great, no more sitting on boxes.....

We started, with Lindy's help, to fit the 'Kingspan' insulation in the roof......What a mess this stuff makes....But it's a million times better that the old fibreglass wadding people had to use in the roof. Plus if Roger get near fibreglass he goes nuts itching, and comes out in a terrible rash, but the 'Kingspan' was ok.

It may seem strange to say this but it really made a difference as each panel fitted......and when we'd finished we had to fix a clear plastic sheet over it all. It really warmed the place up.

Our next job was to fit the wood panelling in the roof, this was 'tongued and grooved' pine planks that we would stain later...We hoped to stain them a 'light honey' kind of colour, and then a clear satin varnish.....This would not only seal the wood, it would be easy to wipe clean.

We'd managed to get a lot done when Lindy's holiday was over, and she had to go...But it was great having her here, and she helped us so much with the work..

Another Christmas had been and gone, and we'd had a fine time at Sheila and Gerry's, but now it was back to work full time on the house....

I didn't tell my Mum and Dad about my foot....Although, to be honest, I could have done with one of those "Mummy Kisses' to make it all better.........Yep even now I miss them, and I always will.

Valerie.

Today my cousin Valerie and her companion Lorna were coming to visit us. They were up here on holiday visiting Lorna's family....

I hadn't seen Valerie for years, so it would be nice to catch up, my Dad's sister, Valerie's mother, had passed away years ago. But I remember her and the family as if it was yesterday..

As you get older the years seems to pass by with a wink of an eye and sometimes it's so easy to let time pass you buy and loose contact with people, although unintentionally.

When Valerie and Lorna arrived I think they were impressed with the house and we showed them around...... As you can imagine there was tons to talk about..

They weren't staying up here very long, so it was just a day visit to us before they were to set off home in a few days time.

We went to the Colquhonnie Hotel just down the road for lunch. We chatted about all kind of things and time past too quickly.

Roger and I had intended to buy them lunch, but Valerie insisted that it was their treat. (Thank you both very much, that was very kind of you.)

After lunch they had to set back, so we wished them a safe journey, and hoped they would come again next time they were up here and off they went...

And Time Goes By

The months had passed and we'd got on well with the wood work. It went together very well, it looked good.

We managed to finish the wood lining/walls, but Roger was now laid up in bed with sciatica, he was in terrible pain. He suffers with back pain at times...I say he's getting old !!! ha,ha.. Only joking..

Our next job would be to dig out the floor downstairs and do the foundations, but with Roger like this we were stuffed....

One day Robert came over to see how we were getting on....It turned out that his wife Pam was learning Reflexology. He said he was sure Pam could help Roger's back.

So we arranged for her to come over the next day. It was like a miracle. Pam did her thing and Roger rested for the rest of the day in bed. Pam also did Reflexology on my feet to help my tennis elbow I'd had for months. I got that when we put the hedge in, all that digging etc..

Anyway the next day Roger was up and about so much so that we went to Huntly for the day and then on to the Auctions at Inverurie.

Roger felt great.....Wish we'd known that Pam had done this stuff a couple of weeks back.

As the months passed we were able to get the back of the roof finished. It was a relief to know it was all finished for the next winter. It was a lot lighter now with three windows, and we had now fitted the last of the downstairs windows....

Digging up the floor

Lawrence and Val Cope Well

A couple of our closest and longest friends came to stay with us this year and yes they knew of the set up regarding the shower etc.

We set up the caravan for them, and we had the awning on the side, so they weren't left open to the elements too much. It gave them a seating area and shelter from any rain as they got in and out of the caravan.

Poor Lawrence (we call him Lorry) is a tall chap, and I didn't realise until now just how tall he was. He never said anything but I reckon it was a bit tight in the bed length wise..

Val is a little older than him, so I was a little worried that she would not take to being in the caravan. But in saying that, if they had shown signs that it was not working for them, Roger and I would have been happy for them to stay in the house...We just felt that it would have been a little more private for them.

However, you have to remember that the floor was being dug out and it could be quite risky walking the plank over any holes and all the rubble. I mean if we fell over, that was our tough luck, but we'd hate anyone to hurt themselves.

We would have done something if we had to have people in the house....Plus the house was very damp...So at least they could put the heater on in the caravan in the evenings, and at night to keep warm.

You should have seen Lorry's face the first time he used the shower!!! Guess it was an experience!!!!!. And Val was so good...Still they mucked in, which was just as well...Bless them both..

On that note, because the upstairs was ok we were able to watch videos in the evening, and eat our meals in the house....

By now I had our small mini oven and microwave upstairs,....so I was able to give them hot food etc.....And they even liked Haggis.

Each day we took turns in driving to different places.....We hoped we were able to show them some lovely places....At night when they had gone to bed, I would prep' up the next days picnic/packed lunch. This was so that we had the choice of that, or if we had a meal in a pub /café, we'd have the food.

I'd put it in a chiller bag that night....It also depended on the weather... Not wanting to sit in the rain having a picnic, we would sometimes just park up somewhere nice, and have lunch in the car, looking at the views.

A Touch of Heaven on Earth

On one occasion we took them to a place not far from Tarland. It was known as one of the 'Queen's Views'......This was normally where Queen Victoria had stopped at some point in time and the view would normally be spectacular.

Well it would have been......There was me spouting on for ages about how when I had first been to this spot, I cried because the view was so moving and breathtaking for me...

As we drove around the country lanes there was always something to point out to them and one was always on the lookout for deer and things in the fields and woodland on route.

We were almost there......Ok guys, I hope you enjoy this......

Damn it,.............As were went around the corner to the spot we were destined for, all I could see were clouds.....What a let down.....

We parked the car, then crossed the road, and stood in the area provided for people to see the view with some safety from the passing cars......It was such a shame...the clouds had come down right across what would have been a wonderful sight to see...

When I first saw this view it was a hot summers day, with a crystal blue sky. One could see a million miles of mountain after mountain after mountain.....Just so beautiful, just so breathtaking. It was truly to me 'A touch of Heaven on Earth'.

Balmoral and the Great Escape

To Her Majesty The Queen, I do most humbly apologise for what happened!

Now what I'm about to tell you, you should take note of!!!!!!! A Warning to you all.!!!!

" *Once upon a time* "..........(QUEUE *the voice of Kenneth Williams.*) "*Oooooo No, stop messing about.*"

Back to me again......Seriously this really happened. It was a lovely summers day and Lorry and Val decided to take us to Balmoral....So we drove over the mountains from Corgarff along the road I called the Val Doonican Mountains Track, and on to Bridge of Gairn, then on to the castle.

We parked up, and followed the signs to the entrance... No public cars were allowed along here.

As Lorry paid, he paid for us to go on a trailer, Val, Roger and myself climbed aboard this smart trailer which was to be towed by a very clean tractor. This we assume was to give us a tour of the grounds!!!

We assume wrong...Once everyone, including Lorry was aboard it took us through the automatic gates into the grounds. It then took us slowly along a small, neatly kept road.

But as we approached some complex of grey buildings it slowed down, and then stopped.!! That was it...Off we had to get....

We were shown the direction of the beginning of the self walked tour!!...So, anyway we went into a room and started to look at the bits and bobs in show cases, and read the history of Balmoral etc, and pictures on the walls.....

Lorry hired one of these hand held sets that you could press the number in at what place you were, and it told you all about that thing, we didn't bother with one as we felt we could share.

Walking around the first part was interesting, all the different ways of transport used over the years etc. then a short but pretty walk down to the grounds around the Castle itself..

The flowers were lovely and considering the amount of people that walked on the lawns, they were very well kept.

Lawrence, Val and Roger at Balmoral 2005

Just Don't Think About It!!!

As we walked around looking at the building work and gardens, I walked off to try and get a full view photo of the Castle from the front lawn area.

Now, if you don't know me by now, I am one for 'sometimes' doing things with out thinking first.

So there I was trying to take a picture, when I noticed an old lady trying to get her, assume husband, to smile for a photo.   She stood about ten feet in front of me to one side.

The women was a large lady, dressed in a coat that seemed far to thick for this kind of weather, and a brolly hooked over her arm, with a rain cap to suit.!!!! But she still had her head scarf on. She looked a true Nora Batty job.

The man in front was so funny, he also reminded me of a character off TV but I can't think of his name. You may know who I mean by this description...I think this character was also in 'Last of the Summer Wine.'

He wore a grey mackintosh, tied in tight at his waste, and almost down to his feet in length, the coat seemed a few sizes too big for him...He had a cap on, just like 'Andy Cap', a shopping bag in one hand and a brolly to match in the other....And spectacles, the thickness of which I've never seen the likes of before.

The old boy wasn't standing right, then he wasn't smiling

enough...Nothing he did was right!!

In the words of Leslie Phillips... "DING~DONG"

Next thing I knew, I was lifting my shirt to *FLASH* my boobs. Guessed it might put a smile on the old Boy.!!!

Suddenly I stopped about half way up... "Wooooooooooops"I thought to myself, as I had visions of being dragged off by the police with the Headlines on the News at Ten being,

"BALMORAL FLASHER CAUGHT IN THE ACT"

I started to giggle, and the old women must have heard me. Nearly catching me I just smiled at her and walked away giggling away to myself...After a few steps I looked back at them...He was smiling!!

I soon caught up with the others, and I couldn't tell them for laughing until much, much later in the day...They must have thought I was on something, as I kept giggling to myself as I thought of what I 'nearly' did. (*Sorry Your Majesty.)*

HEY, don't think that was it for the day......there were one or two other things yet!!!!!

Later on we came across the beautiful gardens lower down and the huge Green Houses. Oh, they were lovely. The shame was the water fountains were not in use....it was a shame to see them unused...that would have really set the grounds off a treat.

We then went into the Castle. That had booklets to borrow while in there to help with description of the paintings etc...

I must say I was very disappointed not to be able to see more of the castle but the structure was very interesting. Plus personally, I think for Americans especially, the chance that they 'might' catch a glimpse of a member of the Royal Family, would surely be an attraction.

But of course in saying that, you have to think of security, it would not be advisable because of the high risk.

In saying that, if someone caught a flying glimpse of a figure, say 'just of someone crossing a corridor in the distance,' just not close enough to be sure who it was, well, it could have been!!??? Or was it !!! Mmmmmmmmmmmmmmm............ just a thought Marm!

Well, we wanted to have another look at the Gardens before we left, so after a cup of tea in the café there, we walked back down to them, but on a different route. Lorry is a keen gardener and works in a garden centre back down south. He is very knowledgeable about plants and things.

After a bit we came across a small cottage in the lower grounds....It looked lived in but most probably empty at that time.....

There were no fences or KEEP AWAY signs, so we had a good look in the windows etc.

I think it was Lorry or Roger who rang the door bell!!! Luckily no one answered!!!!

We suddenly realised that the gardens and grounds looked very empty of people!! So we guessed it was time to head back.

>Now's the time to take note!!!!!!!<

We walked through the grounds admiring all kinds of things, from plants to the odd cottage laid back from the paths, but the place was now deserted except for one man we saw running by in his sports gear. He just waved a polite hello as he passed.

As we approached the gates to the way out and entrance we saw they were closed, but there were a few people walking around outside.

We walked right up to the gates, but they didn't open! We thought they would automatically open on a censor thing of some kind. But NO. nothing happened.

We walked away, and back towards them again and again in the hope that we would trigger something off....But still nothing.

What the hell are we going to do now...!!!!!!!!!!!! There didn't seem to be anyone we could get the attention of anywhere.......

I did suggest that one of us climbed the gate and went to get some help, but no volunteers there I'm afraid...

Then Val noticed a small button on a post a little way back from the gates...Non of us had even noticed it. The button blended in with the wood too much to see, unless like Val you got up close to it.

Val presses it and......HURRAY......open sesame the gates slowly opened before us. As we approached the gates *BEEEP, BEEEEEEEEEP, BEEEEEEEEEEP, BEEEEEEEP, BEEEEEEEEEEEEEP, BEEEEEEEEEEEEEEEP,* came this horrendous sound from the hand set that Lorry was still holding in his hand!!!!!!!!!!!! "For, God sake what's going on" we all cried out...... The hand set was going mental as Lorry threw it to me and me not wanting it I threw it to Val, who in turn threw it to Roger. Sodding thing just wouldn't stop.......!!!!!!!!

It must have looked so funny to the people watching us standing around. We just kept chucking this beeping thing to each other.....And it was so loud. I had visions of the Queen's private *'SAS'* suddenly falling from the sky on a rope from a huge black helicopter, and army men dashing out of the woods, Screaming

"DOWN ON THE GROUND... NOW...LEGS AND ARMS APART...DO NOT MOVE ...OR WE WILL SHOOT'..*EEEK HELP!*

Don't panic...that luckily didn't happen......***PHEW...***(mmmmmm
Shame that, I do love a man in uniform..)   *Oooooooooooooops,   Sorry,*
Did that thought come out loud!!!

Well, we couldn't open the back of the hand set to remove batteries or
anything to shut it up. To top things off the shop where we got the tickets
was shut, and no letter box to even shove this damn thing in.......

Lorry then notice a building next to the shop had a letter box...It looked
like it could be an office. So Lorry and I sneaked (yes, sneaked) up and
shoved the still *BEEEEEEEEEEEEEEEPING* handset through the letterbox.

Thing was as we turned to leg it away, the sodding door opened.!!!!!
And a rather red faced man stood holding the handset!!!!!!!!!!!!!!!

In a very posh, loud and firm voice he said. "I suppose you think that's
funny?????" and he then gave a frown of one that was not
amused.....followed by "I suppose I'll have to deal with it"!!!????

At which point with on lookers in fits of laughter, we just said "Sorry",
and we all ran up the road laughing like a group of school kids.

I did wonder if the spectators around the gate area, thought that it was
all in a days entertainment for them.

Little did they know...!!!!!!!!!!!!!!!!!!!!!!! At least one part could have made
the news.!!

Shhhhhh, I won't tell, if you don't.!!!!!!

We spent the last few days of their holiday having a few giggles over that
and once again we visited some lovely places with them. Before long it was
sadly time for them to leave....

We would miss them, we had known them for years. We hoped they
would come again, but next time to live in the house with a few more home
comforts!!!!!!!

Some roof work!

Mum and Dad are Ill

It was summer again and Mum and Dad were meant to be coming up on holiday again....I got a call from Mum to say Dad was very ill...He'd hurt his back and was in bed and it looked like they may not be able to come up.

Mum sounded odd, I couldn't put my finger on it. But she just wasn't right....I rang my brother and found out Dad was in a bad way....there was no way they'd make it up...And I was right about Mum. Mum was having a hard time coping. You see, Mum and Dad have never really been ill...Well, not like this....

The doctors wouldn't make their minds up what was wrong with Dad.....And Mum had been so stressed to see Dad like it she 'kind of' lost it a bit.'

Thing was the sodding doctor had put her on Diazepam!!!!!!! Good Grief, what were they thinking of....

(We've seen a few of our friends on that, and more importantly my daughter has had 'three' breakdowns because of so called anti-depressants. I believe she was put on the first because of the 'Baby Blues',...Post natal depression,......DON'T get me wrong, thankfully she got off the damn stuff and she's now well again... It took a long time to recover, but you can loose you mind on stuff like that. It was also due to the never ending nightmares she had from her domineering father that still haunts her to this day. I shall never forgive myself for not being there for her, or my son, during those years when she and her brother were in the hands of such an evil man. I must stress she never harmed her son, but it did lead to the final break down of her relationship with her son's father.)

Over the next few months I packed my bags tons of time to go down and help them. but Dad insisted that I stayed up here....He even said he'd never talk to me again, and there was no way I could stay with them.....
(BUT, there was a good reason why Dad had said this, I knew this deep down.....)

Thing was it was Male Pride....Dad was having to be bed bathed and washed etc. and I don't think he could use the bathroom, if you get my drift....so the last thing he wanted was me there to see him like that.

Silly twit, as if it would bother me.....I would have been able to give Mum a break but of course Mum and the nurse would do Dad's private and personal things.

Poor Mum wasn't getting much sleep and Dad was so ill.......I felt totally useless.

They weren't getting anywhere with Dad's back at the doctors.

I begged him to go private, and get to see a specialist now. Not go on a waiting list etc...I tried to explain it's amazing how fast things can move when you're paying for it!

But Dad insisted that he'd paid his stamp etc, so why should he pay for treatment it?

Meanwhile while my brother and his wife were doing all they could.....I don't know if they realised that I was how you say 'BANNED' from coming down......But I didn't want to upset Dad or Mum. Anymore.

Mum became very ill with all the worry, and Dad eventually had to give in and pay to see someone private...

There was no way they would come up this year, and the thing was we were broke, so I could only go down really if I paid on tick...Then we would be in debt, and that's something we wouldn't chance. We just had to hope our money would soon start to come in from odd jobs and my pub work.

I can't thank Paul and Denis for all they did to help Mum and Dad at that time.

A few weeks later Dad found out he had 'Enclosure of the Spine' I think this means the bone tissue is enclosing around the nerves or spinal cord, causing all the pain.

This, he was told, could be helped by an operation on his spine but only might help, and it is a very risky operation.....

Plus to top it off the operation would set him back (a mere 15,000) or so!!!!!!!

But as I said to Dad, you can't put a price on you health, if you feel you need the opp' then have it but remember the risks involved.

Meanwhile Mum's body was addicted to the 'Bloody' medication she was on...That Doctor should be struck off for putting her on Diazepam....The records show what it can do, and for someone of Mum's age. Well she would soon have the biggest fight of her life to get off it.......Each day would be a battle to be won for her......

Getting to grips with the side affects and reassuring herself that it it's the medications that make her feel the way she does.....All the chemicals in her body...It's not her mind at all, it's the pills the Bloody Doctors got her on. Oooooooooooooo, if I could get my hands on that doctor. Well perhaps that's not a good idea!!

So, as I said, they won't be coming up this year......

Tig's Revenge!

At this time we were still cooking food in the caravan and eating our meals there, or some evenings we'd eat in the house.

But this evening we ate in the caravan. Now, Tig was a little scamp, and would keep on trying to jump up at the table...Well, time passed and as the evening went on we got a bit..... how shall I put this... mmmm, 'in the mood'.....and well, one thing led to another...and well, you know.

(Oh come on now, don't look so shocked, it's the first time I've hinted at this kind of thing, we are human.)

Anyway, without any details we were doing what one does, and Tig kept on jumping up etc.....

Well talk about passion killer.......Next thing I saw was Roger grabbing the 'Mustard jar' from the side of the table......

Bloody hell, I thought to myself, what's he going to do with that.?????? Talk about spice up your love live or what.!!!!!!!!!!!!!!!!!!!!!!!!!!!

Thankfully it was the "What".....as he smudged a little on Tig's nose to get rid of him......

Suddenly there was a howl and this ginger thing zoomed around the caravan, running like a cat with rabies as Tig foamed from the mouth.......

Well, that stopped play as you can imagine....   As Roger and I tried to catch Tig, he spat and hissed at us, clawing at anything he could reach.....We managed to get him after a short while and wipe away the remains of the dab of Mustard from his nose.......We bathed him for ages with cold water and Tig calmed down....Oh how awful Roger felt...   it was only a little dab of Mustard, but it had gone up Tig's little nose....Poor little love....

But Tig forgave Roger as he snuggled up to him later that night on our bed in the house...........

We must have dozed off, and Tig was happy and content to sleep beside Roger on the bed. Normally we put the cats on the floor to find somewhere to sleep but our bed was on a makeshift mattress in the floor anyway. So the cats tended to creep back on to the end of the bed at some point....

During the night I felt a warmness come over me, over my head and down my back. It made me think of a Tropical Island, perhaps bathing under a waterfall in the hot sunshine.....Mmmmmmmmmmm.

Then it dawned on me................'YOU LITTLE SOD' I screamed, as I realised Tig had PEE'D on me.................YUCK..........

Roger shot up out of bed, as I jumped and stomped my feet with shear horror at being PEE'D ON.

Guess Tig got his Revenge.!!!!!!!! (Ha, and it wasn't even me!) Thanks to that, I had to do a load of washing in the morning, thank God the summer months are here. So I can get things dry on the washing line...

Tig was his normal self, and running around. He them started to pull the washing out of the bin bag I had on the ground...I kept telling him to leave it...But he just kept pulling stuff out...After a bit I thought that perhaps it was his way of helping..........Oh, how wrong I was....The little Sod pulled out a pair of my knickers, and the little bugger was almost grinning at me as the ran of in to the woods with me chasing him....!!!!!!!!!!!!!!!

So somewhere out there in the wood of the highlands are a pair of my knickers...Knowing Tig, there probable half way up a tree!!!!   He's worse than a kid......Oh'Bless him, NOT ....

The "Arrival" of Bobsky

Bob was the kitchen porter at the Glencove for Peter and Kim, he lived in a caravan out the back of the pub, and over the time here I had often worked with him in the kitchen.....I had to get some income, and I enjoyed working with them all..

Now, to tell you a little about Bob, nick named Bobsky, he was in this late 50's and a retired submariner...Just passing the time until he got his Forces Pension, and he was a very funny chap, a real laugh and a party type of person, but all the time...

He made himself out to be a bit thick, or just not understanding things sometimes. But I think it was just a show, sometimes. It was just his way of getting along in life with lots of laughs.

Well, one night Roger and I popped into the pub on the way home from our friends near Alford, and there was a rumpus going on....

Bob, did like his drink, and this time he'd gone too far.....God knows he'd had a skin full, and to top it off he was meant to have been working. I think things had been brewing for sometime, and what with the drink, Bob said things he shouldn't have to Peter.

I don't know what was said or by who but Peter said he had to go NOW.........So seeing the situation, we said we'd take Bob back with us for the weekend and let things calm down. He could stay in the caravan. It was always made up in case anyone turned up to stay......

We managed to get him back to our place and settled in the

caravan.......He was used to our caravan as, on his days off, he would often come and stay....He used to help us around the place as much as possible and we'd always have a good drinking session.

Bob worked very hard for us, we couldn't pay him, so we never charged him any rent etc, but he would help with food and booze over the time......

Because we were now going to dig the floor out he would be a Godsend. So we plumbed in the loo upstairs behind some curtains.... There we fixed a hosepipe up to the corner so we could fill a bucket of water to flush, and Roger fitted a small electric Ascot so one could wash one's hands....(*ALL THE MOD CONS HERE!!!!*)

At that time we had a TV upstairs and it was detuned, so we could watch Videos and DVD's. We did have a TV License for a while, but the reception was terrible...All snowy etc...Guess this was due to all the trees. So we cancelled it, and told them why and disconnected the aerial from outside.

One night Bob had the usual skinful, but he was ok...As we sat watching a film Bob needed to go to the Loo.. So we turned the TV volume up.. For obvious reasons.

After he had returned back to the TV we carried on watching the film. I notice that the curtain was moving.. I assumed it was Tig 'again' playing around!!

But it wasn't.....To my horror, five minutes later the curtains opened, to spew the hand bowl across the landing on a sea of foam coming from behind the curtains.............Bob had left the hose just on, so over the time any soapy water he had left in the bowl over flowed. Hence now a Foaming Niagara Falls down the stairs.........YOU PLONKA BOBSKY.!!

We had all worked hard over the weeks digging out the old flooring in the house, and by now we were spending a lot of time re-pointing and repairing the granite wall, which was below what was to be the new floor level and above..

The two lower plinths that were in the off centre of the lounge end were proving to be a problem. It looked like we'd have to hire a big road drill to get them dug out.

Frank did try with his digger and a metal rope to pull them up...We put the metal rope through an open window, and then around the plinth in the hope of moving it somehow, but even then they wouldn't budge. In fact Frank's digger was beginning to lean over as he tried for ages to shift them.

We hoped to get the floor in for Christmas this year, time was getting on so we had to work fast...

Plus we had just heard from Lindy that she would be able to come up for Christmas again, and to our delight my son Jonathon wanted to come and stay for a week with his girl friend. They knew the set up here and were willing to muck in etc....

You "Plonka's"

Now>>>>>Remember I called Bobsky a PLONKA. Well this next scene will just prove that having too much to drink can turn most men into 'A RIGHT PLONKA' (You will have to picture the scene as the event unfolds..)

SCENE ONE>

Once upon a time there were two grown men having a few drinks at the end of a hard days work. They had of course had far to much to even contemplate any more work!!!! Or had they ???

As time passed they began to sing a little and mess about as men do...!!!

Watching this, I found it funny as, for once, I was sober... OK' perhaps I was not as bad as them, yet..

SCENE TWO>

Suddenly Bobsky asked when we were to take down the metal shower to make room for the new foundations to go in the house....??

'**BAD IDEA**'   was the thought that went around my head.

But it was too late...............the idea was in their heads.......................

So, they decided 'No time like the present.'

The shower was still on the coffee table, surrounded buy a huge hole where we had dug out.....

Now **Roger** was inside the unit unscrewing the top from the side panels.

Bobsky, had decided to get on his hands and knees, and unscrew the bottom panels!!!!!!!!!

THIRD AND FINAL SCENE>

THE INEVITABLE HAPPENED...... *******C R A S H *****

Down it came, landing Roger head first down this huge hole, with the metal frame encasing him...

As the noise went and the dust began to clear you could just make Roger out amongst the debris as he called out "Bob, Bob, are you all right mate??? Where are you? .SHIT.. Where am I..????"

At which point Bobsky, who I think lost consciousness for a few seconds, began to move at the base of what was left of the unit....."I'm fine,

I think, where are you??" came a groggy reply.

MY reply to all this seeing they were ok was, *YOU BLOODY PLONKA'S !!!!!!!!!!!!!!!!!!!!!!!!!!!!!!!!*

(P.S.).....Does this remind you of something.!!!!!!

All was well, they recovered with mainly their male pride bruised, just a little more that themselves.

Roger climbing out of the collapsed shower

"Bobsky", It's Time to Leave

We went to the Glencove Arms as normal on the way back from Huntly one day with Bobsky and I'm afraid things got a bit heated with Bobsky and Peter. Bobsky had a bit too much again.....So we took him home....He'd really blown any chance of a job back there this time...

When we got home he was in a foul mood, and it really was just the drink talking as Roger tried for ages to get him to go to the caravan that night...

We had tried to give him tea and coffee, but he wasn't having it...He used the loo upstairs and as we were talking to him downstairs....It happened again...Bloody Niagara Falls over the landing.....Yep, he'd left the water running.....

This time I was not a happy bunny.....I was tired and now all this mess...I was cheesed off.......

Roger told him, time for bed NOW.....and Roger marched him to the caravan....

He went ok,..... and Roger turned the gas off to the caravan in case Bobsky woke up still boozed up and blew himself up trying to light a fag by using the gas rings.

The next day Roger would talk to him, but that was Bob, that's how you got him...He was a good chap at heart....He'd give you his last penny.. And one just couldn't stay cross with the guy for long.

Anyway, the next day a friend called Annie came over to collect a book I'd said I'd lend her...Bob was still in bed, but hearing the car pull up must have woken him....

He was fine, and apologized for the night before........Well what can you do....We left the subject alone.......Less said, sooner mended...

The book I needed was in the caravan, so I asked Bobsky if I could get it...... "Fine" he replied I'll just finish my fag and tea...mmmmmm. Sitting on a bench we had against the house, I chatted to Annie whilst finishing my cuppa, and then went to the caravan.........

As I went in the caravan. Phew it stunk!!!!..... Luckily we had got a second hand plastic shower unit last week, knowing we'd have to put it in soon.

(To explain quickly....We had got some second-hand flooring from a house not far from here and they had a shower unit up for grabs.... We would have this in as ours ASAP....)

Back to the caravan...Well, I noticed one of the curtains had come off the rail, so I lent over the bed to fix it... PHEW.....What was that smell???......... 'God Bobsky, you need to change your socks!' I thought to myself.

Now, I must tell you I have had Tinitus for over 20 years, but the hissing sound in my head was louder today, well at this moment in time....

Then it dawned on me..........SHIT....**THE GAS WAS ON!!!** In a split second I turned the gas off, opened a couple off widows and ran like hell from the caravan.......

It made the old adrenalin rush that's for sure........ "What you trying to do Bob, blow yourself up?????" I yelled at him, half in anger and half laughing.....I'm afraid I tend to laugh if I get a shock. It's just nerves......

Well, I wasn't laughing when Roger and Annie pointed out that if I'd gone up there with my fag alight, Well' I would have been blown up, woods and all!!!!!!!!!!!!!!!!!!! *THANKS BOB !!*

Two days later Bobsky moved out......Some friends were going to put him up in Edinburgh for a bit till he found a flat... One of his mates said he could get a job at his firm. So it was good bye to Bob......

It's Set in Concrete

It was now November and over the last few weeks we'd put the rubble in for the foundations and spent many an hour using a 'Whacker Plate 'machine to level it all off.

Today we were waiting for a lorry of Ready Mix to arrive, with Robert, Frank and a friend called Tosh to help lay it....

I could say that for once all went well....... Not really..... The damn delivery man forgot the Long Shoot for the cement to go down into the house.

So the men had to shovel the cement across the floor area at 100mile per hour to get it levelled off as fast as possible before it started to go off..

Within two hours it was all done.....

We'd pulled the make shift stairs up out of the way on hinges from the landing area, and as we went round we propped open the window a little. This was because the cement had a hardener in it, it warmed up....a kind of curing... and it warmed the hole house up. Thus condensation was dripping off walls and windows.

As we left the house we locked up. Tosh stayed for a few drams and we then drove him back home.

We popped in on Frank to say 'thank you' again, and bless her heart Betty had made dinner for us. We stayed for while and on our return home it was back to the caravan for the night.

We decided to have a quick peek at our new floor, God, it was dry. Solid enough for us to lower the stairs and spend the night in the house. Great no caravan tonight....

Over the next few days it dried out great and we were able to put the membrane down and fit 'Kingspan' insulation before fitting the second-hand flooring we had got sometime back.

We laid a cement plinth in the kitchen area for a Rayburn/cooker to sit on, and took the next few weeks fitting the floor.....It was tongued a grooved old pine, it looked great.....

Each day we could see the place coming into shape and it would be done in time for Christmas..

Best of all Frank's daughter Heather gave us her old cooker and Roger was able to wire it to the mains meter we'd had fitted when the wiring episode happened etc....

This Christmas was simply the best. Lindy had arrived safely, and my son and his girlfriend were here....

We had fun and games and the usual Christmas nosh up, with all the trimmings, on Boxing Day. Our friend Sheen, Trevor and their two kids Vicky and Chris came over for our second Christmas dinner. We had a great time.....

Just before Jonathon arrived, Lindy who had been here, about a week by then, had been helping us put the lining around the walls.

This was something called 'TRI-ISO Super 9' and looked like silver tinfoil, with different layers in it. This was only about 20mm thick, but was the equivalent to 150mm (6inch) Kingspan and saved on room. Now, the walls were tanked and a wood frame put up, then the Tri-Iso sandwiched between another wood frame to allow ventilation/to stop sweating etc.

So as we sat eating our Christmas dinners, it was like sitting in a highly polished Doctor Who Tardis. But it gave a lovely glow effect as we had the candles alight on the table. But the time went too fast and suddenly were we on our own again...........Oh well back to work.

Ding, Ding, all Change Your Lives

We were pleased for Peter and Kim as they had now sold the Glencove Arms and were now able to retire. They are a lovely couple, and made us so welcome, they would be missed by everyone

The new couple were also English and had some new ideas for the place. We would save judgment, and see what happens in time.

Their names were Tony and Sally, they seemed a pleasant enough couple with a son and daughter still living down south.

We never went into the pub much, usually only on the way home from shopping we'd stop by. And now of course the good news was that my son Jonathon and his girl friend Louise had decided they would come and live in Scotland, and make a fresh new start in life........Oh, to be young again!!!!

Here Endith Another Year.

The new windows

Working with the Boys

I was now working at the local hotel, 'The Colquhonnie'.... It was owned by a gay couple Paul and Dave..*(guess that blew the brains of some of the locals, a boys !!!).* They were a great couple, and a laugh, there was always a 'bitch fight' of some kind going on between them. But this was all just in play, never anything nasty. All just fun etc.... They were, and still are great.

I used to go and do the rooms at first, then they asked if I could help in the kitchens...

Now I'd always said I'd never go back to kitchens full time, but they were great guys to work with, so I said yes.

As time passed I did more and more work in the kitchens, as well as the rooms and I loved it I would help the chef out and wash-up etc. And as time went on, on the chefs days off, I took over the cooking on those days.

I had the main menu to do, with the special guidance from Ingram the chef, but I was also able to do some of my own ideas as time went on.

But it was always back to the Chef's things on his return...Don't want to upset the chiefy!!!!!

Meanwhile we were fitting the wood panelling in the downstairs of the house, and fitting a panel between the kitchen/bathroom etc.....This took ages, but each day was getting a bit further on.

TV Brian

Our friend Brian came up for a few days to go to an Auto Jumble in Alford. He's known as 'TV BRIAN', as that's what he does fixes TV's and thing...He's an absolute whiz with the things.

He also has a couple of historic motor bikes and was looking for some bits, hence he was here. Brian takes part in the 'Vintage Bike Run,' 'THE PIONEER RUN' from London to Brighton, but I think he joined it at 'Box Hill'. He's won trophies and done very well.

He brought his TV gear with him to see if he could find a signal for our TV. But the only place he got a good clear signal was down on the main road. No good to us..

Next door gets a signal as they are in an opening in the woods, and have a high chimney with an aerial etc., but unless we put a pole 40 foot high forget it.......Still we don't care, to bloody busy for all that. Plus it is only crap on the TV nowadays..... But thanks for trying Brian.

Brian only stayed a few days but he was able to stay in the house, as we now had beds (unofficially) upstairs. Then he too was off back home...

The First of Three!!

Shortly before Christmas the husband of the couple we bought the house from became very ill and sadly in the New Year he passed away. It was a terrible shock to his family, our hearts went out to them all. It was a very sad time.

A Double Blow

A couple of months passed and our friends wife from down south phoned late one night with the worst news we thought we could get.

She told us that ***, her husband had collapsed and died of a massive heart attack at work two days earlier........

We were shocked, and we were very sorry for her and her family, but as you can imagine, that once the reality of it had sunk in, there was the problem of the money they owed us......

On a phone call a week later, she said she was now fully aware that there was the money that was owed to us. She hadn't realised that her husband had so much outstanding still.....

It's terrible to look at it this way but he must have had life insurance, as his wife was able to pay back the remainder with in a few weeks.

However, once we had paid some of the Building Material Account off, and the bills, there was not much left. We were now in big trouble. Nothing would get us to sell the house........... We would survive somehow.

I was working nearly full time now, and some money was coming in. Poor Roger had to carry on building and working on the house on his own most days. We had to get it finished, we had to live. This was our home and we were going to stay. We would just tighten our belts yet again and carry on.

Return of the Prodigal Son.

Well what a turn up for the books, here I was now awaiting the return to the fold of my son Jonathon and I couldn't wait, and his girlfriend Louise would be joining him in a few weeks time. She had a works contract to finish first.

Perhaps selfishly I hoped to try and make up for all the sadness and pain he had experienced at the despicable hands of his so called father in years past and perhaps help him to get a fresh start in life.

I am the first to admit that as he grew up I was unable to be there for him, as his father domineered his life. All I could do was to sit and wait for Jonathon to get free of him in his own time.

Luckily Jonathon was able to break free, and get away from what I can only describe as a truly evil man.

I must stress, I am not an ex-wife full of vengeance for a broken marriage thing. For different reasons marriages break up each day in this world.

It takes two to make a marriage and sometimes, two to break it. Sometimes there are other factors involved, not just a relationship breaking down for different reasons.

The man I once married disappeared and became an evil thing. I never want to see, or hear of him in this world or any other. Nor do his children. They no longer think of him as their father....

Jonathon arrived and all his worldly goods, and soon settled into the routine of our set up here. After a bit he got a job with me at the Hotel, which gave him an income.

I would still do the rooms at the Hotel and now Jonathon was there he started to KP, while I spent more time helping the chef.

I must admit I could see Jonathon was just itching to do the cooking, he was also a good cook. But I'm afraid he takes after me and doesn't like being 'ordered' about. You know the thing. There is a difference between being 'told or asked' to do something and 'ordered.'

Meanwhile in the house Roger was busy fitting the lighting, and fitting ornate frames on the wood around the window. Also laying granite tiles for the window sills..

There was also the 'Fire Wall' to build in the kitchen for behind the 'Wood burning Stove', and the flooring to finish. This was to be covered in granite tiles to match the window sills etc...

As the weeks passed Roger's father had been phoning more than usual, and he didn't sound right. We couldn't put our finger on it.. He had more or less given up hope of moving here as he had recently bought a new mobile home near Yapton...

We had tried to find somewhere near to us for him, but the house prices where just too high for him. But if something came up we reckon he would come up.

Jonathon's girlfriend arrived, and all was well, they were very happy bunnies...Mush, mush..

There wasn't any work at the Hotel for her at that time, but later in the summer things would pickup, and then she could work at the Hotel with us......

Meanwhile she would help around the house, and luckily we all got on ok..............

Dad and Mum to the Rescue!!!

Dad and Mum were able to fly up on holiday this year, as their health had improved enough for them to travel. I knew from my brother that they had both lost a lot of weight because they had been so ill, and had aged in the process of all of it. But I was shocked at how frail they both looked...

It only seemed yesterday that Dad was getting awards for trekking up the mountains in Switzerland faster that some of the youngsters. And Mum was always doing something, as well as them both being in good health. There was such a change.

But on the whole I think they were getting better than they had been. And they had made such an effort to get here, we hoped the weather would be kind to us.

Roger and I were in money trouble and we knew that we couldn't hide it from them anymore.

Dad, being conscientious about money matters, always asked how our savings were doing, and hoped we were getting the full interest etc. He was well into accounts over the years, and always did ours for the business, and checking I had done it right. We were very grateful for his help and advice....

Well, the day came we had to tell them. We were in a quiet hotel lounge having some soup for lunch and a cup if tea

I was the one to tell them. So I started by saying that Roger and I had something to tell them. Reassuring them first it was nothing drastic to do with our health, but to let me talk, and finish what I had to say, because if they interrupted I wouldn't be able to carry on. And that then, they could tell us what TWITS we had been........

Dad and Mum both piped up that they had felt something had been wrong for some time, and asked me to continue.......

I felt sick to the stomach as I told them about the money we had lent our friends, and all the troubles that had happed because they were only able to pay so little back at a time. And that because of them we had no money to spare. We just managed to pay house bills as we went along, with me working and owing some money. But that as the money came back, we were slowly paying off the Builder Centres where we luckily had an account. Thankfully we hadn't run up debts though God knows how we managed, we just did it somehow, but it was getting very tough at times.

As soon as I had blurted all this out, I was so choked up I thought I was going to faint or be sick.

So I asked to be excused, and went to the bath room....

I balled my eyes out. I felt such a fool for what we had done, and the relief of telling Mum and Dad after trying to hide it from them, it was as if a huge weight had been lifted.

We hated not telling them the truth for so long, but there were two reasons. One of course was that they were so ill, it would have been to unfair to tell them. They had enough to cope with, without us worrying them. The second being that we felt such 'IDIOTS' at what we had done in the first place...

We knew we would be told what Twits we were, but that was to be expected. So it wasn't that..

When I came back from the loo I could see Roger too, was upset... His eyes were all red.... It was also very embarrassing for him. And I know he doesn't like to see me upset so much...

Dad and Mum said they were relieved that we had told them what had been wrong at last. And to our amazement, Dad said to let them think things over....perhaps they could help in some way ?????

The next day my Dad took myself and Roger, one at a time, to talk in private in our car...

I really thought that I was in for an carful...(most deservedly, I might add). But after a firm talking to, and answering some money questions, I was amazed that Dad, with Mum would help us out......

Our conversation was private, between us. He would n talk to Roger, which would also be private between them......................

We were then able to get on with what was a lovely holiday, and the weather was great. So we were able to get to see some beautiful places..

A few days after they got home safely, Dad sent us a cheque, with a letter, this also said they would find a way to help my brother at some point. As they always treated us the same with everything.

We can never thank them enough for what they did for us... *THANK YOU BOTH xxxxxxxxxx.*

The Passing of Roger's Father

(It nearly always happens in threes!!)

One day we got a call from Roger's father as usual, but this was a very strange call. He was very low!!... Something was wrong!!!!

He started by saying to us not to forget that he still wanted to move up! And as soon as possible so he was putting his place on the market.

That was fine, but trying to find somewhere quick was pushing it. So we suggested that he move up, and leave the mobile home in the hands of an agent to sell. That way he could be here to view places as we found them.

At the end of the conversation Roger's father said a very strange thing. He said "I don't want to die alone down here." !!!!!!!!!

Now, Dad had been feeling low, we knew this, but we put it down to him being lonely etc... But this last comment rang an alarm bell in us, deep down we felt something was wrong!!!!

So we rang Dad's friend Chas. He'd know if Dad was ill, they'd known each other for many years, and would meet most weeks for lunch. However not so much since Dad moved to Yapton.

Chas said it wasn't his place to say anything as Dad hadn't, but he did say Dad had lost a lot of weight.

This was perhaps his way of saying Dad was not well...Mmmmmmmmmmmmm.

We started to make arrangements, and look for a place for Dad, and about two weeks later Dad phoned again.

It was unusual that Roger answered the phone this time. He's no good on the phone he gets tongue tied with his words.

Anyway, it was Dad. He told Roger the pain had got so bad the doctor had been called out to him....But what pain was this I could hear Roger asking Dad?????? It turned out Dad had not been able to go to the 'loo' for about a week and the doctor thought he had a small blockage in his bowl. So Dad was going into hospital now by ambulance. He said he'd ring us as soon as he knew what ward he was in...

Roger was very concerned, me to, but all we could do was wait.........

Later that evening Dad phoned and gave us all the ward details. He was to go to theatre the next day for them to have a look inside....

The next day I rang Dad and spoke to him before he went to theatre. He sounded very tired and weak. Again all we could do was wait.... We'd go down as soon as we could arrange things if necessary.

There was no way of knowing at that moment what was wrong. Perhaps, hopefully it was nothing serious and as soon as Dad could he'd join us up here.......

Little did we know what was about to unfold, and how our lives would be shattered in such a short space of time.

I phoned the hospital, and although I explained who I was, they would only say he was as comfortable as possible???!!!!!

After two days I was able to speak to Dad on a phone beside his bed......
He sounded terrible.....

He said he had a 'Bag' thing below, and they had taken something away!!!!!!!

Now this sounded very serious. I tried to sound cheerful for him, not wanting to let him know how worried we were...... .I remember saying to him something like "Well Dad, just think how much loo roll you save on !!!!!" Not very funny I know, but I couldn't think of what to say to him......

After I spoke to him, saying we'd come down soon, I rang the ward Sister. I didn't get much out of her. They can't disclose anything on the phone with out Dad's say so. Thing was even he didn't know what was going on.......

I assumed this was because they were waiting for results. But it was very frustrating for us, because we were so far away......

I phoned as much as I could to speak to Dad, but I didn't want to upset the staff by phoning every two minutes....

Also for nearly a week I kept phoning to talk to the Doctor about Dad, to try and find out what was happening.

In the end I got to know one of the staff by name, she was always helpful and comforting to me. Letting me know how Dad was, even though he was so ill. She was so sorry that she couldn't tell me what was wrong with Dad. It just wasn't allowed etc. but she told me what she could..

She said she would talk to the doctor/surgeon and ask for 'consent' to tell me on the phone what was going on with Dad, because we were so far away.

To be truthful, deep in our hearts, Roger and I knew what news was possibly coming, but one hangs on in hope that the gut feeling one gets is wrong.

The next day I phoned and spoke to the nurse...........

It was bad news, the worst of it kind...........Dad had Cancer...

We were numbed, even though we had a good idea this was to be the answer, it hit us like a sledge hammer.

I pushed the nurse to tell us what stage the Cancer was in and asked what we should do.

She told me what type it was and her personal advice was that if it was he father she would come down immediately.

Thank God Jonathon and Louise were living here. They just told us to go. They would look after the animals which included Sam our new dog......We'd only got him a few weeks back and he was still a puppy, but rather a large puppy..... He was a cross Wolf hound/bearded collie, or so we were led to believe.

The Boys at the hotel were great. They said to go now, and come back whenever. Bless them. Paul told us how he had not made it to his mother's side when she passed away and how it has upset him ever since... So he said we must be with Roger's Dad if and when it happened.

We arranged train tickets to pick up at the next day, and arranged a taxi from here to Huntly to get a train to Aberdeen Station.... God what a panic........

The next day we set off with just a rucksack each with a few things in.... We just didn't have time to worry about anything.... We knew we had to get to Dad as soon as possible......

All went well and we made the trains on time, then we began the long train journey to London where we had to change at King Cross. Then to Victoria and on to Barnham.. .

We had a straight forward trip to London, but a bit of a panic from King's Cross. As we left the station we took a wrong turning and had to run like hell to the underground to get to Victoria, but we just made it in time.

The hospital knew we were arriving after visiting, but said we could go straight there to see Dad... We had told Dad we'd be there that night to be with him...

When we arrived at Dad's, a neighbour, who we had contacted by a number we got from Dad, was there to give us a spare key to his place.

We let ourselves in and got Dad's spare car keys from his rack...We jumped into his car and set off for the Hospital.

Bloody Hell, have you ever got on the road to find yourself going in circles.... Well we got there in the end..

As we eventually found the correct door to get in the hospital, after trying about five, my heart was racing.

We went to the front desk and they told us where the ward was..... So up we went.

When we got there we were met by the night sister on duty... She was the one I had been speaking to on the phone... She took us to one side and talked to us about Dad.... She was very sensitive with us...

Thing was it was a shock to us how bad Dad was, let alone how much we were to see he had deteriorated. The sister warned us to be prepared for this.

But worst of all Dad hadn't been told yet..... They were waiting to speak to us before breaking it as gently as possible that he hadn't got long...............

"OH Bugger, Bugger", is the only way I could think of at the thought of telling him!!!!!!!!

As we went in to see Dad, it was a shock, although we had been warned..... Dad was propped up in bed resting.

We tried our best to look 'cheerful', and made conversation, but Dad was very tired, so we said we'd return in the morning. At least he knew we were there...

The ward sister said we could visit any time... They were all very kind..

When we got back to his place we made up the bed settee and went straight to bed, we were exhausted.

Over the next few days we tried to find the right time (*as if there is a right time to tell someone they don't have long !!!)*

God it was so hard, I mean, what do you say, and How.....

Perhaps 'we' were in a kind of 'denial' ourselves..!!!! As we decided that as soon as Dad was well enough we would get him transferred up to Scotland to a hospital near us, and in time to a Hospice if needed.

We wanted him to be near us, and with us when 'IT' happened..... We would not let him be on his own.

When we had first found out Dad was ill, I pre-cooked some meals and froze them down, in anticipation that he may come and stay with us while recovering etc but little did we know at that time.

Roger and I had hours talking about when, and if we should tell Dad he had Cancer.... In the end we talked to the sister again.

She told us the truth.... The news 'we' deep down knew.... Dad had not got long at all, maybe only days.............

Well that made our minds up. We weren't going to tell him!!!??

This decision was not a 'Cowards' way out by any means. We just felt that if Dad was told there was no hope of him getting better, it would break what was left of him etc...

It would be bad enough to know you only had a short time left, be it years or months, but to know you only had days left to live. Well, I for one would be terrified...

The sister said that there may be things that have to be said between us and Dad, but we felt there was nothing he or we could say. We loved him, and he loved us, and we all knew this.

As far as we were concerned, now knowing Dad could go at any time, if he slips away in his sleep believing and dreaming that he would be coming to Scotland, which had been his dream, then let it be...

Who were we to destroy that, we had no right to take that away from him....

'Oh God' it was so confusingly upsetting, I wanted to hold Dad in my arms forever... Kiss his forehead and make it all better, like when you were a child and your mother would kiss your grazed knee and make it all better. But this I knew I could not do.... What should we really do?? I just wanted it to all go away like a bad dream....

We talked to the Sister and Staff and told them our decision, and why. We asked them to respect this, and making sure we were 100% sure, they agreed.

Meanwhile Chaz, Dad's old friend had been to see him. It really upset him, but he knew, he kind of came to say his goodbye

Dad had also had his friend from the site visit... They all knew not to say anything to him.....

There was one couple that were very close to Dad, Derek and Carol. It was hitting Derek very hard..

Dad was going down hill fast... We would be in and out during the day. I would feed him, Ice-cream was all he could eat now, and drink slowly..... Oh God it was heart breaking......

Then the sister wanted to talk to us in private.!!!!!!!!!!! She explained that Dad really needed to go to a Hospice now........ There they could take care of all his needs........... And it would be more comfortable for all of us.........

They were very good and arranged things for the following morning..... Meanwhile I told Dad we were getting him into a Private HOSPITAL.....not a HOSPICE...... We felt the name would alert Dad to his state of condition etc....

We phoned the Hospice and begged them not to tell Dad he was dying, and the reasons why, as it was so near.... They agreed, although they said it was against policy.

They believe people should be told the truth, because they may perhaps have things to say, or make their peace.....

But they did state that, if Dad asked, they would have to tell him, but they were trained in this situation and it would be handled sensitively.

When we arrived at the Hospice we were shown to Dad's room, he was resting..... But as the nurse was leaving Dad opened his eyes and said.... "I've seen the doctor,......He's told me the worst."....

It was as if I could hear ten thousand doors slamming in my head. Dad then just closed his eyes........ I could have hit that doctor at that moment....... All I thought was 'how could they break his dream'......

I lent over and I gave him a gentle hug saying "we know Dad, we're sorry."......

Dad was so tired after the ambulance drive, it had taken it out of him. He was sleepy, so Roger gave him a hug, and said we'd see him in the morning and talk then, and just to rest......

As we were leaving a nurse asked if Dad went down hill, did we want calling in.........

Well, we decided that if Dad slipped away in his sleep to call us in the morning. There would be no point in driving in when it was to late. However, if Dad started to slip away, to call us straight away even if it was during the night....

We went home to Dad's and spent some time with his friends.....then we went off to bed....

We couldn't sleep much, it was horrible.......we just talked about Dad and things until the early hours when we must have dozed off.

Then the phone rang.............. we knew before answering it, it was about Dad......

He was slipping away... we had to dash in now. We dragged our things on and left for the Hospice.

On arrival they were waiting for us and we were shown into his room. The nurse asked if either of us had been in this situation before????? Did we know what to expect??????

I don't know what made me lie, but I said I had... Roger was just quiet... he said nothing...

The nurse spoke gently and explained things to us, and left us alone while she got us a cup of tea...

We asked her on her return if Dad would be able to know we were here for him... She said that some people believe that Dad would know we're here, and more so, that the hearing is the last thing to go... so we should talk to Dad as much as possible......

'Blood Hell' what could we say.............. Anyway I got a paper from the nurse and began to read it to Dad.... I talked all the time, about the news, and anything I could...

I told Dad we'd look after Misty his cat. She was meant to go to a lady at his old site if anything happed to him...but Misty had begun to cling to Roger's every move......

I had my hand on Dad's head all the time, gentle stroking his fore head, in the hope that he could feel I was there.

Then the doctor came in to check on Dad, and to see us....... I was no longer mad at him for telling Dad, they did say if Dad asked they would have to tell him the truth.

As the hours passed we thought Dad had gone, but then he would start breathing again. It was horrid to see. We didn't really know what we would see when it eventually happened... It's nothing like TV...... This was the real thing........

A short while later the doctor returned..... Roger spoke to the doctor, he asked because Dad had for a long time been taking so many pain killers then indigestion tablets, could it have contributed to his condition..... The doctor said, not really.

But as he said this, Dad seemed to shrug his shoulders as if he heard what was being said!! This happened a few times, in time with what was being said!!!!!!!!! I really believed he could hear them talking.

Suddenly Dad opened his eyes and turned his head to look straight at me..... In a split second I asked if he was going to see Mum now?? Then Dad turned to look at Roger, and as I called out to Roger that Dad was awake... Dad closed his eyes again...

The doctor just stopped talking to Roger and said he would leave us alone now ?????????

Guess the doctor knew that Dad was now leaving us....... So he left us in private......

About twenty minutes later it was over .... Dad was gone.......... Roger said his goodbye, gave him a hug, and promised he would take him to Scotland. That's what Dad wanted...He'd be with us....

I leant over and gave him a hug goodbye, and kissed his forehead telling him I loved him..........

A nurse must have been just outside and she came in to check Dad had gone.... She asked if I'd like to help lay Dad out nicely before we leave.... No, I would leave Dad some pride.....

We left the room and went into the gardens with a lady to do the necessary paper work.... Best to get it done now ....

After that we went to say our last goodbye to Dad...... He looked so peaceful now... All the pain of the last few weeks had gone from his face...... Perhaps he will find Mum.... I truly believe now that this life is not the end of it...... I know we will all meet again one day.....

It was a strange mixture of feelings, overwhelming sadness, yet relief that the pain was over for Dad......................

Next were the phone calls to make and the funeral to arrange..... It was very difficult to tell his family and friend of his passing etc.. But it had to be done......

The day arrived for the Funeral and all went well and to plan... They played The Flower of Scotland as Dad's coffin was taken in... And after the short service they played the music from The Dam Buster in memory of his years with them in the war....*xxxxxxxx REST IN PEACE DAD xxxxxxxxx*

Dambusters ground crew

It was a small gathering of close friends, but Chaz didn't come. I think he just couldn't face it. He'd known Dad for so many years, they were good friends....

After the 'wake' I was talking to my Mum, she and Dad had come down for the service. Mum was still very ill herself and in a moment of sadness she said that her last wish would be to see Roger and I married!!!!!!!!!!!! (*I said we'd have to talk it over. We knew Roger's Dad had often spoken about it.*)

Everyone left, and we had lots to sort out over the next few days or so.......

Over the next few weeks we packed Dad's things and arranged a removal company.... We also had to arrange things with the estate agent.....

We spoke to the agent that Dad had already spoken to. They agreed to sell the property on our behalf for a small fee. This was good news as we had to get back to Scotland......

We were able to visit friends down in Brighton and go to the Tavern, and go to The Lanes, plus the Market we used to go to..... It was great to see them all again....

But back home to Scotland we had to go...... We now had Dad's car loaded up, and his cat Misty........ So off we set.

(I would like you to know, that what I have just finished typing, was the hardest part in this book to do.) It seems only yesterday, yet as you will see from the following events, Dad was still unable to rest in peace for some time to come!

Saying Goodbye to Our Old and New Friends

It was hard saying goodbye to our friends, believing that we may not see some of them again for some time, if at all. We loved seeing them, but we just hated the hustle and bustle of towns. Even in the short space of time since we moved away, every thing had changed.

We had a fab time at the Brighton Tavern, and meeting all our old friends again. Walking around The Old Lanes was great fun. We bought lots of things to bring home with us.

Shame we couldn't bring all our friends from Brighton with us, (but I guess Strathcove wouldn't be the same again)!!!!!

We also popped in on Alan and Heidi at 'THE FLEE MARKET', this was where I sold my antiques and oddities with their help. They're a sweet couple with their young son. They have a good business going there. I miss the chats we used to have with them on our regular Sundays outing to Brighton.

We'd also made some lovely friends at Roger's Dad's site, they were all so kind, they helped us so much. We can never thank them enough. They were a great help when Dad was so ill, they gave us some form of normality in a world of sadness and chaos. And such comfort, at that time.

Derek and Carol were some of Dad's closest friends. Derek would go around to Dad's door every day and they would put the world to right. Derek used a mobility cart to get around on, his legs were bad. He had a number plate on it "OLD GIT".. apparently there were three old boys in their area (all pals that met up) and they were "OLD GIT 1, 2 AND 3."

It hit Derek very hard when Dad died. Derek did visit him in the hospital a couple of times, but it was very upsetting for him.

Carol his wife worked in a care home not far away. She is lovely, and is a good friend. I should keep in touch more. But time seems to fly by.

There was also Cynthia and Alan from next door, they were also a great comfort and help to us. But Alan was at work a lot so we didn't get to see so much of them.

And of course Mike and his wife Margaret who lived opposite. He was a character on his own. He always had a joke to tell and cheered us up. Sadly his wife was very ill and blind, so he spent his time looking after her..

There were others too. A chap called John, and others, who without them all, we would have found Dad's passing even harder.

So we thank you all for your love and kindness at that time...

Leaving family was tough, but leaving Mum and Dad again was heart breaking. Still, we hoped to see them next summer if they are well enough to come up on holiday again.

We had arranged to go and see some old friends Chris and Sue, with their daughter Ellie. They had moved up near Castle Douglas some time back. A little diversion on our journey home would make a welcome break. It would be great to catch up.

We set off home late one evening after what we hoped was knocking off time for the main workers.

I suppose it wasn't too bad, but the weather started to change rather for the worse. As we travelled along the motorway you could see black clouds gathering above, and a strange yellow tinge in the sky.

Then it hit..... The skies just opened.... There was flashing and banging all around us and driving was hellish.

What with the black clouds being lit up by the lightning, and now the night skies were in, it was like a scene from a spooky horror film.

There were a few nasty pile ups happening, so we tried to find somewhere to stay overnight. But most places were fully booked, or we had just missed out, because so many people had the same idea of getting of the roads. Then we found a place to stay, we didn't really know where we were on the motorway and to be honest we didn't care.

There had just been a nasty crash on the road, and a car was upside down on the embankment... We counted our blessings that we weren't involved and hoped of course that whoever it was would be ok... But it didn't look good from where we were.

So we were very glad to get off the roads for the night....

Plus I think we were tired. It had been a very stressful time and to be going home was a relief in some ways.

There would be a lot to catch up on...We were behind getting the wood cut for winter and all kinds of things....

I didn't have to worry about getting back to work, the Boys had been great and were great in giving us as much time as we needed.

Once we were in the hotel and settled in, we studied the map and found we were near Birmingham, or as good as.

We had a great nights sleep and set of early the next morning to our friends.

Seeing Old Friends

We managed to find them fairly easily, down a very long narrow road to nowhere..

God, their place looked fab. It's a huge house with outbuildings. And a fair bit of land.

Sue had written a few times and told us of some of the work they were doing. It was a big renovation job.

Chris was there when we arrived, but Sue was still at work, so yes you guessed it, "Pub Time" ... But first Chris showed us to the guest room they had prepared for us to stay in that night. What a spectacular place. It reminded me of a Royal House. Full of wooden corridors and wood panelling and a magnificent wooden stair case to suit.

He showed us in this one room "the play room." It had the biggest snooker table I'd ever seen and again wooden panels to suit the building with a huge drinks bar etc.

They had done some fantastic work around the place, tons of renovating etc. Oh, and as for the bedroom, it was beautiful, with a huge old bed fit for a King. The views from the windows were out of this world..

Chris took us to a pub in a small village near them. It was great and everyone was very welcoming.

After a few beers we set off back to their place and Sue was soon home with their daughter from school.

While Sue cooked dinner we were shown around the house by Chris in more detail. It was unbelievable. The hard work they had been putting into the place was a credit to them both and there was still work to do on the building in the kind of courtyard area.

It was a fab nights sleep, the bed was so comfortable we didn't want to get up. But too quickly the morning arrived and we had to leave for home...

The rest of the journey was normal and we arrived home in the afternoon come early evening. Louise and Jonathon had good dinner for us.

Now we were back it was back to work for me and time to also catch up with all the chores for the winter months to come. Time was passing us by.

Also Louise was having to return back to the south for an operation. She was to have her tonsils out. The poor girl had been very ill with infections for years, and at long last they were going to get them out.

Meanwhile Louise was now in hospital and Jonathon was looking for a " live in" job where they could both be together.

Down at the Glencove, Jonathon was offered such a job but he was to live in an old caravan. It had been lived in before, but needed to be cleaned and done up i.e. also electric put in plus painting and repair work.

He was offered a set wage with food and rent over the winter months, then a review in the summer and a job for Louise. So he took up the offer.

Now this meant that they could use one of the showers in the pub and the washing machine etc. But he managed to reduce the rent as he said they would get their own food in.

He left the Hotel and set about doing up the caravan. He spent a lot of time getting it nice for Louise. Yes, it was going to be hard, and we hope they would make a go of it...

It was to be tough over the winter months, but come spring and summer it would be good fun for them. Well this is what we all hoped for them. It was a start anyway...

As time went by Louise was due to arrive back and start their new life together in the caravan.

We went to the airport to collect her and on the way back we stopped at the pub and Jonathon was able to show her their future home...

They would move into it in a week or so. Her brother and dad were bringing her things up in a van then.

Now Louise is a typical young girl. In the sense of all youngsters, they seem to think they have done every thing, and know it all. Please don't get me wrong, I love her to bits and wouldn't want her any different. It's just her way...but some people don't like that kind of thing...(hence the next bit later).

You must remember at this point I didn't know Louise very well as she had only just moved up here in the last summer when Roger and I had to dash off because of Roger's dad etc...

So you can imagine how embarrassing the next event was in the pub!!!!!!

Well, as we sat at the bar having a drink Louise asked me very quietly that if her panties showed at the back as she sat at the bar, would I let her know!!!!!

OK, came my reply..........but I'm sorry to say, that being me, that was like waving a red flag at a bull!!!!!!!!!!!!!!!!!!!!!!!

In the sense that when the inevitable did show, as I lent over to whisper in her ear that her panties were beginning to show, I instead just gave her a big 'Wedge'!!!!!!!! Ooooops.

But to top it off as Louise shot in the air and took a deep

breath.......TWANG......

Her (as I found out) G-string panties SNAPPED. We just looked stunned at each other. Me not believing what I had just done to someone I didn't really know well enough to even think about doing such a thing to.

And Louise was just...shocked I guess......but after a few seconds of silence we both burst out laughing. People just didn't know what was happening. Thank God, well, that is until now.

As for Jonathon, he just couldn't believe I'd done it. But he had a good laugh about it and well, I am his mum. He should know me by now!!!!!!

Well, life returned to normal, and we all got on well. In spite of my moments of insanity!!!!

Jonathon and Louise soon settled into their new home and Jonathon seemed to be getting on with his new job although there wasn't enough work for Louise yet.

They made new friends at the pub but there was some friction. Not everyone gets on with everyone..!!!!

Tony and Sally seem to be having problems!!! You could tell by the atmosphere something wasn't right. And now there was their daughter Jane.

She'd been here for some time and I felt that she resented Louise, i.e. Jane wasn't always centre of attention. Kids, eh!

And I felt Jonathon was having problems in the kitchen!!!!! But I do know that Jonathon can be funny to work with at times. So I won't make out it was all plain sailing.

They began finding it harder to get their washing done, as the machine was always in use.

Normally with Jane's things! Jonathon began to think that if by chance he had mentioned he wanted to use the machine, it was then full when he went to it. Funny that! Still, maybe a coincidence! But it was just little things like that, that seemed to be happening more and more.

One night Jonathon and Louise were in the pub and Jonathon stepped out for a fag. He began to throw a stick for Tony's dog Buster. God knows how, but he managed to pick a bit of wood with a nail in it and, yep, as he went to throw it, it lodged in his finger.......OUCH...!!!!

I don't know the line of events, but an ambulance was called to get Jonathon. The nail had gone up his finger and out the top. Impaling his finger to a point of no return, wood and all.

Now, what happened next I don't rightly know but there were a few words between Louise and Sally?????

This confrontation, or whatever, left it that Louise would 'never' get work in the pub!

Well, that stuffed it really for them both in the end. What money Louise had in savings was going fast and Jonathon's money was not enough for them to live on nicely. So the rot began to set in big time.

I'd help them when I could i.e. when out shopping, I'd give then a few quid to get food etc.

It was hard for them, believe me I know what it's like.....

Plus Louise was feeling homesick and now feeling more isolated by some people, although she had made some good friends here. But as I said I don't know what was said or done. I wasn't there so I can't judge.

I did ask Louise what had happened, but she felt she had apologised to Sally for whatever she said that night!!!

Sally has never told me 'What' was said or 'Done'...So who knows??

And to be fair Jonathon stood by Louise's side on that subject. Which I admire him for. It is right that he stood by her.

Visitors

About this time we got a call from an old friend called Cathy, she and her family were staying in Scotland for a holiday and she asked if they may come and see us before they return down south.

Roger had known Cathy since she was a young child. So to catch up would be great.

Cathy had two daughters, the eldest was Hannah, and the younger one Jenny and then there was Tim, her partner.

Our pending civil partnership came up in conversation while they were visiting us, and we said we had already asked James, to be Roger's best man.

The children got very excited about the news, so Roger and I asked if they would like to come to the service, and make it a holiday.

They said they'd love to be here with us on our special day and Cathy said that she and the girls had some lovely dresses they could use, but they may be a little bit too bridesmaid like for them to use. She would send me some photos when they got back down south to see what I think.

"Oh what the hell" I said, "you may as well all be matron of honour and the girls can be proper bridesmaids. Lets go for it,."

After catching up on all the news it was soon time for Cathy and her family to leave. So it was set.   And we would be in touch on the phone to arrange things later on.

We phoned James and told him that Cathy and Tim were coming with the children and he in turn told us that Adam and his girlfriend would be able to come along with him. The invitation was for all the family, so it was now going to be a much bigger affair than we had planned. But that was great by us, it would be great to see them all again. Unfortunately James and his wife were having problems, so she would not be able to come along. It was a shame, we would have loved her to be here as we'd known them all for so long. Still, may be it was for the best.

Now knowing there would be a group of them coming up, James said that he would talk to Tim and Cathy about things. Perhaps they may get together and hire a mini bus to save on fuel etc. He would keep us posted. We would leave it in their hands to arrange.

Meanwhile I would try and find a place for them to stay near us. It would mean 8 people, so self catering may be best, I'd have to find out.

I just wouldn't have the room at the time as others would be here and my Mum and Dad would be staying near us on holiday at the same time. So I would be a bit busy.

But we just couldn't wait to see them all and there would be plenty of places to show them. Oh, and hopefully a good few parties.

I Will Miss the Boys.

Meanwhile after a few weeks I left the Colquhonnie Hotel, I must admit that some of it was due to Roger's dad passing which meant that I needn't have to work full time. But also now with the summer season over the work was slowing down a little. Plus David had his family there now working, so to be fair on them it seemed silly to employ me, when you have family to help do the work. The winter is just too quiet for full employment.

But I left on good terms and said if they needed me they could call on me at any time.

I would miss the Boys very much, it seemed only yesterday Roger and I had the honour to be at the Kildrummy Castle, for their Civil Partnership.....

It was lovely to see them making their commitments to each other, and the whole day was great...(apart from the sprouts being a bit "SOLID", a Paul) note.. This was Not my fault........

Another thing about leaving the Hotel is that I won't have to feel that the ghosts were watching me at my work in the rooms. 'Oh Yes', the place has about three, I think." I've only seen one." That was enough!

Anyway me leaving left a good job for Jonathon to step into in the kitchen side of things. He took over my job cooking with the chief...

About this time Roger and I decided we would have a "Civil Partnership", which as I understood it to be, was like a Marriage, but not religious. But it's the next best thing.

So I rang my Mum and Dad and gave them the news...They were over the moon. I told them it would be next summer.....

So Mum and Dad would get there most wanted wish. Plus I reckon it was about time.

Roger had never been married before, but I had, and I had to find my Divorce papers. God knows where they were after all these years.

Still, plenty of time to get things ready.

Beware of the Rampant Rabbit!!!!

Christmas came and it was a family affair. Jonathon and Louise came to stay, and it was lovely.

A white Christmas is something time has lost, but not here, it was chucking it down.

We had a fantastic day and after lunch we were still just about sober enough to open our presents.

We gave them little gifts, but mainly some money to help out.....

Roger got a book on Dirty Pub Jokes and some other little bits.. Then it was my turn to open mine!!!!!

Talk about Louise getting her own back for the Panties thing!!!!!!

As I opened the outer paper I could see an 'Anne Summers' bag!!!!!! Oh my God, what has she got me ?????????????????????????????????

As I opened the bag this THING fell to the floor in its box.!!!!!!

I burst out laughing, as I saw their faces, as I realised what it was...'Anne Summers' latest in technology 'THE RAMPANT RABBIT.'

Note. FOR THOSE WHO DO NOT KNOW WHAT ONE IS...WELL...I'M NOT TELLING YOU!

Talk about scream with laughter, I nearly wet myself.......COW........ha, ha.

But I 'guess' Louise thought she'd got one over on me. But it takes a bit more than that to fluster me.

There be a Trouble Brewing

With Christmas over they returned back to the caravan and back to work...

By now things were defiantly not right between Tony and Sally, and as for Jane, God she was impossible. She was so rude to people, it was beginning to cheese every one off at times.

Maybe because she knew what was going on behind the scenes, and that was part off her problem.

But her rudeness and grumpiness was now not just in the sight and ears of regulars but people just coming in for a meal. I'm surprised some people just didn't walk out at times.

Jane is a nice girl at heart, but sometime she can be outright bloody rude. Perhaps she just didn't realise. Guess that's the younger generation for you nowadays. Still, I suppose she has her reasons.

But she's always gone on at how she hates the pub, and working there!

Mine is not to reason why. But I just wish she wouldn't bring it into the pub.

When I worked in pubs over many years, on the 'Bar' you 'Never' brought a grumpy face along, or any problems you had. You gave a smile to all, no matter who they were or what you may secretly think of them. They are your customers, and without them you have 'NO BLOODY JOB.'

I mean, people go there to enjoy a pint with a friendly atmosphere. But that soon goes when the person behind the bar looks like she or he is 'sitting on a cactus, sucking on lemons.'

But in saying all that, she can be the life of a party, 'when she gets her head out of her arse, she can be so nice. Deep down she must be deeply unhappy about something in life?

I must say that, as things began to unfold, and things became common knowledge, I felt very sorry for Jane, as you will see. It's true to say that if you live and work in a pub, you have no private life.

Jonathon and Louise Leave

Because Louise was unable to find work, and Jonathon was not managing on the money side, they decided to leave and go back to her parents until they found a place to live and work.

It was heart breaking to see them go. So I have to admit I didn't go for a farewell drink with them before they left. I just couldn't face saying goodbye.

Then in February a job in a million came their way. But this meant they would have to move far away. They took a gamble and went for it. (Good for them.)

Before they left we talked about it and I said they should really go for it.

On the day they were to leave I got a call from Jonathon to say they were at the airport in London and flying off to their new jobs in Spain, and they would keep in touch via email.

I will miss them so much, but they had a good chance of going far with their new jobs.

There be Infidelity in the Village

WELL, it's all come out that Tony's been a naughty boy and been playing away from home!

Sally's, understandable is a bit 'Peed Off ' to say the least. Worst of all, we all know about it now.

Now before anyone judges anyone, I have only this to say.

Firstly, for whatever reason, Tony was not happy, hence he played away. It was obviously not a one night thing. It had been going on for some time.

Second, for what ever reason Sally wasn't 100% happy with the buying of the pub in the first place and that showed at times.

Thirdly, you 'never ' know what goes on in a relationship behind closed doors.

I should know because I've been there in my last marriage. So one should 'NEVER' judge on appearances.

And finally, but delicately, fourthly, whoever the woman, one should not blame her 100% because in my view, if a man...(*I'll try and put this delicately*) removes his trousers, (*then in my view*) 'he' has made the choice to do so. And will no doubt pay for his infidelity in the end.

This event in turn made Sally so bloody mad and ill she took up walking, I think to let off steam.. She would walk miles every day, sometime twice. She would hardly eat, and was a bag of nerves. She had always been a 'well rounded woman' but the weight was falling off each day. Many of us were very worried about her.

I felt so sorry for Jane, to see her parents at war like this.

This would be the beginning of the end, as far as the pub was concerned!!!!! Let alone the marriage......

Wedding Plans!!

Plans were now getting together for our special day. I had already been to the registry office in Huntly and got the paper work to find out what we had to do for a Civil Partnership.

We had wanted the service to be at our house but there was so much involved. You had to have insurances to cover all kinds of things.

If you had over a certain amount of people you had to have fire insurance, and insurance to cover personal injury in the house.

So we said we wanted the service out in front of the house. Still it was a non starter, because if you had it booked for outside, and God forbid it rained, you had to stay out in the Bloody Rain!!, as you would not be insured in the house.

This was getting Bloody Maddening....

Then came the biggest hitch...

As I went to the offices in Huntly the women behind the desk called me to one side. She then proceeded to say the following 'in a very embarrassed hushness'.... "Oh, we are very glad you came in, we have been wanting to speak to you!!!! I have to ask you, *Is your partner of the same sex??*"

WELL.............., after a few seconds of it sinking in, and trying not to laugh, I managed to say the most embarrassing thing in reply......

I just blurted out a bit louder than I should have done in view of the fact that there were others in the room...... "*Not when I looked this morning, madam*" Oooooooooooooop.

Well, that put the cat amongst the pigeons. We could not have a Civil Partnership as it was for GAY couples only. It would have to be a Civil Marriage. Mmmmmmmmmmm.

I wasn't sure if Roger would be up for a Marriage!!!!! Something he felt was not necessary after all this time. We both felt the same on that after all these years. We thought the Partnership would be enough!!

I'd got everything else on the go by now, I'd even had to send off for a copy of my divorce papers..

Plus we had now booked the service for July 9th and we had told everyone it was to be a Civil Partnership.!!!!

We talked it over and to my surprise Roger was up for it. Deep down I had always wanted to marry Roger, but I knew he was kind of against it 'the marriage thing' and all the fuss. Roger was not one for speeches. And as for standing up in front of people....Well, he'd run a mile first.

But here he was saying lets get married then. So it was arranged to have a marriage.

When I phoned and told Mum and Dad, they were over the moon even more and couldn't wait to get up here for the now "WEDDING".

There were invitations to do to tell everyone of the change of venue. It was met with great excitement by everyone. And everyone I had invited on the phone would be coming up. It would be a great day.

As for a dress, well white was out but cream looked to be the next best thing. I had a skirt I could do up and a lovely top to go with it......

Anyway hopefully now I would make things right. I would make Mum and Dad proud of me, and involve them as much a possible, considering they were so far away, I'd have to do this on the phone, and send photos of the dress to Mum etc.

So planning and all was to be done, and then I suppose, just wait for the day to arrive.

We had been able to book the Glencove for the reception, but then we had the idea of having the wedding there. A dream come true for Roger, and most men I suspect. Well, I mean A PUB, what heaven.....

This we were able to arrange with a Special License to cover the pub, plus it saved on insurance costs for us, as the pub was already fully covered....

I was able to ask Sally if she would make The Wedding Cake as well as doing the buffet for us... Cool, all was coming into place....

Dad very kindly said he would contribute to the cost of the reception as a wedding gift. We didn't expect anything from them, they had been so helpful to us over the years. Bless you both.

One problem remained, my weight. I had to do something fast.....I didn't want to look like the Michelin Man in my dress on the day. So here starts another Sodding diet!!!!!

Meanwhile we were now working for Sylvia at the Manor House, doing the gardens and odd jobs. This was a little income well needed.

There would be tons to do there over the pending months as her daughter Tanya was to be getting married in September and that would be a grand affair.

The grounds were huge, there were flower beds and all to do as well as planting special flowers for the day itself.

Plus not forgetting I had my own planting etc to do for my own wedding. Thing is, nothing really grows here in the wooded area so perhaps silk/ fake flowers will be in mine.

Penny Pinching

Great news came our way. Roger's dad's old house had a last been sold. We could do with the money now...

The agent dealt with it all for us at a small fee as arranged. But something was not right!!!!

First we had to re-send our details to the agent as it was something to do with Government protection of Money Laundering!!!

So this we did......Then we only received (weeks later I might add) about half the money from the sale!!!! Mmmmmmmmmmmmmmm.

Something smelt about this but we were assured the money would be in the bank soon....

As the weeks passed, we received a cheque from the agent but still not for the full amount.

On talking to him on the phone, his explanation was that by splitting the money up this way (!!!) it would save on us getting mixed up with 'Inheritance Tax ' costs etc, etc !!!!??????

Well now I knew that was 'Bull Shit' on his part, as he knew Roger's father didn't have anywhere near that bracket of money.

So I rang our solicitor on the matter. Now because Dad had already chosen this agent, that's why we stayed with them, plus being a Mobile Home we were informed we need not use a solicitor in the sale side of things.....

However our solicitor, (who was also Dad's) was horrified at what was unfolding. He would look in to the matter 'a.s.a.p.' and get back to us....

Then blow me down, the cheque Bounced!!!!!!!! So they sent another one.......

Which, you guessed it again. It also bounced...

We kept on at this agent time and time again......and time again there was always some 'good' reason for everything .....

He even tried to pull the wool over our solicitor's eyes but you don't want to mess with them. So now we were in 'Legal Land', and the solicitor was on the case....

God if I could get hold of the agent I'd give him a flea in his ear. But now the solicitor would do all the talking.....

A Flea in Who's Ear?

One night we were fast asleep in bed and suddenly I was woken by a loud buzzing. I jumped out of bed so damn fast you would have thought I had been bitten on the bum.

Roger nearly had a heart attack, as I terrifyingly looked around for a wasp or bee in the room. Or worse still in our bed. Roger stripped the bed and we found nothing, then the buzzing seemed to stop.....

"You were dreaming" Roger proclaimed, and we remade the bed and settled down to sleep again.

After a few minuets I heard it again, and again shot out of bed......

Again we stripped the bed...Nothing....So we made it up again, and settled down again....

We must have dropped off, when I awoke again to this buzzing sound!!! This time I lay there a just listened, .and listened........

I slowly nudged Roger till he woke up. I told him just to listen. He couldn't hear a thing!!

After five minuets or so I became aware of a tickling in my ear!!!!!!!!!!!!!

I began to feel that familiar feeling of sheer panic, as whatever it was, was in my bloody ear hole.

God, I shook my head around like a crazed women, trying to shake whatever it was out!!!

In the end Roger held me down on the bed and looked in my ear. He could see it......

You know what...it was a tiny Nat....buzzing away, very happily in my ear. Well until Roger got it...... Now we may get some sleep!!!!!!!

How can something so small sound like a huge bee......????? Hey, STOP laughing at me!!!

IT'S NOT FUNNY.......ha, ha.....Well, I suppose it was looking back. !!!

So hence the saying 'A FLEA IN THE EAR' I think NOT.......

It was now getting on in March (2007) and the Wedding Plans were going well, but there was something I couldn't get my head round....The dress....What ever I did was just not right..

I mean the dress itself was fab, just something, then it dawned on me. CREAM...

My dress before was cream, so I didn't want that reminder, so I began to add colour to it.

I sent some pictures to Mum and Dad. They loved it....so I was to get it dry cleaned and I was set.

I had got Ghillie shirts for Roger, James and Tim to wear and changed the neck laces to match the colours in my dress. The collars needed a good pressing and the packaging creases ironed out, so they went to the cleaner with my outfit.

But when I went to collect them, I didn't notice until we got home what a mess they were in......I had to iron them all myself, I just prayed I didn't scorch them...They were like silk.

The skirt was ok, but again I had to press it...but my top was round, all it's shape had gone. I just cried. What could I do now?

So I frantically went on the Net and after weeks I was able to find a dress that would fit. It was coming from China. It didn't cost much, and looked beautiful...and not cream (tell you later).

Otherwise everyone who was coming now had a place to stay and best of all, my daughter and my grandson Erik were coming up and staying a whole week. I couldn't wait to see them, I miss them so much....

Sad thing was Jonathon and Louise would not be here to make the day complete. Still they were getting on well in Spain...

I was able to get a self catering place for Tim and the crew. They had arranged to bring James with them by car now as Adam and Lisa had found out they were expecting a little bundle of joy. In fact twins. So it would seem to make sense for them to save the money and come by car...

James was going to stay on after the wedding for another week when Tim and Cathy go on somewhere else or back home. I can't remember which it was....

So once Tim and family had left, it meant Roger and James could catch up on old days and stuff.

I was having to arrange payment for the place they were going to stay at but James and Tim had been made redundant from the same firm we were at and their cheque hadn't yet cleared in the bank.

So I arranged to pay, and they would pay me back when they came up....seemed easier that way......

When I phoned to confirm the booking and arrange payment, I booked the place in James's name, as I didn't know Tim's surname at the time. Still the receipt would come to our place in James's name (c/o, me at our address) saves messing around and they would lose their weeks booking if not paid soon.

Weeks later Cathy phoned to say they too would be staying on for another week. So, as James was to stay in the caravan, I said James could stay in the house as my Sara and little Erik will have gone home by then and then Cathy and family could have the use of the caravan at night...and use the house facilities in the day...they could just use us as a base, so they could go out on outings etc. Cathy did however say Tim didn't like caravans!! So I said we'd swap around to suit etc at the time.

(A Letter to the Chief Angel for the Attention of God)

Dear God,
Yes I'm afraid it's me again, and I'm on my soap box ...... again.

The reason I am writing to you, is that a recent encounter with one of your tiniest inventions has made me wonder about the following things.

I was wondering if my thoughts are valid, and if not, could you give me the correct answers?

Although as I said before, I love 'all creatures, Great and Small' this is *apart form Wasps and stingy things, and come to think back, I must say I'm not keen on Bats and sodding things that dive bomb you, that includes the Wood Wasp from Hell.*

*Oh, and then there's Slugs...and ...Snails...*I mean for God sake (*sorry*) lets face it, how on earth can one find it in oneself to be in anyway endearing to something that resembles, only what I can describe as a tiny slimy alien form.

A snail is just a 'Posh' SLUG with a house on top for housing. A slug...!! so I guess some are homeless !!!! *poor things?*

OK, so maybe their purpose on this planet is to clean up waste mater in the garden. However I wish God had told them to leave my (*shouting this >* BLOODY VEG PATCH OUT OF THE EQUATION<

While I'm on my soap box again, SPIDERS, why did God give them so many damn hairy legs?

We get around on two easily enough, so why give them so many?????

I think God knew Mankind would one day invent BOOZE, hence 'God' knew humans would then have trouble enough with TWO legs, let alone the troubles we'd have with SIX or EIGHT.......Can you imagine that in casualty.!!

And as a runner up for the most insane, and wacky ideas, THE GIRAFFE..... What was this all about ?.....Legs so long that when giving birth, the poor baby is dropped at 900miles an hour.

Oh, then if it has survived the G-force, it's bashed into life when hitting the earth below by the hard scorched and dry grounds of Africa. Then to add insult to 'possible' injury, it's then expected to be able to walk perfectly within the hour on what only resembles four long stilts!!

And why the long neck one asks? Is it just so they can eat what's left of the greenery on the very tops of the trees, as everything below has been eaten by others...?

But what is it with those two things on their heads ?...(Not the ears, the other two things) I mean to say, they look like a pair of small alien antennas ...!!!!! Sorry but they just do.

And finally .....PINK FLAMMINGOS !!! WHAT, was someone up there smoking when they had that idea.????? (Yer, ok, I know it's what they eat, or something like that, that causes the colouring, but still BLOODY PINK>!!!)

P.S.> Just one other thing I'd like to know. It has just come to my attention that the one domesticated animal your friend Noah didn't take on the ark was 'The Cat'. I ask you to tell me, did Noah not like CATS.???

Yours Sincerely Susan.

P.P.S.> If however you do not reply to these letters by post, and I can only get the answers if I meet you personally, I am quite happy to wait many, many years, to get them. Thank you....XX

Let's Just Call Him "Bungie"

Again we got a cheque from the Estate Agent that had this time gone to the Solicitor regarding Dad's Mobile Home sale, then on to us, and yet again it bounced...

We now know he hadn't got our money?? Spent it, or what I don't care. It was not his to have in the first place. He will go to court for this...we were hopping mad....

Plus it was hard enough losing Dad, with out being unable to lay him to rest with all this upset going on. One never wants to loose anyone, and the grieving is hard enough, but this is a daily reminder being rubbed in our faces. I can't believe this chap is slapping us in the face like this. It is so upsetting.

So it's up to the solicitor now to do his bit...

158

Our Wedding

All was now ready for the biggest day of my life. I love Roger so much, I want him to be proud of me on our day. The build up had been tremendous, the planning was great fun but a little frustrating at times.

I did all the arrangements, (making sure I had Roger's input and approval on everything except the girl bits). I also made all the invitations and place setting cards for the seating in the room where we were to be married......

I took weeks making all the button holes. Some were cream or blue silk roses set in imitation diamond set hair clips. This way no-one had to stick pins in there clothes. There were also some normal ones with just pins as I ran out of clips.

The bouquets were also all made by me. Cathy's in particular took weeks to get just the right look I was looking for and all the 'Bling' I got together myself over the months before. So all was ready for the day.

You know what, I still tingle all over when I think back to that day. (however there is a small dark cloud over some of the after events which I will explain later) but the wedding was a dream.

OH' come on, you should know us by now....there's nearly always something that turns to Poo.!!! I sometimes wonder if life could be boring, if nothing was to happen to liven things up..!!!

Anyway the garden was the best I could do seeing as nothing 'flower wise' would come to much and it all had to be covered in wire until the last second because of those "lovely" little fluffy BUNNYS. ***Grrrrrrr!!!.*** ....And our geese would have a lovely time if they got the chance.

Life was sometimes bloody annoying on those points.

So I confess to cheating. I bought tons of fake and silk flowers from the charity shop in Huntly. Good old Eric, in our favourite charity shop, he got tons for me. He's a great chap, always full of jokes and fun. He has a real cheeky smile and the ladies there are so sweet, and always there to help.....

We also, at long last, had got the granite chippings to finish off the drive in and around the house. It's a mixture of colours. It looks all shades of grey but when it has rained they match the house. The wet chippings really show up a pinkish at times (matching the house).

Well everyone was booked in to their respective dwellings for the big day, and the Glencove Arms was up to date on all the arrangements and Sally, as I said was doing the cake. I had found a fab centre piece for it.

Instead of the traditional Bride and Groom, We had a Dragon Bride and Groom....Which was fitting, as Roger calls me "His old Dragon " Mmmmmmmm......As well as Crab /Crabbie and other such like 'endearing ' things..!!!!

My dress had arrived two weeks ago and with some added shoulder straps (thanks to getting an odd suntan) it looked FAB.....

Thank You Mo

My friend Mo and I set off to Aberdeen City, for a Girlie Day. You know, getting those naughty things for the wedding nuptials etc.....But I'll keep them a secret......*AND YOU WILL TOO MO...WON'T YOU.......!!!!*

We had a great time looking around all the shops. Sometimes just window shopping. It was just great being able to stop and look at all kinds of things without the "NAGGING" or "PULLING ON THE ARM" to move along by out other halves.....

At Christmas they have the right idea here for all concerned. The men folk drive us into town and park up. We then 'PARK' them up in a 'MEN' Creche. .....Where they can read the paper, or watch the footie with the other men folk......Leaving them there, leave us to go and get the Christmas shopping with no Nagging at how long we take,,, OR how much we spend.........Suits ALL..Mmmmmm

Then we return to collect them and they in turn take us back home. All done and dusted...

Anyway, Mo and I had a couple of chances to go to town and we just met the men folk back at the pub.

We will do this again at some point. It's nice to go with Mo, she's a laugh and we get on well.

Wedding Gifts and Traditions

The Tradition ***BLACKENING*** This is a time held tradition here, something we did our damndest to escape....

It's not always on a stag night or hen night...It can happen at any unsuspecting moment.!!!

You can be grabbed and Tarred and Feathered. This is not real Tar, it is grease of some kind and anything else the mob decide to do is done in true fun.

Luckily we were let off this event.....Due to Roger being on blood pressure pills, it could cause trouble.....He's not into that kind of stuff, and his blood pressure would go sky high.

Me, well...I'm all for a good laugh but not any 'de-bagging' stuff....I'm too old for a 'beautiful baby shot on a fur rug' kind of thing....!!!!!

But I have to admit we did tend to watch our backs for some weeks before hand......

We didn't want a Stag or Hen night so we just all met up for a drink at the pub. Mind you I have to admit we left early although we were promised nothing would be done to us.... *just in case !!*

The Wedding Gifts Just Kept Coming

We had told our friends and family not to get any wedding gifts for us. Just being there, on our day would be a precious gift in itself.

But to our amazement wedding gifts started to arrive from everyone! No matter what we said everyone started to deliver gifts! Oh please, don't misunderstand me, it was truly lovely of them all.

We were politely told it was tradition so we had to accept them. This we were told in a loving way.

I was at Pam and Robert's one day doing a rehearsal for their son Sean, who was to be the Ring Carrier at the service,(standing beside Roger, guarding the ring which was to be on a small gold cushion) and Loran, who was to be the Flower Girl. She was also to throw a small Bouquet at the wedding instead of me. That way they both had a little something very special to do and had to have a practice etc..

As we were doing this Heather, Robert's sister, came in with some wedding gifts which I thanked her for. I said we would wait and open them on the day.

As she left I felt she was a bit 'put out' by something..!!!

It was a day or two later when talking to Betty, Robert's mum at the farm, it transpired that it was tradition to open the gifts straight away, and put them on a table in your home on display, then offer 'whoever' a dram........Oooooooooops

Then when someone else arrives with their gift, you do the same, and also show them what others have given you..........Bigger size Oooooooooooooooooooop

Hence that night we opened our many gifts, and placed them on a table on our best lace cloth ready for our friends and family to see......

So please forgive us for we just didn't realise, and we hope you understand nothing was further from our mind than to offend.....

On such a day our friend Angie phoned to see if we were in, as she had got her and her husband Sid's gift to bring around.!!!!

This I knew would be a 'TEA POT', as they insisted on getting something. So I had agreed on a modest gift.

'Bloody Hell' was my thought, as when Angie arrive, she produced such a huge package. If it was a TEA POT it would be filled enough for an army. She didn't stop to see us open it as she was to meet Sid somewhere and time was getting on..

When we opened it our jaws hit the floor. It was a wicker lined washing basket full to the overflowing point with goodies. Champagne with glasses to suit, candles, chocolates, smellies and all kind of things. Well, what a thoughtful couple........Oh...AND A TEA POT.....

There were just so many gifts. All we can do is say THANK YOU ALL SO MUCH..the list is so long, it would fill a page to thank you all again and again....... *THANK YOU.....XXXXXXXXX*

Count Down

Mum and Dad had arrived and we had plenty to tell them and show them. We were now just waiting for the day.....

They stayed at Bill and Mary's B&B opposite the Glencove Arms. They had a beautiful room, and Bill and Mary took great care of them. Bill and Mary used to own the Glencove Arms years ago so I guess you could say they have seen a few changes there...

It must be sad in some ways now as the atmosphere is a bit 'tense' due to all the upset between Tony and Sally. Some days Sally would look so down and the strain is showing on Jane. I felt, and still do, feel sorry for her.....

It can't be much fun for her to see her mum and dad splitting up, and in public for all to see and hear..

There's no privacy in that kind of work, your life is on show at all times...

I was also just a bit worried it might all 'kick-off' on the wedding day......

But I did ask if it would be a problem. You know.....upsetting for Sally etc... but she had said it was ok....

When I had spoken to my Mum on the phone I thought she said she had a cream outfit. This would be great as the Boy's shirts were cream but it turned out to be Green.

So I asked if we found a Mother of the Bride outfit in cream, would she be offended if I bought it for her. Perhaps something she could use again

162

would be practical. Mum was fine about it.

The green outfit was lovely, but I felt a little dark for Mums complexion. 'Hold On'

*(**How spooky is this, as I am typing this very part, our Wedding Music has come on the radio.** Sorry got to stop for a min'...I'm having a weepy moment.............................) Oh God and another to follow......you'll have to forgive me.....just talk among yourselves.* Sorry about that.......as I was saying.....*(sniff, sniff).*

To continue,

As it was we found just the job, a beautiful cream outfit and a Mother of the Bride Hat to suit. She would look more beautiful than ever, if that was at all possible.

I ran through what was to happen on the day as Dad was giving me away. My heart was full of joy and pride that my Dad was to do this. There was a point when we didn't think they would make it here at all due to their ill health.

This is where some friends of ours would have to come into play. At Christmas last, we met a lovely couple called Harry and June with June's mother Betty....

Harry, I believe was, sorry I have learnt, a bit of a 'Nutter' when he was younger, from the tales he and June let us in on. (HE still is......In a nice way......)

June is more controlled but she can let a few things slip at times. Well, we're all human.

I've come to learn that June is a damn good Golf player. Perhaps one day she may teach me. I'd love to have a go.

And then there's Betty, June's mother. She is simply a lovely lady, all Grannyish, I could just hug her. She is so sweet and quite funny at times. When I say Grannyish, it's not her maturity in years.....it's her 'Orra' it just so scrumptious... Oh, I'm sure you get my drift...

Anyway we asked Harry, that if my Dad was unable to be here to give me away, would he do us the honour of doing this in his place....

To our delight Harry was very touched, and would be delighted to do so....

But as you can see my Dad and Mum made it and now it was all systems go.....

My Mum helped me arrange the flowers outside the house the day before the wedding and we just prayed for a sunny day.......

Everyone was now here and I was in a dream world. There was so much racing through my little brain cells....It was a crazy time.......In a nice way.....

This Is It!

Morning arrived and it was a beautiful day, the sun was out in full form, and all was going to plan...

We got everything done at home and set off to the Glencove Arms, where I was to leave Roger with James to set up the rooms, while I went to get my Mum ready. I said I'd help her and see them both before I went to the Glencove Steading where I was to get ready with Sara's help and Cathy with the girls and little Erik was to get this suit on etc.....

Oh, and one thing I forgot to say ******* *IT'S ALSO MY BIRTHDAY* ******* 21 again, and again... Plus a bit, I hear you saying....*Ouch.* THAT HURTS..ha, ha,..But true. (*Anyway, If Roger ever forgets my Birthday, not that I'd let him, it would mean he had forgotten our Wedding Anniversary, so a double thump would be heading his way.!!!!!!!!!!*)

Now I went to their room at Bill and Mary's and found Mum and Dad getting ready. After hugs and kisses Dad gave me a Birthday present I will never forget. It was a painting he had done of our house.

It was lovely, and spot on to bring the tears.......and a beautiful card...plus a cheque as a wedding gift in a beautiful wedding card......

I had to stop myself from crying, I was so touched. They had done so much for us over the years. This was so loving of them...but if I cried, I'd get all red eyed for the wedding in just a few hours time....and look all bug eyed..

I helped Mum with her new outfit, and then she put the hat on to see how she would look. Mum, you looked so beautiful and that hat finished it all off fine..

I was and am so proud of you Mum.

I know you had been so ill, and still were, but you were here. Dad took a picture of Mum....

Then I just had to leave to get myself ready. Besides our close friends for many years Don, our old school teacher, and his wife Janet were staying at the same place and could keep them company until later.

Meanwhile, everything was ready at Cathy's place waiting for me to get ready.

At the Steading we put the music up and opened Champagne but I didn't dare drink too much. I may mess up my lines. I'd been reading the words over and over, so I didn't mess up!!!

Roger is not one for all the fuss, but we choose the words together. I was surprised at which ones he chose because they are all so 'mushy,' as he says. But these are so meaningful, and truly say how we feel.

There is also an added bit...which Roger chose....where we join in sharing a drink from a "shallow cup" made from pewter or silver called a 'Quaich' and this is done as we make a joint promise to each other. It was a traditional Scottish thing at a wedding.

However there was one thing I was unable to get Roger to do and that was to get him to practise, or even read through them before the day. He said he'd say the words then, and only the once. His nerves may go and that damn cough would start, and that would be the end of that. So I didn't push the subject...

Sara helped me with getting ready and was now waiting to help me last thing with my dress which had been under wraps until now. It was crazy, I was a bag of nerves, I was so emotional, so excited, I was at bursting point with joy......Weeeeeeeeeeeeeeeeeeeeeeeeeeeeeeeee.

Cathy was great. She did my makeup, my hand we shaking too much and she also did my hair. She did all this, and getting herself and the girls ready. *THANK YOU CATHY. Xxx*

The girls and Cathy all had Tiaras and plenty of 'Bling' I had given them for the day, plus the bouquets I had spent ages making for them.....

(I'm afraid 'I WILL' blow my own trumpet for doing those things. As it was the first time I'd do stuff like that....and I think, I did very well. So I give myself a pat on the back...........)

Then on with my 'Bling' and lastly the dress. I didn't mean to, but I did snap once at my Sara. I couldn't do my necklace up, and she was all thumbs. Guess looking back she was a bag of nerves in case she broke it...(*Sorry Sara*)......And she had to keep an eye on little Erik while she was helping..

Well, this was it...We were all ready. I felt very guilty as Sara was really the one who should have been my bridesmaid, but I never thought that she would be able to afford to get up here. I did however offer to get her a dress or outfit of some kind but she insisted not to. She had a perfect outfit she brought along for the day. (*She did look lovely, and Erik looked so smart in his suit....I was proud of them both.*)

So we all went outside for, I'm afraid to admit, a much needed fag break before my Dad was due to come and get me.......

As I stood there waiting I felt a tickle on my ankle!!!!   Not really daring to look, I had to check what the hell it may be!!!!!

As I lifted my dress a little, I got Sara to look for me.....*Oh please God, don't let it be a wasp.!!!!*

" It's ok Mum, it's a tiny spider" came her answer...... ....

"OH NO YOU DON'T, NOT TODAY THANK YOU" I said as I brushed it off ....*Phew........*

Then Dad arrived. He looked so smart in his suit I was and am proud of him......

I apologized to him for me smoking!!!! Yep, even now at my age, I know how he hates it....

Just peeking down the road at the pub we could just see that tons of people were walking around. So we waited for them to go in...and waited and waited.... but still they were outside ??????

As I said, we had invited all our new friends from here, but I never dreamt that they could all make it. Most are farmers!!!!! Of course we wanted them to all be here on our special day but we didn't want to take it for granted that they would be here because of possible farming commitments. But from what we could see, it seemed like hundreds were waiting my arrival.....God I was in a tiz'.......I'm the first to admit I'm one for showing off sometimes, and one to be outwardly confidant....But when push come to shove; I'm the first to back down.....In the sense that I am quite shy deep down.....

Anyway the reason people were outside, I found out later, was because there just wasn't enough room for them to get in the door. Which goes to prove what great friends we have made, for them 'all' to be here.

Dad said we really must go now, as Roger will think we're not going to show up. So along we went...

As we got to the car park I heard a cheer, as cameras flashed. I felt like a 'Film Star' on the famous 'Red Carpet' ....

I was so touched, and I could feel myself getting butterflies even more, as I felt very shy at that point. Tears began to well in my eyes as I saw all our dearest of friends smiling and waving at me as I crossed the small car park to the pub. *(It felt like a hundred miles wide.)* I had a quick look down at my bouquet to double check I had remembered to fix a small photo of Roger's dad pinned inside.

I knew Roger had his late father's pocket watch with him........

I had no idea at that point, that poor Roger had been waiting so long. I was a bit more than the traditional 5 minutes late....In fact about 20......Oooooooooooooooooops *Sorry Roger.xxxxxxxxx*

While people were waiting music was being played by a girl called Tansy and her group. Just a few tunes we had chosen to pass the time. Etc......of which they must have played a dozen times by now.!!

Here We Go

(Now before I start, with hankies at the ready. There were 2 songs going though my mind, (first was the main song with me walking in.) But there was also an old song which starts 'close your eyes'..... by a coloured group, I think,......(Only they seem to have the inner vibe.... The inner thing.!!!!.) sorry not P.C. ..(darker than white people.!!).. (O' who you are, who you are!!! Black, white, green, or blue, who care's...I for one don't give a damn... weather you believe in God, Buddha, or whatever.* **LOVE.... is Love,** *and music that ....'moves your soul' is* very special, and,......anyway it was something Roger once said to me ...and this song is the B's and E's. It's all about making love etc, it's so Mmmmmm. Find it and, you girls will know what I mean. Anyway where was I.......*

As the Bridesmaids went in the door, the Special song I had chosen to be played began. (THAT NEARLY DID IT. I WAS NOW REALLY HAVING TROUBLE HOLDING BACK THE TEARS.)   It was called **Endless Love** sung by **Lionel Ritchie & Diana Ross.** This song has great meaning to Roger and I as we were each others first love. It's our song.

Dad and I hesitated at the door for a few seconds, then Dad walked me in on his arm. I had such pride with Dad at my side and a sigh came from the family and friends in the room. It was all a blur to me, I was so emotional, I felt so overwhelmed with pride for my Dad' and the whole day..

Then I saw Roger. Oh, how I love him. Now, I felt I'd be ok. He looked so smart. Then the music was turned down and we began.

The Registrar introduced herself as Frances, and explained why we were all here. She explain what was about to happen in the service, and what it's true meaning was.

She asked who was to give me away and Dad proudly came forward, and said "I do" then passed my hand into Roger's waiting hands.......

After passing my bouquet to one of the bridesmaids, we were then asked to face each other and hold hands again as we were to take our vows to each other.

As Frances spoke the words, Roger looked straight at me, straight into my eyes as he in turn repeated them.

I remember getting a glimpse of my Mum out of the corner of my eye. She was a bit tearful....

However, looking into Roger's eyes I felt myself welling up inside. Then I was to say my vows to Roger. Now, normally I'm the first to have a big mouth but as I went to speak......nothing much came out.!!

My voice was like a whisper...!!!!   And I had to keep looking at Frances to stop looking into Roger's eyes as I knew I was going to cry at any second........

After we had said our vows, and made our promises to each other, we had one more thing to do...

A small joint speech and commitment with the Quaich. This was a good bit, because we needed a swift drink....'Well I know I did' and 'Boy' it was a strong one. It was then passed to James to share and then on to my Dad (I think).....

After we signed the register, Frank and Betty Taylor then as witnesses signed the register.

Then as Roger and I were asked by the Registrar to stand facing all our friends and family, that had been able to get in the room, apart from those who had seats.

Frances, the Registrar then asked for silence.

She then said "Ladies and Gentlemen I would like to introduce, for the first time....

MR AND MRS PETTY"
AND EVERYONE IN AND OUTSIDE THE ROOM GAVE A BIG CHEER AND BURST INTO APPLAUSE.

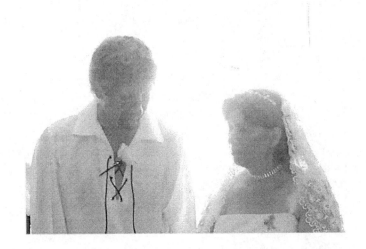

Our Wedding Vows

I will cherish our friendship
and love you today, tomorrow and forever.
I will trust you and honour you.
I will love you faithfully.
Through the best and the worst.
Through the difficult and the easy.
Whatever may come, I will always be there.
As I give you my hand to hold,
so I give you my life to keep.
These are my solemn vows.

The "Quaich"

Trust me not to leave you.
For where you go, I will go.
And where you stay, I will stay.
Your people are my people.
This is my promise, now and forever.

A Fantastic Day

The rest of the day was out of this world. All our friends were with us as we celebrated and danced the afternoon away.

Dad did his speech, and he called Roger by the wrong name !!!!...Which everyone felt was so funny. It looked like he had done it on purpose, as the timing was just right in his speech. But that's a little secret we shall keep. Well until now!!! *sorry Dad, but it was funny*, and you got a good laugh.

Poor Dad, he didn't realise how nervous he was and you know, it didn't matter one bit, Dad did us proud.

Then outside we posed for photos. We didn't have a professional photographer, but friends took pictures.

And little Loran threw a little bouquet I had made for her special part of the day. *Bless her xxx.* Cathy's eldest daughter Hannah caught it. Poor girl just burst into tears??? When told it meant she would be next to marry, Bless her, she thought it meant now. Poor kid !!!! Arrrrrrrr.

Inside they laid a nice spread for all the guests to enjoy, the usual sandwiches and cakes etc.

The cake was beautiful, and Sally gave it to us as her Wedding Present to us. *Thank you Sally xx.*

* *

Note: (The one thing that did go wrong on the day was the photos. It was only when we got back to the house we realised we hadn't had any with all our friend together !!!!! And to think of all the effort people had gone to, they must have thought us so rude but we were having a BBQ at home the next day, perhaps we could get some photos then and fix things then on the computer.....!!!!!!)

Anyway still at the pub we joined in with some dancing. Well, put it this way 'I tried to dance, but not any luck with my dress etc. Poor Steve, who is Heather the architect's husband, must have thought I was a demented octopus as I got tied up in knots. Roger seemed to get the hang of it dancing with Heather, he looked great and for once didn't seem to mind being centre of attention.

My Mum retired early as she was tired. It had been such a big day for her, she had done so well....

Roger and I were to leave the pub and go back home with family and friends for drinks etc. As we left Martin, who had entertained us with his Accordion for some hours, started to play a few bars from 'The Funeral March'. Cheeky git....and all burst out laughing as it was done as a joke. Then he played 'The Highland Fling" as we walked to the car. Without thinking Roger and I started to do the Morecambe and Wise dance down the driveway. *There were hoots of laughter and clapping as we left......*

And the bride and groom danced into the sunset.

A note to all · ****Thank you all for making our day simply 'THE BEST'****

Back at the house we posed for photos in front of our house with family and friends. My brother Paul and his wife Denise (who were also here, if I hadn't said already) had stayed at the Glencove Arms overnight, so they got changed before joining us.....

Thing was when we got home there was a bag tied to the gate!!!!   In it was a bottle of Champagne and a card from some of the neighbours?!?!?!

Now this was very kind of them, but considering how some of them had been with us since we arrived here, we didn't want to be hypocrites and invite them to our wedding. I mean THEY had until this moment made things very clear to us how THEY really felt.

But we felt that MAYBE this was a good time to break the ice. So after the photos were done, Roger and I popped over to invite them over for tomorrows BBQ and it wouldn't be too much of a 'face to face' thing as others would be there. However, although they thanked us for the invite, they had their excuses!!

But we made the effort. It was up to them!!!!

In fact we had a small BBQ after we had got changed that evening......

Later that evening one of our friends call Nick, who is a Helicopter Pilot, popped in and left a DVD full of photos for us of the wedding as a gift.. So we put it on the computer.   The photos were just great, all our friends were on it at some point, it captured the whole day. (*Thanks Nick.*)

Thank heavens for him.....Lucky for us he'd been kind enough to do this, as he really did get some smashing moments, which we will cherish forever.

However then I saw a side view of myself dancing with Steve. I just burst into tears. I looked like a giant sized pink STAY PUFT MAN from the film Ghostbusters.!!!!!!!!BoOOOO HoOOOOO.

I was told not to be so daft, it was just the days events showing on me, and I was just all emotional. And I was told that I looked a beautiful bride. ....

Just between us though, I know I'm big, but 'Bloody Hells Bells.' Not just my bum looked big in that dress. My whole body did, still, can't change it now, what's done is done...OR can I change it??? Mmmmm computers are good!!! Mmmmmmmmmmmmm.

That night there were still some presents to open, which we did and put them all on the display table. Then we found one that we had missed.......

It was from Steve and Heather. When I opened the box I just burst into tears with emotion. It was our very own "Quaich" cup. I believe it was the one we drank from each side at the wedding. *(I may be mistaken on that, but it means the same.)*

Inscribed inside are the words "*To Love and Cherish*" on one side, and on the other it had *"To Have and to Hold."* All the lovely gifts were wonderful but this was so touching, it just made our day complete. *Thank you Steve and Heather so much. Xxxxxxx.*

Xxxxx In fact, Thank You All for everything xxxxxX

Dad was ready to go back to the B&B, so Paul and Denise offered to take him, as they were to leave for the airport soon. However we insisted Roger took him back, that way Roger could thank Dad again for everything in private.

Later that evening after everyone had gone Sara suggested she could stay in the caravan so we could have some privacy on our wedding night. Roger and I had to laugh, and said we wouldn't hear of it. Besides we'd been together too many years to worry about one night. We'd have our 'wedding night' when we have our Honeymoon!!!

Probably in a year or so's time when all the building work is done and we can have our first holiday since coming to Scotland. We wish!!!!

Anyway tomorrow we celebrate, and also we have a cake for Iain, a friend from the pub. It was also his Birthday on the 9th .

So Good Night all. Thank you for sharing in our special day.
XXXXXXXXX

P.S.....If I find the name of that song I'll put it at the end for you girl's. It is Mmmmmmmmmmmmm.

Some wedding photos.

The Day After the Day Before

As morning arrived it dawned on us that we were now husband and wife. We'd done it after all these years. It felt wonderful...

We had to get a move on as people were arriving at about 12 and time was getting on.....

The marquee was up and thankfully the wind had not got up during the night, and the day looked set to be a sunny once again.

Time went by fast and people began to arrive. However, our neighbours did not take us up on our invitation. Which was a shame, as the kids would have had fun. And as I said, it 'could' have been the ice breaker. Mind you in saying that, when one breaks the ice, one can often sink!!!!

Still we all had a great time, and I'm sure Iain enjoyed his surprise cake to celebrate his birthday. Which in fact was yesterday, but we made up for that!!!!

I know I keep saying it, but Roger and I can't thank all our friends and family for all the love and kindness when they made it such a wonderful time.

The days past by so fast and now Sara, Erik and Mum and Dad had returned to the south. It was a very tearful time for us all saying goodbye again.

Friends to Stay!!

James was now to stay with us for a week, and as Cathy, Tim and the girls were staying on another week as well, we were to still be very busy. We looked forward to spending time with our friends now all the fuss was over with.

James was to stay in the caravan and Cathy's family in the house with us. We had a double bed upstairs for Cathy and Tim, and the girls could share a bed-settee downstairs.

We also had another small caravan that we were going to use ourselves if the house was too crowded with our friends staying in there with us....But to be honest we were just too busy to get it empty and set it up (as you can imagine we were a little rushed off our feet!!) But if needed, I'm sure our friends would have helped us clear it out.

However during the first week we found out from James that he suffers with bronchitis and can catch a chill quicker than others. So without thinking, I made up the other double bed, in the bigger that was first set up for James, for Cathy and her family to stay in. I did my best to make it homely for them.

They would have a key to the house so that if they needed the loo, or anything in the night, they could let themselves in etc. Although there was a port-a-loo in the caravan closet, sometimes one needs privacy!

Cathy and Tim had a free run of the house and could come and go as they pleased for the next week.

James came out with Roger and I, and the 'boys' were able to catch up on old times. It was nice to see Roger having a laugh with James...

When the subject of the money owed to us from when we had advanced the fees for the steading came up, Tim explained that his redundancy cheque hadn't cleared yet. So we left it that he would send a cheque as soon as it cleared. This was fine by us......

We had a lovely time and it was all too soon when they all had to go back down to the south. We'd miss them all. The girls had been so well behaved, and Cathy is very funny. Good thing she liked a booze up like me. We had a few giggles.

However weeks passed and there was no sign of the money heading our way. So we phoned a few times. There was something up because Cathy had said they had encountered a few problems on their return home and she had been in hospital. We hoped she was ok....so we tried to make allowances for this.

I'm afraid things go a bit nasty then. We needed the money and now it seemed to me Tim was avoiding us.....

We tried to get Tim on his mobile and we sent texts asking him to contact us. He only returned one or two phone calls. When we were able to leave a message with the kids for them to ring us back they rarely did.

So after weeks and weeks I sent a text to give him 'a kick up the arse kind of thing'. Saying he'd get an official letter from us if we didn't get the money by a set date. (*We had no intention of going to a solicitor, for God sake it was just meant to get Tim on the hop.*)

Perhaps that was a bit harsh in some ways, but hell, we wanted the money they owed us back. They never really told us what was up. (*Not that they should tell us their personal problems*), but it might have helped us understand the delay etc....

(God, why does anything to do with us and money always turn to shit one way or another.?)

During all this we got a couple of nasty letters from them. In one Tim had the cheek to say *"why should I use my redundancy when you have money from the sale of your late Dad's house?"* unquote! We were absolutely disgusted at this comment.

They also clamed that we only invited them, so they could bring James. Now, 'that' was hurtful, as we invited them as our friends and the travelling arrangements were up to them.

(You have to remember the money they owed was for the rented accommodation, and '**not**' for their holiday with us.)

Anyway, in the end we got the money.

Apparently the main grievances they had, was that Cathy 'had' told me Tim didn't like caravans ??

Ok, well, I'm bloody sorry, I FORGOT. I/we were a tad preoccupied with just a few minor events that were taking place !!!!!!

Besides, if it had been that intolerable, why didn't they say something. Or go and pay for a B&B...

They stayed here as our friends and guests. I truly thought they had a good time.

I was so happy to have them here I gave Cathy and the girls all the Bling, and the 'Tiaras', which weren't cheap 'Bling', as a thank you gift for all they had done.

Now my memories of our wedding are ruined, by this painful slap in the face. Every time I looked at the photos of us all enjoying the day. Tim and Cathy are in them, and it hurts deep down in my heart.

But I have to confess, I have now edited them out...But not the children, they are innocent in this matter, and they looked beautiful.

P.S. Tim heard that we had shown our friends up here his letters, (*this I add, was purely, to clarify if we, or they were in the wrong*) he then threatened 'me' with his solicitor and to have me for 'Libel and Slander.'

If he cares to look up their meanings up in the Oxford Dictionary it reads.

Quote:

Libel: *the crime of publishing a false statement that is damaging to a person's reputation.*

Slander: a *published fake statement that damages a person's reputation.*

Un-Quote.

I stand by all I have said, I have not lied, or bent the truth in any way. I have the evidence, and will swear on the Bible it is the truth, the whole truth and nothing but the truth, so help me God..

This matter was dealt with, NOT from my 'SOAP BOX' this time, but from my 'Bloody High Horse' !! So there.!!!

I have inside me to this day a mixture of anger and sadness. As now instead of remembering our wedding as the happiest day of our lives with joy, I get so upset about all the bitterness from our so called friend. I would burst into tears at the very thought of the wedding day being over shadowed by the aftermath.

Because of all the upset, weeks later we decided to retake our vows. We would have a blessing next year on our first anniversary. That way it would be like having our wedding all over again. But with no upsets.

Friends back at the house

Spooky

As the months past we found a lovely sunny spot to put Roger's late father's ashes to rest. We had waited until this summer for two reasons, but this act would seem to make it more final, so we had kept putting it off. Kind of not wanting to let go

We had kept his ashes in the urn in the grandfather clock that he and Roger made together when Roger was a young lad...

The first reason was that we had made a promise to Roger's father on his death bed that we not only would take him to Scotland with us, but we would put him somewhere sunny. But until the later part of the summer we would not know where he may be over shadowed by the leaves of the trees.

Secondly, we were hoping to put him to rest knowing all the 'unrest' caused so far by the Estate Agent regarding the money that they had not paid us would be settled.

But I am sorry to say the Estate Agent was still owing the funds and it would appear they have misused it for their own purpose??

However we felt that the time 'had' come to let go, and put Dad to rest.

Now, something I have kept quiet about to you until now, was that since Roger's father's ashes had been here in the house, strange things had been happening!!!

Things would be moved from where we had put them the night before and I would loose things I knew I had just put down.

But, the main one was that each time I used our shower it had a life of its own!! I would get in and the temperature would suddenly get freezing cold, then boiling hot!! The freezing water would make me jump, and as for the hot, I would have to get out of the way of the water damn fast or get scolded.

Now, Roger used the shower every day, and never had a problem, and Sam our dog would have a shower most weeks as he was always getting muddy and we never had a fast temperature change when doing Sam!! Roger said I must be doing something to make it change temperature. I said it was his DAD playing silly buggers...

Now this had gone on for a year, and nine times out of ten I had a strip wash from head to toe. Only getting in the possessed shower if I had to, or if doing my hair. But I would always get in such an upset state, because I only wanted a nice shower, I would always land up in tears...

Roger found it funny, *BUT I DID NOT.*

The day we put Dad's ashes to rest it was a year to the day of his passing, and I had been in the garden working all day. So, I just had to have a shower.

When I got in this time I told Roger's dad, to leave me alone! That enough was enough and it was no longer funny. So he was to stop peeking at me from 'where -ever' and to leave me alone. So please let me shower nicely!!!!!!!

You know what, that shower was the best ever.....I stayed in there for hours....THANKS DAD??

The next day the weather had changed and we had showers on and off. Between them I took some silk flowers and put them beside a large stone we had out to mark Dad's spot. I noticed a shape on the top of the stone, but couldn't work out clearly what it was.

I had heard that if you took a photo of this kind of image, it can come out clearer and when made wet. So I got my camera and I as I took the photo I said jokingly, "Come on then Dad, show me if you are looking after us, and if there's an after life??"

When I looked at the digital photo on the camera, I nearly dropped it. There was clearly an image of a man's head. You can see it in the photo, and judge for yourself....

That night Roger realises the grandfather clock had stopped. It must have stopped the day before as thinking about it we hadn't heard its chimes.

It was spooky. It had stopped at the exact time Roger's Father had passed away. Mmmmmmm, makes you think a bit, doesn't it.

Another Year Comes to a Great End!!

It was Roger's birthday on the 13th of September, and sadly it is over shadowed by the fact that his dad had died just before it the year before. So Roger's birthday was a little more low key than I would have liked for him. We just had drinks with some friends at the pub instead of a big party. Even though life carries on, it is something you never forget.

The year had gone by so quickly, with the wedding done and dusted and Roger's dad's ashes in their resting place, all settled back to the normal work on the Doocot.

There was still plenty to finish off indoors, the final touches before we could get the house signed off the building regs.

These were jobs we had put off during the summer months as there was plenty to do on the land during the nice weather, so why waste time on stuff we can do indoors over the coming cold winter months ahead.

The Beginning of the Last Straw

About this time we were really looking at getting plans drawn up to submit to the council for an 'Agricultural Building'. This was to be behind the house on the farm land and used to store all our farming equipment, and animal feeds etc.

There shouldn't be any problems as it is a straight forward 'Notification' thing with regards to any planning, basically because we are registered as a farm.

So we went to see our architect Heather Smith, and got the ball rolling, leaving things in her hands. She said we should have no problems, as you don't need planning permission for an agricultural building of this size.

Part of the 'Notification' process involves having to put a 'Notification Notice' up at the end of our lane, and also a 'Neighbour Notification' is sent to all the neighbours. This is so that everyone has the chance to ask any questions concerning the building. Plus if any complaints/objections are submitted they in turn can be noted and looked into. People are given 21 days to do this, and they can go 'online' to view any plans etc. if they so wish.

We were half expecting some neighbours to fire-up with something, as so far they had complained in one way or another about other things in the past.

But the weeks passed and we had heard nothing, so by November all was ready for the building to be put up,(because we hadn't heard of any complications or objections from the council planning offices, we, as you will see, foolishly assumed all was well). We got a contractor to put the main frame up and the roof joists in place ready to start work. We would now be trying to beat the coming winter months, and for once all to be going to plan. *(Yeah right, I hear you thinking, as if things would be plain sailing !!)*

Yep, you were right. We then got a phone call from Heather and she explained that an inspector had been up to view the site, and is now saying it must all go to 'FULL PLANNING' as the structure was to be close to a Listed Building.!!!

So assuming that the inspector had meant our house was the 'Listed Building' concerned, we took measurements from the house to where the agricultural building would be, and took the information to Heather. Surprisingly it was the 'Walled Garden' which was nowhere near our place!!!!

So this simple 'Notification' for an 'Agricultural Building' was beginning to get more involved. It was crazy, since when have you had to have 'Full Planning' for a building like this??

So we dotted all the 'Is' and crossed all the 'Ts' and sent all the information to the council again.

There would now have to be another 21 days Full Planning notices put up and sent to neighbours

Here's Hoping for a White Christmas
(Say Hello to.....Jezz-a-bean, knickknack and the boys)

Meanwhile, much to our delight, we were going to have friends to stay for Christmas and we couldn't wait for them to arrive. They were close friends from the south that had lived near our old house, and had moved to Maplehurst a few years after we had move up here.

We hoped to be able to give them an 'Old Fashioned White Christmas'!! This was because their two young sons had never seen REAL snow. You know the kind...The ones from the Christmas cards and movies...

So let me introduce you to our friends.

First there is Jezz, known as 'Jezz-a-bean'. He is a 'LOONY', an absolute nightmare of a chap. In the best possible way....A Hyperactive 'NUTTER' on speed.....and loveable with it. (IMPORTANT: *Please take note that 'He does not take drugs, he's just JEZZ-A-BEAN')* Jezz is on the go at 100 miles an hour from the moment he opens his eyes to the time he goes to sleep. He is the funniest and kindest person I have ever had the good fortune to meet.......Oh, and *'As if I could forget '* Jezz is...wait for it...' A FIREMAN '....Mmmmmmmm,Mmmmmmmmm,Mmmmmmmmm.!!!!!!!.

Then there's his long suffering wife Nicky, known as ' Knickknack '!!!.(*Only joking, she's not suffering at all, she just loves him as he is!)*

Nicky is so sweet and kind, she's just all round great. She is also hyperactive, buzzing around after Jezz and their two boys Luke and Harry, doing the day to day running of a home as well as working part- time, and looking after the dog and their horse.

And last, but not least, THE BOYS. First there is Luke the oldest, he's 'The Charmer' of the two. He is a lovely lad and will break a few hearts in years to come. He tends to take after Nicky, in the sense that he's quieter and more reserved at times.

Then there's Harry. He's just like his dad. A real 'Jackal-Bunny' and so cheeky with it. But never rude, just full of beans, and on the go 24/7.

We had as I said hoped to give them an old fashioned Christmas but in more ways than one! We were to arrange, a kind if 60's Christmas....(*In case any children read this next bit)* we would send Santa a Christmas list for the following to put in the boys stocking 'from Santa'. We asked for Dandy, Beano and Sparky annuals from the old days. Chocolate coins, an Orange and an Apple for each and some little bits and pieces to top the stocking up with.....

All we then needed was for them to ask "why are there no computer games???", and we were ready with a great answer. This was "that in the 'OLD DAYS' there were no such things"......

(Har-de-har boys.!!!) *Note: One can save a fortune, with the real Old fashioned Christmases.!!!!!!!!*

Well Christmas was almost upon us and still we awaited some heavy snowfall. It was part of the deal God.....We must have lots and lots of snow for our friends children to see when they stay..

There had been a few snow falls, and the higher mountains had a coating in places. But none really stayed here very long.

We had given Jezz two routes to choose from to get here, depending on the weather forecast. If it was to be bad weather they were advised to go around Aberdeen and stick to the main roads to Huntly, then on to us. If it was good weather, i.e. not snowing heavily, they could chance going over the mountains from Perth, then along the backroads.

We had to put temporary banisters around the top landing as although it had been ok for us without any, it would be too unsafe for the children running around. Everything was set, the two double beds were made-up for them upstairs. Roger and I would sleep down-stairs on the bed-settee. There were plenty of warm blankets and quilts for them. We had tons of wood chopped ready for the fire, and some coal...

I had warned Nicky to bring plenty of warm underwear and clothes for all. They would not be used to the extreme weather changes that we had, over the years, learnt to be so unpredictable.

The day before they were due to arrive we had got most of the house tidy and on retiring to bed fairly late, we had only to hoover and wash the floor before they were due the following afternoon at some point.

The next day as Roger was in the shower, and I was still in my jammies I heard a car.....OH, MY GOD", I screamed as looking out the kitchen window, their car was pulling up along side.

I ran and called to Roger that they were here and then went and opened the door to our friends, who were now standing in front of their car.

Sam our dog was going nuts, because they had brought their dog Mazy and he knew she was outside.

I just grinned from ear to ear as I screamed in a laughing manner "What are you doing here??? Sod Off, and come back this afternoon...We're not ready for you...Go away. Go away..."...At which, seeing the boys faces were indicating to me that they weren't sure if I was joking or not, I flung my open arms around them, giving them a hug, and kisses each of them. To show I was in fact delighted to see them here.

I got them indoors and made a cuppa while Roger finished in the shower. Shortly after he emerged to welcome our friends.

Sam, our dog is a very jealous thing. He's used to it just being him here with no other dogs. So we were worried about the fact that he may get 'putout' by Mazy being in the house. Some dogs he just doesn't take to. I suppose like people, you don't necessarily get on with everyone you meet. But we need not have worried. It was as if a romantic song had burst into full volume as their eyes met across a crowded room. (Actually, that's a good old song, not that I'm old enough to remember it. My Mum used to sing it to us. One of many songs she sang as my brother and I were in bed at night going to sleep.) It went something like "one day you may meet a stranger across a crowded room."

As the days passed, every time we couldn't find the dogs just guess where they were??? The little minxes would have crept off and gone upstairs, and we'd find them laying together on Jezz and Nicky's bed. Arrrrr.

It was great to have them here, and we were ready for the best Christmas. Just waiting still for the snow to make it complete.

We went out and about to places over the next few days leading up to Christmas Eve, and they were very comfortable in their beds at night. The boys were so well behaved, you have to remember our place is very small, and we don't have TV. But we had videos and DVDs coming out our ears to entertain them, and Nicky had brought games along for them.

The night time arrived and it was time for all good children to go to bed, so they are asleep when Santa comes.....(*I don't know who was more excited, Me or the kids'!! I love Christmas and all that goes with it.*)

Jezz and Nicky had told the kids that they were to stay in bed until they heard the alarm clock crow!! This clock was a wedding gift from Sheila and Gerry. Mmmmmm. As if we didn't have enough cockerels of our own, this bloody clock lets out the loudest 'COCK-A-DOOLE-DOO' you have ever heard!!!! So off to bed the kiddies went.

Nicky wanted to help get things ready for the pending feast the next day. I was grateful for her help, she also made some vegetarian food ready for herself and for us to try. But I so much wanted her to rest, it was meant to be a holiday for her.

We all had a few drinks and watched a movie before retiring to our beds, and we just couldn't wait until the morning to see what 'Santa' had brought the kids.

```
        *              *              *
   *         *
              *              *              *
   *              *         *
        *                   *         *
   *
              *    *    *         *         *
   *         *
           *      *    *                 *
   *         *
                      *      *    **         *
   *         **
        *         *         **         *
***
           *    **         *         *         *
**
```

A hush fell on the house this Christmas Eve night, as all slept peacefully until dawn.

When morning arrived, from downstairs we heard Jezz whisper to us from upstairs "are you two ready for this!!!!!!" Then in full volume of his voice he cried "COCK-A DOOLE-DOOOOOOO."

This was followed by a sudden shuffling of bedding from the kids end of the upstairs and the patter of feet, as the kids ran across to find Santa, had in fact left some presents for them with Mum and Dad.

Shortly after I guess you could say I got 'my' Christmas present!!!!! *Now, .hold on, it's not what you may be thinking!!!*

(Ha....Just thought I'd make you wait, and have to turn the page to find out what.)

And Guess what, Mmmmmmmmmm. No, I won't tell you after all.

Ok, Ok, I will.

As I lay in my bed sipping a lovely cup of tea that Roger had made for me, Jezz came down the stairs wishing us a happy Christmas. "So what" I hear you say "is that it?"

In true Pantomime form "OH NO IT'S NOT" I say.

Jezz-a-bean was only in his undies!!! He then proceeded to clamber across my bed to give me a smacker of a kiss, saying "MERRY CHRISTMAS CRABBIE" !!!!!!!!! *MMMMMMMM,* MMMMMMM, mmmmmmmmm.

Blimey, what a Christmas present!!!... all my dreams come true!!!! A Fireman, on my bed, and only in his undies, giving me a kiss. I blushed terribly...

You could hear Nicky laughing her head off upstairs, and Roger just creased up. I reckon Nicky set it up. She knows I love firemen, but knew I'd be the first to do a runner, and so did Jezz, *the little minx.!!!*

When Nicky and the kids came down a few seconds later, Jezz went and got dressed....

"Shame that" ..Oooops, did that thought come out loud.!!!!

Anyway we gave Christmas hugs and kisses to each other and then gave gifts all round, before getting washed and dressed for the days events to come.

It was fantastic. We all had a lovely day and a feast fit for a king. By the end off the day we were exhausted, the kids were so well behaved. It was a delight to have them all staying here with us.

The next few days passed by with outings at times, but before long it was time for them to leave us. We hadn't had snow up at The Auld Doocot, but we took them out and about to places and they saw it all over the mountains nearby.

It was very emotional to say goodbye to them, we wished they could stay longer, but duty calls for Jezz and the Brigade, so they had to leave.

I couldn't believe it, when less than three hours after they had left it bloody started snowing, and didn't really let up much for weeks. Also adding insult to injury, they had snow down south for the first time in years. Bloody typical!!! Guess I didn't pray hard enough before they came up. But at least the boys saw some snow.

We hope they will come again for a Christmas, this time hopefully with lots of SNOW. But they can come and stay any time they like at a moments notice......

XXXXXXX THANK YOU ALL FOR SUCH A WOUNDERFUL TIME..XXXXXXXXXXX

Happy New Year to You All

Well we saw the old year out and the New Year in, and in true tradition we enjoyed a few drinks by the fire. We watched some funny videos until midnight and then engaged in the wishing of a good year to each others. We raised a glass to friends past and friends a-new, and hoped their coming year would be full of love and good health.

We thought of my Mum and Dad all those miles away, and hoped that their health would turn for the better, and bring them the strength to come and see us later in the year. It wasn't just for that reason we hoped they would soon be in better health. It was also because it is heart breaking to see them so down with ill health in their later years. When they should be enjoying the luxury of going places together, and putting their feet up when they like, or just pottering around in the garden. We pray each day that they get better and better.

There was a lot of planning and things to do this year.

First was to get the agricultural building up and running but we were still waiting to get the final go-a-head from the planning department of the council. Then there was a party/wedding blessing to arrange for July. This was to be our first anniversary celebration and my birthday party all in one. Remembering the wedding blessing was to make up for last years 'dark shadow' that still, in my mind, hung over our wedding day.

Days passed into weeks, then nearly into months, and we still had no news from the council. But I was able to look on the net each day to see 'if', God forbid, there had been any objections posted.

From our first Notification back at the end of November 2007, to the Notification being posted for Full Planning on 15th February 2008, it had been 3 months.

Now it was approaching the end of the 21st day Notification for this second one, and again so far there had been no comments/objections received by the council planning.

It was not just here the Notification had to be 'Posted'. It also had to go in a special paper in Edinburgh as the new Barn/Agricultural Building was near a listed building i.e. The Walled Garden!!!

It seemed all was going well, and should be plain sailing this time. We'd done everything by the book. So we hoped to be able to turn the page soon and get on with the work.

We still had lots of building materials under covers in the woods, so it would be nice to get the place looking tidy after all these years.

This IS the Last Straw!!

About the 6th or 7th of March the closing date passes for any problems, so fingers crossed any day now.

Then, (I know what your thinking, God 'Not' again!!!) yep it's happened again.

***3 DAYS *** before closing date one of our neighbours phoned!!! They expressed concern about 'possible' noise that may come as a result of the building?

I informed them that there would be a minimal amount of noise as the building would be insulated, as we had taken every possible step to consider all our neighbours.

I gave them an open invitation to come and talk to Roger and myself at any time, so as to put their worries to rest. This meant they could also ask any questions.

The days passed and we heard nothing from our neighbours, or the council. That was until we got a call late one evening from our architect!!!!

She was to say the least bloody fuming!!! It was now '12 DAYS' after any complaints could be registered and some bad news had come to light!!?????!! She had dotted all the (Is) and crossed all the (Ts), there was nothing she hadn't done.

Yet it turned out that there had been some complaints just put in!!!!!! It seemed that some neighbours had complained to the councillor, (AGAIN)........

"Oh, for God's sake, can't people just talk to each other." This was the bloody last straw as far as we were concerned.

Understandably, because issues had been raised, they now had to be looked into. It didn't seem to matter two hoots that the time allocated for all this to have been submitted, had expired nearly TWO WEEKS earlier??????

We also felt at this moment, that it may not be in our best interests, as Roger had, how shall I say, 'had a confrontation', with the councillor involved a few months back, over a private matter. We felt this may have had an influence on things, plus we had had dealings with him before!!!!

Well we were right, and all hell let loose. We were sick of this! Just as before the councillor was not looking into things, thus digging his heels in.

I know he has to do his job, and I know we have had confrontations between us. But if he was to just come and talk to us, face to face business wise, we would have welcomed it. Or if he didn't want to come to the house, he damn well knew he could use a thing called the PHONE. It would have saved a lot of hassle, and time, if our neighbours had only the decency to just talk to us in the first place about all this. (*Oh but I forget, we are aliens from Zorb, with 2 or possibly 3 heads!!!!*).

I'll tell you what, over the next few weeks I had to avoid any chance of communication with the neighbours concerned!! This was because I was scared!!! In the sense that if I was caught at the wrong moment, I may well just (with good reason, in my view) blow my top at them.

But as I said before, as far as we are aware, we have done nothing to upset or offend anyone. If we had, I wish they had told us at the time, and put whatever it was to rights. But if, as it seems, it is just because 'we' or 'someone' else had bought the 'then empty building', well we are sorry,!!!!! but we are here to stay. There was no reason for back stabbing when we could have talked things through.

A Long Awaited Moan?

If I can blow our own trumpet for a moment. I think you would be hard pushed to find neighbours as good and considerate as us, and they should count themselves lucky that we try our very best to respect their privacy, and be good neighbours. Even our hens and cockerels are put in sheds overnight, we never let them out before 9am. So this reduces as much noise as possible. We are registered as a Small Holding/Farm and could leave them out, as we want them to be as *Free Range* as possible, but I do feel we are doing our best to be thoughtful.

While I'm having a long awaited moan. When we were doing the work on the structure outside, we tried our best at all times not to let it look like a building site. We cleared all the tooling away each night, and didn't leave a mess for anyone to have to look out on to.

We never had the famous radio blaring away all day, like builders so often do. Or shout at the top of our voices in making conversations when working on opposite sides of the roof.

We took all the rubbish to the dump/recycling point in Huntly. So there was never any burning of smelly rubbish wafting over to the house.

Anyway, it would be bloody stupid to have a fire outside here, as we are in the woods. It would only take a spark to catch the whole lot alight. (*And I don't think the Cairngorm National Park would be very pleased with us one bit.*) Plus I expect there would be a heavy fine. (**Perhaps our neighbours should note this as they often have a fire in the woods, even if it is in a clearing. As I said it takes only one spark.**)

Also over the years we have tried to turn a blind eye to a couple of things that they have done. The first one that just sticks in my throat is going back a year or so now

One morning when I went to collect the eggs from the hutches, I became aware of someone moving around a little distance behind me!!

To my surprise and disbelief, there was a chap on 'our land'. He was knocking fence posts into 'OUR LAND'???????

Not knowing who he was and not wanting to jump the gun, I nipped back pretty sharp to get Roger.

I don't really know what I would have said to the chap. I was a bit shocked to see anyone there in the first place. I suppose I could have told him to 'GET OFF OUR LAND', as he had no right to be on it in the first place. But I 'did' realise that he would have been working under the instructions of the neighbours.

Roger and I decided not to say anything, as it was to our advantage that they put some kind of fence up. It would stop them looking at what we are doing all the time. So it was left at that. But what a cheek coming on our land and doing this without asking first. If they had asked, perhaps we would have said ok. But it was the principle of it all.

I can't tell you how many times I've felt like getting the chainsaw to the posts on our land, and lobbing them back over their side, to 'their land'. Because they have wound us up, (i.e.) over the Planning issues etc, but I will not lower myself to that level......Yet!!!!!

So anyway, back to the complaints about the Agricultural Building. Well, they were soon sorted out. As there was nothing we hadn't already been through. But as we have said before, the councillor concerned hadn't done his homework, thus he didn't even know we were registered as a 'FARM'.

So in his eyes, and the neighbours concerned, why have an 'Agricultural Building' in the first place? So they got egg on their faces again and I guess much to the councillors embarrassment!!!! I often wonder if they speak ENGLISH or SCOTTISH. We do!!!! (*CONTRARY TO WHAT THEY MUST THINK !!! (i.e.) That we speak ' ZORBBISH ' form the planet Zorb.*

In one of the comments made, it was claimed that the building construction was nearly finished???

All we can say is **'WE SO WISH IT HAD BEEN NEARLY FINISHED'.** As it would have been done by now, if it hadn't been for all the hassle......._**Bloody thanks for nothing.......!!!!!**_ sorry, I'm just bloody mad at them all for the stress and crap they caused, instead of talking to us.

In time however all was passed in the end, with conditions on the building. Guess what? It will be the poshest 'AGRICUTRUAL BUILDING' in history!!!!!!

It's now June 2008, so, we had now started with the building work, and it is a slow old job. Over the past few months we had Robert and his dad Frank here to use a 'cage lift thing' on the end of Frank's digger arms to lift Robert and I up to fit the roof panels on. Poor Roger took one look at it, and there was no way he'd even get in the thing. You know, him not liking heights....

Roger did all the ground work while cutting the panels to size etc, he had to run around like mad to ensure we had enough screws and drilling equipment at hand at a moments notice. Ha, and for once he also had to make sure we had tea and coffee when wanted. This was a nice change for me, as I felt I was doing something worth while. It's all too easy to watch the men folk do the building work. Anyway, I was used to building work, from when working on the house. It was nice to feel useful again. Not that making tea is a woman's job only...!!!! *(and to be truthful, although I'm not keen on heights, having a 'fireman' next to me made a Big difference)* I felt totally safe if anything was to happen, as Robert was a 'First Responder' with the local medic team.....

The only time I did feel a little uneasy, was when I 'happened' to ask Robert what the weight capacity was on the cage and lift???? *I mean, I am a big lass...!!!*

There we were, Robert and I in the cage, and about 20 foot or so up in the air **"not a good time to think of this one", I hear you thinking.**

I said to Robert, "Maybe this <u>is</u> not a good time to ask you Rob, but what is the weight capacity of the cage??? His calming!! reply was...... "No, don't ask "!!!!!!!...... Don't worry, I was ok, and not fussed at all,.....I'm cool....., I'm fine............ I'm......Mmmmmmmmmmmmmmmmmm!!!!!

A Day to Stay in Bed!!!

Today is Friday the 13th of June, and what a day it was!!

It didn't start well by any means, it was to be a miserable wet and cloudy day on and off. Poor Roger had to keep dodging the rain showers while trying to get on with the work on the Barn. I will call it a 'Barn' from now on, as to keep typing 'Agricultural Building' is getting on my nerves. So we all know what I mean. (Just in case the neighbours think we are building another one.!!!!)

I had to clean out the chicken pens and sheds, which is a weekly job, or sometimes more if the animals have been kept in the runs because of bad weather. Anyway, today was the day. However, have you ever had the feeling you should have just stayed in bed??

First the hose pipe end on the tap outside shot off at 100 miles an hour, soaking me in freezing cold water. So I went indoors and got changed, then slipped down the stairs landing on my big bum. Although you could say it has a 'good' amount of padding, it damn well hurt.

Then as I walked out the door I trod in 'Dog Poo'. "OOOoooooooo" came my tantrum scream. Oh yuck, a dog with upset guts, that's all I need today. This in turn made me dash to the loo to be sick, as on top of it I was feeling unwell today.

I have been a little poorly for some time now!! Nothing too bad, (I hoped), but I am seeing the doctor regularly to keep an eye on things. I had developed what I would call 'a stomach ache' some time back, just below my ribs. Stupidly, like most of us, I put of going to the GP. Or saying anything much to anyone except poor Roger, who put up with my whingeing.

In the end our friend Mary told me I must go an see the doctor because I was looking so pale and dark under my eyes. She said if I didn't make an appointment that week, she would damn well take me.

I have to say, that without makeup on, I am usually pale, but even I had to admit that I was looking a bit rough around the edges.... *"Nothing unusual there"* I hear Roger thinking!!!

I did go to the GP, and she thinks it's a stomach ulcer giving me all this hassle. So she did the usual blood tests and all is well there. It cheesed Roger off on one test. 'My' cholesterol level is '4.2', ha,ha,ha..

I was more worried that my liver had been damaged, due to the large amount of alcohol I've had over the years!! But to my surprise and relief it's fine, and working well.

However, for over a week I worried until the results had come in as one of the tests was for 'Ovarian Cancer'. It had crossed my mind, but I had pushed that thought to the back of my mind. Well that was until I was told about the test. This again was clear, thank God.

So all was pointing to a stomach ulcer, and as tests came back clear it was eliminating anything really nasty. Not that I particularly enjoy the symptoms of the stomach ulcer, to be honest, it's bloody hell at times. But at least I'm on medication for it, and it helps. And for the first time in years my weight is going down, and down. Just wish I could loose the weight, without being ill....

I have had to change my diet completely, OH YUCK..All low fat stuff, and so much salads I can feel my ears twitching!! But I am enjoying what I eat. Although Sunday lunch isn't the same. Steamed or boiled chicken and boiled tatties.!!!

You just can't replace a good old SUNDAY ROAST. MMMMMMmmmmmm.

But I'm learning fast, sometimes the hard way, what I can eat without getting terrible pains in my gut. I don't eat any spices or curry type of meals, because even a little will set things off shortly after eating it. Also keeping off citrus fruits helps. Luckily I love bananas, and they don't have any side affect.

As for the wicked booze, I have to confess I do indulge sometimes. But then I never learn, as it's always followed by a rough night. So perhaps I should stop completely, for two reasons. My health, and poor Roger who is kept awake by my whingeing. Mmmmmm *Sorry Roger xxxxxx*

I still have to have some tests, but I'll be fine. It took 30 plus years to get Roger's wedding ring on my finger, so he's not getting rid of me that easily. There are two options in life, the first option is the favourable one, it is to get well.

The second option is 'NOT' my option.. Thank you God, I hope you are listening!!!!

Oh, and as if I'd forget to say, going back to when I rushed into the loo, I had forgotten to remove my boots. So now I had 'Doggy Poo' all over the wooden floor from the main door leading to the loo. Oooo!

The day however did get better as time went on. That was until my Dad phoned, and asked me to talk to my Mum!! Oh, poor Mum was in a hell of a state, she was in tears on the phone. She'd got so down again, just hearing her cry tore my heart in two. I just wanted to be with her and hug her.

I'm convinced it's all the chemicals in her body from those damn pills the GP keeps giving her to take. She has never been right since then. It seems to suddenly swim over her and apparently for no reason at times it triggers of this over-whelming feeling she gets. I gather she gets very sick with it and doesn't feel like eating when we know she must. Mum has lost so much weight since being on these pills..

Dad of course is a tower of strength for her, but there is only so much he can do. Just being there for her, holding her in his loving arms and comforting her, is the best medicine any loving husband can give. I feel for Dad, as at times it must be heart breaking for him to see Mum, the woman he loves more than life itself, being in such sorrow and despair to the point of crying. But knowing it will pass, is of some comfort to them, although at the time it may not seem like it .

And there was me wigging about my problems, guess I'm very lucky compared to what they are going through....*PLEASE dear God, help them to get well.*

At a later hour of the day things did turn out nicely. One of our neighbours rang to say they had one of our hens marching about outside their cottage, with a brood of babies. So we went up and managed to retrieve them safely and bring then home to their pen.   It was our black bantam, and she has 10 little black beauties.....Arrrrrrrrrrrrrrrrrrr.

June 15th..Fathers Day.....

What a lovely surprise for Roger. Both Sara and Jonathon had sent beautiful Father's Day cards for Roger. (I had hidden them as they arrived the day before.)

I phoned my Dad to wish him a good day, and to my delight Mum was much better, and seemed positively cheerful. Dad thanked us for his card, and we talked for a bit, even he seemed a little brighter.

I put some more silk flowers beside Roger's Dad's resting place, and said a few word to him!!!

Roger had been outside all day working on the barn and was now in for his supper. But first Sam has to have a well needed shower, as he'd been up in the woods with Roger, and was now covered in mud due to all the wet ground.

The next big event is Mum and Dad coming up at the end of June if they are well enough, and then our wedding blessing combined with my birthday party.

We are having the whole thing at The Colquhonnie House Hotel just down the road. Paul and Dave are going to do the place out beautifully for the Blessing etc. We wouldn't dream of going back to the pub as before. The bill made our jaws hit the floor, we were bloody fuming.   Not forgetting that we had to pay for the rooms that people didn't turn up for. Although we had told them to let the rooms out to anyone, (i.e.) other guests apart from wedding people. The whole bill was nearly a grand!!! But because we paid cash we were very 'kindly'!! let off the VAT.

The room we had the service in Roger and I had fixed up, apart from some lovely flowers that were on the table in front of us. But nothing was done in the bar for the reception!!! We were very disappointed. There was of course a table with a white table cloth on it, with the beautiful wedding cake that Sally made for us, which later had the wedding food on.

The first round of drinks must have been laced with gold champagne!!! Even if there had been 60 people there at 3 pounds a head, it would only have been 180 pounds not what they charged!!!

Sorry but it still gets us cross, never again will we book a function there.....

But the wedding itself was great, and the weather was beautiful. *Thank you again to all our friends. Xxxx.* '

A Change of Plans

We went to Huntly today, just to get some corn for the animals and some odd bits we needed for the building work on the Barn.

We popped in to Cheers, out normal stopping point for lunch, and our friend Sheena and her son Chris were already there having their lunch, so we joined them at their table. While talking to them I began to see that perhaps retaking our wedding vows was a bit pointless. I only wanted to do them again because of the upset we had following the wedding. But as Sheena pointed out, that whatever happened was a good 3 weeks after our wedding, not on the day itself. The wedding had been great, and as I had already told her, I had in fact edited Cathy and Tim out of the Photos, because it was a constant reminder of all the upset. She felt that no more could be done, and anyway, it was after the wedding itself..

Although this was true, and still hurts to think of all that followed, she was right. So we are now just having a First Wedding Anniversary Party with all the trimmings, and my birthday party in one. We hope to get some good photos this time.

(Deep down we will 'NEVER' forgive Cathy and Tim for the upset, and hurt they gave us. We opened our lives to them, and gave them a place to stay for their second weeks holiday. Free, as our friends (so we thought) but in return they seemed to slap us in the face, by holding back the fee's for the previous weeks rented accommodation. So 'YES' it has left a bitter taste, and dark shadow over the wedding

It could have all been avoided if only they had kept in touch, instead of not returning our phone calls. We didn't want to know their personal problems, but if they had just explained 'something', and kept us informed, it would have help us understand. But after their rudeness to us in letters they sent, they will never be welcome here again.

There, I've said it.!!!

Now, Sheena had told me last week on the phone that Chris was joining the Army, and that Hannah, Cathy's daughter who is going out with Chris, was coming up to stay with them for a while before Chris goes in, so they could have some time together.

So I hope I made it very clear to them that Hannah is more than welcome to join us for the parties. Hannah is a lovely girl/young lady and is not responsible for he parents actions in any way. The subject would not be spoken about with her, it would not be fair on her to discuss it. It would be nice to see her again.

XXXXX Congratulations Dad and Mum XXXXX

June 19th 2008

Today is my Dad's and Mum's *** *60th Wedding Anniversary* ***. What a day to be proud of, all those years spent with the one you love, must feel wonderful.

In some ways I envy them!!! To have had 60 years together is what I envy. In the sense that I would not be able to have another 60 years of marriage together with Roger, simply because of our ages. It would make me, from our wedding day last year, plus the 60 years the grand old age of 109. If you get my drift, it is not meant in a nasty way.

If it is possible I believe they truly love each other more each day, and we are so proud of them. They have had good times and bad, yet I have never heard them complain. Ok, they have been fed up with the getting 'Old Age' thing in life, and they have also had a rough ride these passed few years but as I so often say, it is better than the other option!!!

Dad and Mum are taking my brother and family out for dinner tonight in celebration of their anniversary. I wish Roger and I could have been there with them today. But hopefully they will be here next week if all goes well, and if they themselves are well enough to travel

Dad and Mum seemed in good spirits today, and I was pleased that their parcel arrived early in the morning from us. I had arranged flowers and Champagne to be delivered, with a card from Roger and I.

Mum and Dad

Thank you Pam for Being my Friend

Pam was due over today to carry on with helping me and my spelling, but I nearly phoned to cancel. I had gone to bed early last night feeling unwell, and didn't think I could manage a day typing. Trying to get my brain cells going is a challenge when I feel rough.

All night I'd had terrible stomach pains, and today it wasn't much better, but hey, what the hell. There are people far worse off than me in this world and they carry on, so on I must go...

Pam arrived after she had finished work and after a much needed cup of tea we started on the book.. Poor thing, she must be pulling her hair out with me sometimes, as she tries to correct things. I am very grateful to her, and Robert for letting her help me. She must be very busy with family commitments, and working part-time, yet she still makes time to help me. She also has her own business to work at in-between all this called 'Taylor/Made Reflexology', and she's very popular. Not only is Pam what I would call 'my best friend'. I would also call her my saviour at times over the years. Pam is a qualified 'Reflexologist ', and damn good at it. She has helped Roger and I out many times. It's all to do with 'pressure points' on your feet or hands, that can control different parts of the body when stimulated. So far she's been spot on each time with her diagnoses, and treated it successfully.

However I hadn't told Pam I was ill until recently, as I hoped it would be a short passing thing. I don't like to abuse out friendship by asking for help at every slightest thing. But as soon a I know what's wrong I will get her to do her stuff. I just hate taking pills and things. I'd rather try natural remedies, and I trust Pam, because I have experienced, and seen the results of their handy work. Pam has said what she thinks is my problem, but because I am under the GP, she has said it's best to wait and see what they say. Pam says that because I am on medication from the GP, it's best that we wait for now. If only I'd gone to her first, daft cow that I am, I just didn't want to trouble her with my silly aches and pains.

While Pam was here the post arrived, and in it was an appointment for me at the Gastro-enterology clinic in Aberdeen. Great this has come through quickly, problem is my Mum and Dad will be here on holiday, and to top it off it's on my Mum's birthday July 1st. But I don't want to cancel it, I want it over and done with, and to find out for sure what's wrong. Plus I don't think Mum would want me to cancel, I feel sure she would understand. We can go out for a meal in the evening, or even the next day. Plus they are here for two weeks, so we'd have plenty off time together.

Winding down to the end. Will summer ever get here?

God what crap weather we are having for this time of year. It seems to be raining most days, and it's so cold at times you'd think it was autumn, and on a windy day like winter.

Yes, I know the seasons here differ from England, but for God sake, give it a rest!! Besides, even though we're used to it now, it would be nice to have a little more sunshine for the end of June.

Still on a happier note, my Mum and Dad are due to arrive on Saturday, and we can't wait. It seems forever since they were here, yet it was only a year ago at our wedding.

I've just spoken to Mum on the phone and she seems happy today, and I believe Dad has got over a recent neck strain, which I thought might give him some discomfort when driving.

Meanwhile everything is going to plan for the party on the 5th of July, and we are looking forward to having a knees-up with all our friends.

I also hope to have some good news regarding my tummy problem by then. Because the other day I was a bit concerned. I had rung the doctors to see if my scan results were back, and said that if everything was ok I would make an appointment after my next lot of tests had been done. If however the doctor wanted to see me, could they ring back?

As it was Roger needed a repeat prescription and as we were going out, we may as well it pop in. When I arrived it turned out that one of the other doctors had tried to ring me at home. The scan results had come back and where the hospital doctor had first said there seemed nothing to worry about, there was in fact a problem. The doctor at the hospital did however say he couldn't give me a guarantee that all was well, but he seemed to think it was all ok i.e. there were no Gallstones to be seen, and all seemed in the correct places etc. So that was a relief.

I assumed all was well, as the GP hadn't phoned before with the results. Anyway, it turns out my Gallbladder has a problem. (It's dilated or enlarged.?) The GP said it could be that there was a Gallstone, which has now passed through? (*The human body is weird.!*)

*So this could be some, or all the pain etc.....*I wonder.??? But surely if there had been a stone, why am I still ill?? Surely I should be getting better, not worse by the day. Well, I shouldn't really be so dramatic, I have good and bad days, only it does seem to be getting worse. Perhaps it will pass away soon.

One good thing that has come out of it, is that at long last I am losing weight. About two and a half stone since I first felt ill. I'd been losing weight before I went to the doctors, and now I've changed my diet to salads and no fats, it's coming off nicely. If nothing else, I feel better for getting rid of the excess fat I've carried around for far too long.

Otherwise in myself I'm fine, still as nutty as ever, and doing the garden as much as possible. I find digging is fine and doesn't cause any real pain, unless I go stupid on things. *Sorry to describe this*, but sometimes I get so much 'bile' in my mouth I feel sick. I say 'bile' but I don't know if that's the right word. It's just like when you are going to be sick,.... your mouth gets all watery.... most unpleasant.

Sam our dog has just come over and nudged my leg and jumped up on the chair next to mine. You know, it's as though he knows what I'm writing. He definitely knows when Roger or I are ill, he's so loving and gentle in wanting to be at our side. Almost pushing himself on our laps at times, just to be near us.

I guess that's his way of telling us he senses we're ill, and in need of some T.L.C.

Sleeping Well

June 27th 2008, Friday

Well, first thing this morning my Mum and Dad set off on their two day drive up to see us for a two week holiday. I have to be the first to admit, I was very worried about Dad driving all this way with only one night stop-over in Richmond. It is such a long way for someone of our age, let alone for Dad, who is now 89, plus Mum being so frail now, it must look very daunting to her..

However after me pacing the floor most of the day, in-between doing the last minuet hoovering and dusting, Mum phoned to say they had arrived safely in Richmond.

She sounded very tired, in fact she said that they were both exhausted. But they were now having a lovely cup of tea in front of an open roaring fire at their accommodation. Mum said they would arrive tomorrow as planned, but could not give a specific time.

Next day they must have set off as planned, as the understanding was that they would ring if they were delayed in any way.

However as the day passed I did tend to stay near the phone, half expecting Dad to ring and say that they were to break the journey up by stopping off again overnight at a hotel. But as time passed I assumed that they would arrive at any point in the late afternoon.

At about 4.15pm Dad phoned to say they were at Blairgowrie, which is about 33/35mile from Ballater, then a drive over the mountains and last bit to us. This drive would take them over what I called the Val Doonican Mountains, and then to our place. But they were to continue on to Bill and Mary's B&B, and ring us from there. This was simple because I didn't think that Dad would want to drive up our track in his car, because of all the potholes and stones. In the end we decided to go to the Glencove pub and keep a watch out for them, as the B&B they were to stay at is opposite.

We left our place and drove to Roger and had a beer while awaiting their now imminent arrival!!!.... and waited...... and waited.... and waited!!!!!!!. It was soon 6.15pm and we were getting worried. But we know it's is a windy road, so perhaps Dad is taking his time.

I was outside pacing the ground having a ciggie when Roger came outside to give me my mobile phone that was ringing away. It was a call from Mo and Hughie, to say that my Dad and Mum were at the Colquhonnie House Hotel down the road. So I in turn rang the Colquhonnie and managed to speak to Margaret, Dave's mum, and she told me that Dad just couldn't drive anymore. He was too tired, and could we come and get them.

Well, we shot down to the hotel and found Dad outside talking to Paul, looking tired-out. After saying hello, Roger stayed with Dad, and I went into the hotel and found Mum sitting at a corner table having a cup of tea. We hugged and said hello, and cried a little with relief to see each other until the men folk joined us shortly after.

Dad and Mum were both exhausted, but after a little something to eat, the colour came back to their cheeks. I think Dad did wonderfully, but hoped he wouldn't do it again by car. Or if he did, to take at least 3 days.

A little later we drove in front of them to refresh Dad's memory on where Bill and Mary's place was, and then left them in their room. Bill and Mary are a wonderful couple, and I know they will look after Mum and Dad well. The place is spotless, and so lovely, with a friendly atmosphere, *NO SORRY, I'll add to this,..* lovely, friendly, and homely.

We were to ring in the morning before 11am to see if they were ready and able for us to pick them up for a day at our house.

As arranged next day we rang, and then went to pick Mum and Dad up. They were both still very exhausted from the drive, but wanted to get to our place and have a good look around.

It is great to have them here, and Roger and I looked forward to taking them to some lovely places. In-between looking over our place and catching up on all the news, they both slept on and off. I think the long drive has really taken it out of then both this time. We just let them rest, and I did a

Sunday lunch. It made a change for us to sit down during the day, so it was a rest for Roger not to be working on the barn. Which by the way, is coming on nicely now, and Roger was pleased he managed to get what he wanted to get done to impress Dad just in the nick of time.

......*June 30th ..Monday*

I was looking forward to today as we were taking Mum and Dad to Leith Hall, which is not far from here. The attraction for me was that it is said to be haunted, and I just love all that spooky stuff. Even if sometimes it scares the pants off me.

But what a let down!! When we got there to we found it wasn't open to the public until the next day. Now was only for school trips, but Mum and Dad had a walk around the outside of the building. I didn't even want to do that until I could go in and have a good look inside. I just felt that if I'd found an open door I'd be tempted to creep in and get ghost hunting. But then I may get in to trouble, so I didn't want to put temptation in front of me for a second.

By now it was lunch time, we went back to our place and I did a light lunch and then prepared dinner for the evening. Mum and Dad rested and I think they need it, as they slept most of the afternoon.

Happy Birthday Mum

July 1st Tuesday.

Well, what a birthday for Mum!!! They come all this way and today on her birthday I'm at the hospital. (Bloody *great!!!*) I did say to Mum that I could try and rearrange the appointment, but she understood that it could mean I may have to wait some time for another. Hopefully I would be back in time for lunch, if not we could all go out for a birthday dinner.

Dinner was arranged for 6pm at the Colquhonnie, and we hoped that June, Harry, and June's mum Betty would be able to join us.

After my appointment at the hospital, which was only a consultation to see if I would need a 'Gastroscopy' *(which basically, if you don't know, is a small tube passed down your throat, so the doctor can see what's going on using a camera)*. Unfortunately, I will have to have this done. *Oh' whippy-do-dars!!!*

When we got back home we had just enough time to get changed and dash to the hotel to meet Mum and Dad. So for the first time ever, I didn't listen to my answer machine for the phone.

If I had, I would have got some bad news, and some great news. The bad new was that June and Betty were too ill with a type of flue, so they would not be able to meet us as arranged. But the great news was that Cara, my brother Paul and his wife Denise's youngest daughter, has had a baby girl. This would have made a wonderful birthday for Mum.

Even so, Mum had a lovely birthday dinner with us at the Colquhonnie and she looked lovely too. Even Dad was now beginning to perk-up a little after his traumatic drive here a few days earlier.

We arranged the next days outing before they went back to their B & B down the road, so we'd pick them up in the morning.

We only went to Huntly today as Dad was a little under the weather, and we needed some shopping, so it would be an easy day for them.

While we were out I managed to persuade Dad to let our friend Pam do a session of Reflexology on him, to make him feel better. Up until now Dad has always been a believer in the 'GP', but today he had no hesitation in taking my advice, and letting Pam try to help him. Older people tend to shy away from things they don't understand. But I do feel that Dad is getting a little more open-minded at times like this, when he feels so ill, or is in pain.

We arranged to pop in to Pam's on the way back to our place.

Mum decided to wait in the car with Roger, while I went into Pam's with Dad. Pam did her Reflexology on Dad's feet, and Dad was very interested to see that Pam was spot on with her diagnosis. She put Dad at ease, and did her thing while Dad relaxed in a chair.

Dad was a bit sceptical, but he was the first to admit that he felt much better straight away, and improved over the next day. Two days later Pam came to our house and did Reflexology on Dad, and Mum, and they both enjoyed the experience.

Pam was able to show Mum where to apply pressure on her hands when she feels sick and unwell. Also the points to massage when Mum gets that over-whelming panic and depression so that may help Mum when she is back home.   *(THANKS PAM)*

Party Day
July 5th 2008

Today Roger and I are celebrating our first wedding anniversary and my birthday (*all be it a few days early*) as it was the closest date we could book the party.

Originally we were going to have a big BBQ at our place, but with all the rushing around last year for the wedding, and the expense I decided '*Bugger it*' I wanted us to relax and enjoy the day. Let someone else do all the work for a change.

All our friends that had been at our wedding were invited, and some new friends we had made since, plus Mum and Dad.

The weather was in our favour, just like our wedding day, and it was truly to be a lovely day all round. We arrived at the Colquhonnie at 2.30pm, and the boys and staff had done a lovely job of setting up the rooms. They did us proud. *THANK YOU ALL XXX*

Dad and Mum arrived, and shortly after a mini bus arrived with a crowd from Glencove. We never expected any gifts, as it was just a party for all our friends to enjoy. But it was truly over whelming, the gifts and cards were never ending. Plus the biggest bouquet of beautiful flowers I'd ever seen from all our friends in Glencove. It took a lot for me not to just burst into tears with pride, to know Roger and I have made so many true and caring friends.

I was able to get into a dress I had bought two weeks earlier that I couldn't fit in. Ok, so it was a bit tight in places, but I got in it. However I was unable to wear my shoes for long as the foot I had hurt when we first arrived here just was not having any of it. So I slipped them off and tried not to slip over on the polished floor. (*Later I must have looked the height of fashion!!!!!!! As I borrowed a pair of Dave's trainers to walk around outside with...for some reason they didn't quite match my dress!!! but thanks anyway Dave, they were a God send XXX.*)

As the afternoon went on I tried to mingle with everyone, talking to as many people as possible, thanking them for all the wonderful gifts etc. Later Paul, from the Colquhonnie, gave a small speech on our behalf thanking all our friends and family for sharing in our celebrations and explained that the reason that Roger and I didn't have a blessing in the end, was because we both felt that we were truly blessed already by having them all as our dearest friends. (*Oh' mush, mush, I hear you saying!!*)

Later our friend Martin played his accordion and people began to have a sing song, a couple of people had a dance.

Now for one second did you think I'd let the day go by without just a little event!!!! Well, we'd all had a few drinks, and the moment took me!!!! I mean, something possessed my hand, which was holding the camera and as I stood behind Martin, my hand took the camera down to the back of his knees, and took a look up his kilt, and with me having no control of the said camera, it took a picture!!! *Ooooops, you naughty, naughty camera!!!! (this of course had nothing to do with me!! honest!!! I'd never think of doing a thing like that!!!)* Sorry Martin, *but I must say, It's a damn good picture!!!* Just in case you are wondering, I did have the decency to get Roger to check the photo first, just in case. Also in case <u>YOU</u> were wondering if Martin was, how shall I say, <u>A TRUE SCOT</u>   *I'm not telling!!!!!!!!!!!!*

*But I do have the negatives, and you can call me on this number..........................**AS IF...!!***

Later Mum and Dad went off back to the B&B, while we all partied on into the night, until about 9.45pm when the minibus set off back to Glencove with the majority of the partygoers. We stayed until about 12.30pm talking with Susan and her husband from the Glencove post office, and Jamey and his wife. It was a lovely day and evening and we were tired when we got home. But I took ages going to sleep, as I reminisced over the days events.

XX Thank You All for Another Wonderful Day XX

On July the 9th our anniversary and my birthday, I spent the day at the hospital again. I had my GI-endoscopy. All I will say on the matter is, go for sedation. They offer you the choice of the spray in the throat, or sedation. I tried with just the spray, and it just was not going well, so they sedated me. Then all was a blank. Best way in my view....OK.

I got my results as soon as I was compos mentis after the events. I now have to go for a CT scan and then to the hospital again in a few weeks.

Found out I have a Hiatus hernia in the Oesophagus (sliding), Stomach Gastritis and to top it of with the icing, Duodenitis (basically erosions in my stomach....Ouch. *(I never seem to do things by half.)* But although it all sound technical and scarier, I believe it's all something that can be sorted with diet and medication.

Luckily my own GP had already said it could be an ulcer, so I had already started on the road to recovery with medication. Plus I have already changed my eating habits. Although I was still drinking my Cider, that has now stopped. Also crisps, peanuts and spicy food is a definite no, no. Bugger, all the things I love but I know that when I do eat them, I suffer later for it. So that's that.

Plus they are all the things that kept me fat, so again, that's the end of them. It has been trial and error finding what I can, and now can't eat, but once bitten, twice shy, as they say.

But in myself, I am as nutty as ever, just this 'gut ache' gets a bit too much, some days more that others.

The days were going by, and although we had been able to go to a few places with Mum and Dad, now into their second week the weather had changed to rain. So apart from the odd day or two the second week was a restful one at our house for Mum and Dad.

Too suddenly it was time for them to leave, and as we said our sad goodbyes it was decided just to say "See you soon", that way it didn't seem so hard when they left.

Dad of course, now fully recovered, and forgetting how exhausted he was on the drive up here, was hell bent on driving back with only the one overnight stop!!! But he did promise that if it got too much for them, they would stop off at a hotel!!!

Anyway in the end I got a phone call when they had arrived home safe, and apart from being totally exhausted, again, they were ok. However, they will not be driving up next time.

'I Don't Believe It!'

(In the words of Victor Meldrew)

Life returned back to normal, and we continued the work on the barn. The weather was beautiful and all was at peace with our world. *(The neighbours were away on holiday!)* So we were able to get on with our work, and not have to worry too much about the noise we may make, because we do try to keep things down when they are around.

However, the neighbours arrived back a few days later, and now we would have to try and keep the noise to a limit, which is understandable.

Anyway on this occasion, which was a Sunday, we were working on the barn, Frank phoned to say he was to bring some gravel and stuff up for our drive. This was because it had sunk over the years where it lead into the woods, from the house to where the barn now is.

As we carried on our work our friend Martin arrived, *he was the chap in the kilt at the party,* so at that time of day one just had to open a bottle of the bubbly stuff. It would be just rude not to!

We chatted to him, and while he was here Frank arrived with the first of what was to be about six or seven loads of the drive foundation mix.

We got through the old booze nicely, as the heat of the day was needing quenching! And very nice it was too.

Martin is a great chap, and a chap that seems to be able to tolerate some of my wilder side. In the sense that I can be 'a bit' O.T.T. at times to say the least. And I am the first to admit that I can be more than a little suggestive at times. But Roger knows there is nothing in my remarks to worry about. It's just my sense of humour, and my sometime outrageous thoughts come out loud. Usually when I've had a few drinks, and my mouth just says it, before my brain says not to. But then that's just me.

Getting back to the events that where to unfold.

On one of the trips that Frank was doing Martin, Roger and I had been sitting chatting to Frank when Roger went to the barn for something. As he did this Martin and I stood to one side out of the way, while Frank went to lower the back of the trailer after it had unloaded. When suddenly, 'BANG', and in a flash a shower of glass rained down from the air, and at the same time, the trailer began to wildly sway out of control. Martin grabbed me to one side, as the trailer swerved around, and then luckily stopped, a little closer than we liked!, but we were not hit.

It certainly made us all hop a bit, and Roger came roaring back to see what had happen. Luckily no- one was hurt.

It turned out that the trailer had somehow come un-hitched at the back of the tractor, hence all the drama.

You'd think that was enough drama for one day, but not here! It always seems to happen in twos, or on a day like today in threes, again.

The second was a minor thing of me bashing my big toe on a huge rock, but the third thing to go wrong was a biggie.

Later that evening after Martin had gone home, we carried on working on the barn. As Roger fitted the huge panels along the side of the barn, I held them in place while he put a holding screw in them to temporarily hold them in. On the third and fourth ones I assumed that Roger was done with my help holding them in place, as he went off to the other side of the barn.

Oh how wrong I was. As I let go of the side panels and bent down to start picking some tools up off the floor to put away, I saw stars!! I vaguely remember hearing Roger shout, "Crab". Now, whether that was before or after, I don't know. But the fourth panel had fallen down on to me, and hit me full blast on the head. The only thing I really remember was the horrific pain as this thing hit me on the head. Then me nursing my head hoping it hadn't been split in two, and wondering if my brains where about to spill out!!! *Because believe me, that's what it bloody felt like. And yes I cried like a baby, but God, it bloody hurt.*

It turned out that when Roger had gone across to the other side of the barn he had said it was to get some more screws to hold the fourth panel. But I hadn't heard him, so that's why it all happened.

After all this I'd had enough, so I went in doors, leaving Roger to clear up. Roger did try to help me, but I was best left to get my senses back in peace. That night I went to bed with a stinker of a headache, and I think it was 5am when I last looked at the clock when taking my fourth headache pill. *Talk about a base-drum being played in my head! I had the whole sodding band doing the Twenty-one Gun Salute all bloody night!*

That was on Saturday, and it's now Monday afternoon, and my head still pounds away nicely to itself, but the tune has no base drum, just a normal drum kit!! Roger has been great during all my 'excitement', bless him. If it carries on, the headache that is, I'll see the GP, but they'll probably only tell me what I already know, I have no brain to damage!

Ok, I think I'll end my book now before 'ANYTHING' else happens!!

So, really that's it until the next time from me, when perhaps you may want to see the next adventures and antics that happen. Because believe me life is never boring, and

d
    d
d
      d
        d
       d
    d
     d

Bugger, I fell of the chair!!!

THE END

(Just for now anyway!)
P.T.O.

And They all Lived Happily Ever After

Hughie & Mo

They are happy and seemingly in good health. And are now settling into their new home not far away, so we still meet up in the pub from time to time. Thanks again Mo for all you help.

Sid & Angie

Are doing fine, and always make us laugh. They are true characters in their own right. Thank you both for the TEA POT!

Harry, June & Betty

Thank you all for being such good friends...Thank you June for reading my book, with such enthusiasm, that encouraged me to hurry and finish the next chapter for you to read. And Harry, just for being your chuckily self, and for all your help. Keep up the good work in the garden, it's looking great.....The mini Niagara Falls is looking spectacular.

And not to forget Betty, June's mother, you are a true Granny in the best ever way. You are so sweet and kind... Bless you.

Charles & Ruth

Charles is a joyful as ever and full of energy. I believe Ruth is suffering with back problems. So we hope she will soon get sorted, and soon be in no more pain.

Nick the helicopter pilot

He's fine as far as we know. Thank you so much for the wedding photos. We will always cherish them forever. And thanks for being our friend.

Paul & Dave...From the Colquhonnie House Hotel

They seem to be enjoying married life, and business is blooming....I believe there are some 'Civil Partnership's' booked for the coming year. The Gay scene is to me, seemingly becoming more open here, and good for them...The place is a credit to them, and all the hard work they have put into the place. I miss working with them, and I often wonder how many others have seen the Ghosts....SPOOKY....

The Neighbours

John & Marion, Brian & Doreen

They and their families that we have come to know over the years are fine as far as we know. We enjoy meeting up with them when we can.

Which isn't as often as we would like because of commitments. They are all very nice people to know.

Unfortunately some of the neighbours are still not as friendly! But Rhubarbs to them...Life is too short for all that silliness! I have a feeling it will continue which is a great shame.

Gerry & Sheila

Gerry has just had a hip replacement and seems to be as normal, 'overdoing things'. He's not one for sitting around. Sheila has had some health problems and we hope she will soon be better. The windows are looking fine now with the wood oil and sealant on ready for yet another long winter.

Trevor, Sheena, Vicky & Chris

They all seem to be well. Trevor was very ill some time back, but he's ok now. Sheena too has had a spell of illness, but she's now fine....Vicky's moved out and is now living with her long term boyfriend. And young Chris has grown into a smashing young man, and is hoping to go into the Army soon. They are some of our closest and dearest friends, they mean the world to us.

Mary & Iain

Unfortunately their marriage came to an end a few years back, and Mary recently sold the B&B from down the road, and moved away. We wish her all the best in her new adventure, and hope to keep in touch. We owe you so much for your kindness. As for all those hot baths, long weekends and for a warm bed to sleep in, it was just heaven. Thank you so much XXX.

Bobsky

Well, bless him. Where ever you are, we hope you are well. And yes, we do miss you in spite of it all! Lets face it we did have a few adventures. Love You XX,

Peter and Kim

We speak on the phone from time to time, and they seem to be enjoying their retirement. We do miss the old days in the pub with you....COME BACK !!! please.....

Frank & Betty Taylor

I wish I could find a word for them to sum up all the love and kindness they have given us. To somehow say 'thank you' for all the work and help they have done for us. We have never met such a wonderful couple. And could never repay them for everything they have given us. Friendship like they have given us is something so rare it is to be cherished for life.

They welcomed us into their family, wanting nothing in return. They have made us feel part of life here, when at times we felt some were hostile towards our presence. They are wonderful.

Robert & Pam

What can we say? They are the best ever friends you could have. They also welcomed us into their lives. And I feel that they are family to us...This last week they have been away to Disney World with their two children, and all their family on Pam's side. I would have loved to have been there to see Loran and Shaun's faces at seeing from Mickey Mouse to Winnie the Pooh, to Peter Pan in Never Never Land. They are just at that age when Fairy Tales still exist, which is a time to be cherished for ever. However I have to say we have missed them all so much, and can't wait for them to get back home again. I feel as if part of me is missing. It's a strange feeling. They all mean so much to us.

And I have to thank Pam for all her help with my book. Just hope she will help with the next one!!!!!! (Yes Pam, there's another one on the way. But very different. Shhhhhhhhhh. Don't tell anyone yet!)

In fact, 'Thank You' to all the Taylor family, it's great having you in our lives.

Heather the Architect, Associates, and her family

Thank you on a professional note for all your help, and batting the ball back at certain parties during our times of trouble.

On a personal note, thank you and Stevie for the wonderful Wedding gift of the Quiche. And thanks for being our friends. Your two 'Cheeky' boys are a credit to you.

Thank you also to Nicky her assistant for all her help. You and Andrew have a wonderful family, we wish you love and happiness in all you do. Oh and sorry I gabble on a bit after a few bevvies.!

Tony & his new partner

They are very happy, and have now just bought a house together. We wish them all the happiness and good luck in the world for their new lives together. And at least now we can all have a drink together like before, as things have settled down.

Sally & her new partner

Sally eventually moved away with her new partner. We wish them health and happiness.

Jane

Jane is looking as if she runs the pub single-handedly most of the time. She does all the cooking and works very hard. She can still be a little moody but we all have our off days. She seems to have coped with the break-up of her mum and dad in the end. Good Luck Jane.

Bill & Mary from the B&B.

Thank you both for the wonderful care and friendship you gave my Mother and Father on their stays with you. You have a fantastic place. You are lovely people.

Martin....and a long awaited apology!

I apologize to Martin here and now. Here is a man who seems to ooze testosterone from the merest beginnings of a gesture of a smile. He, I'm afraid to say, has been the brunt of my leg pulling and teasing for far too long. Much more at times than a now married lady should do. However Martin gives back as good as he gets. He is such a funny chap, and takes life in his stride. Which is just as well as I still have the negatives...

(Ooooop's, Did that just come out loud....dam.... I told him I'd got rid of them!!!)

Iain the Birthday Boy!

Here is a great chap who sadly gets the brunt of the barman jokes. Unfortunately there's always one who gets it. But sometimes it goes too far in my view. Iain is so sweet and is a really nice chap to talk to. I personally haven't seen a young lady on his arms but I'm sure if he had a bonnie lass he'd never bring her to the pub because of the constant barrage of what is sometimes quite insulting. One day I'm sure he will be pushed too far by the barman and land him a good one, which would be followed by many a cheer!

Thank you all for being our friends and may all your lives be blessed with Love, Happiness, Fortune and Good Health.

Just a few more and that's it, I Promise......!

All of the friends who have stayed here...

Lindy, Charlotte, Brian, Lawrence and Val, Jezz, Nicky and their boys Luke and Harry (not forgetting Mazy their dog who our son Sam fell in love with).

Thank you all for showing so much interest in our work, and for bearing up to the living accommodation on your stay with us on your visits. You are all truly wonderful friends.

And thank you to all our family and friends who travelled so far to be with us on our Wedding Day.

To those we have left behind in Brighton. The likes of John and Robert, and all our friends from The Brighton Tavern. We miss you all dearly. xxxx

And FINALLY.

My Mother and Father hope to come up on holiday again next year. Their health is much the same, be it that some is due to life's cruel journey. But the other option is one I have said is not one I would recommend!

My son Jonathon, and his now fiancée Louise are doing well in their new life in lands far away, and we keep in touch.

Sara and Chris are fine, and hope to come and see us next year for my 50th. Erik my grandson is just 'Scrummy'.

My brother Paul and his wife Denise seem ok, and seem to be taking to being Grandparents. And I believe the girls are growing up and doing fine.

Roger is fine and carrying on regardless with his wonderful work come rain or shine. I am so proud of him and love him so much. He never stops working on the house and is always full of new ideas and projects that seem to be constantly whizzing around in his head for the next day's work. If he ever sits still too long I know instinctively something is wrong with him. He just never ceases to amaze me with his energy....

I believe I am beginning to respond to treatment for my tummy troubles and I'm helping Roger all I can with the work still to do on the house.

Dear Roger has put up with me as I always seem to be in the wars. Bashing myself or things falling on me! But hey, life would be boring otherwise! The latest being that I had a fight with our 'Big Red' Honda trike! It won and I now have a lot more than my pride bruised!

The house is almost completed. The kitchen and stair are the projects for the long coming winter months. The house was, and still is, on hold whilst we build the Agricultural Building. Which has been yet another battle, thanks to some interference, but we have almost completed the main work on it. Just in time for winter.

AND FINALLY IF YOU DARE TURN THE PAGE

GOODBYE

X